1933
E.D. GOMME
W.T.R. MEDLOCK
I.O. ABRAHAM
T.T. BAIRD
J.L. HUGGAN
P.G. HARTLEY
A.B. UNWIN

1934
H.G. ROBERTS
F.J. SEABROOK
H. DAWSON
J.L. ELWELL
P.G. EVANS   C.C. WELLS
D. ROBERTSON
J.M. HAYWARD
R.V. STONE   J.M. EDWARDS

1931
J.T. BERRIDGE
H.M. MATTHEWS
J.W. GREEN
R.T. PELLS
N.W. NEWTON
G.K. HASELDEN
J.H.H. WILLIAMS
R.W. SODEN
P.A. HEALD
A.T. EASTON
B. GLEDHILL

1932
J.N. PRENTICE
C.P. MARKHAM LEE
J.A. ROEMMELE

1935
P.D. McENTEE
M SYMES THOMPSON
G.S. GILL
A. WHITEHEAD
A.D. RUCK   G.P. LINCOLN

1935
M.S. ROSS   HAILEY
DAWSON, J.P.
S.W. FRASER-SMITH
I.P. HUNTER
H. FERGUSON
W.J.P. MASH   HAILEY
R.R. TRUMAN
P.H. PETTITT
T.S. MORGAN

1935
H.G. SOUTER
E.D. INGHAM
COPE   HAYLES, C.V.
J. McMILLAN
J. BEAUMONT
R.C. BLAMEY
C.G. FINCH
J.S. WATSON
T.W. MILLER
C.J.B. DINGLEY
P.G. Hartley
H. PALMER
R.D. MORTON
L.L. BAITHES
P.R. HERBST
J.H.S. MOWAT

1933
A.I.S. DEBENHAM
J. GOYNE   R. BURN
H. LETANG
M.W.H. SHEPHARD
I.P. MORE   F.E. BELL
H.B. GIFFORD
I. NELSON   R.T. JOHN
J.S. ELDRIDGE
A.A. CLARKE   Irish Free State
K.L. DE RIVAZ
D.H. RIDLER
G.F. WOODS
H.J.L. MARRIOTT
H.G.J. CODDINGTON
C.C.A. GREENWOOD
W.B. EVANHAM

HAILEYBURY

A 150th Anniversary Portrait

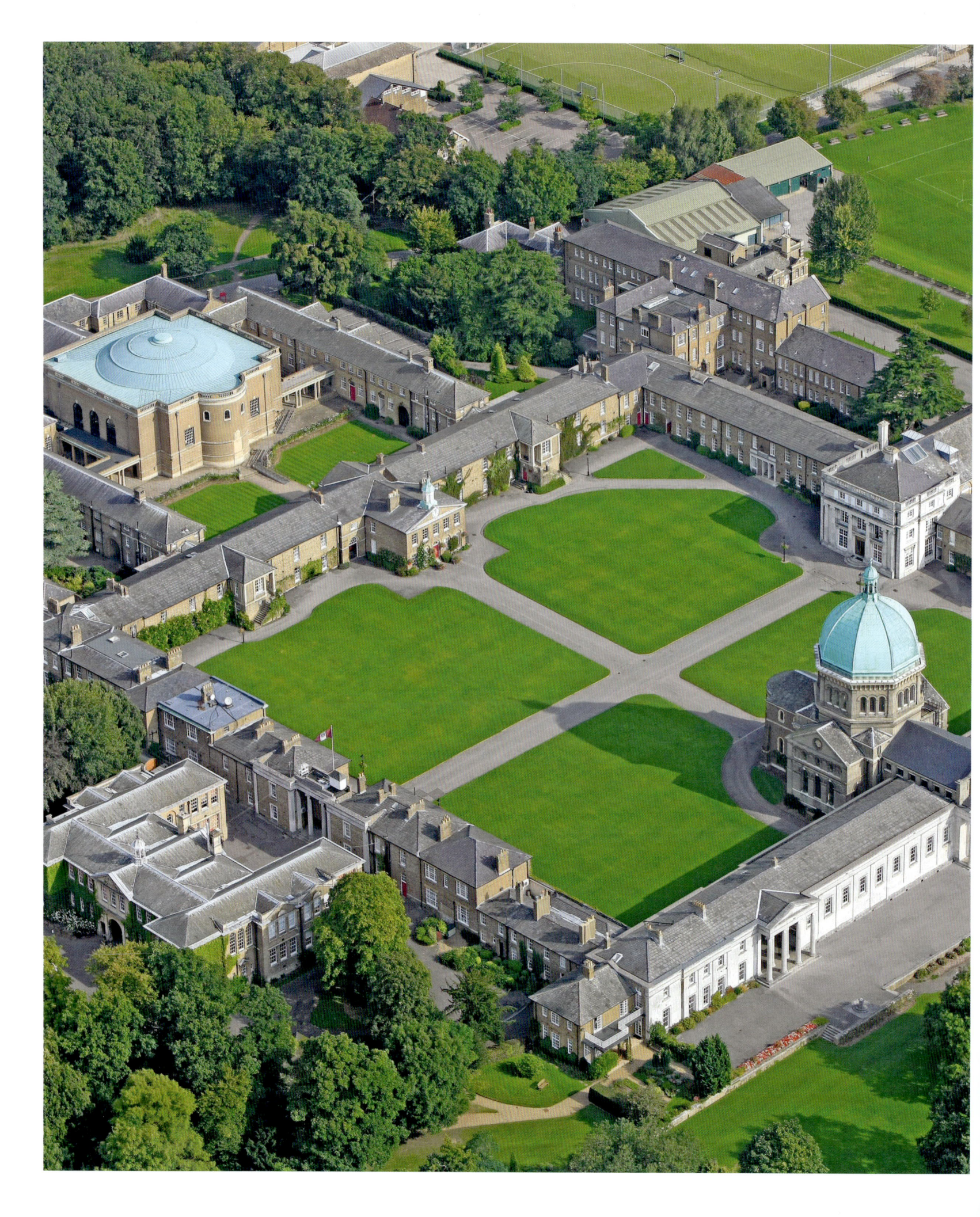

HAILEYBURY

A 150th Anniversary Portrait

Edited by
Roger Woodburn, Toby Parker and Catharine Walston

III
THIRD MILLENNIUM
PUBLISHING, LONDON

Haileybury: A 150th Anniversary Portrait

2012 © Haileybury and Third Millennium Publishing Limited

First published in 2012 by Third Millennium Publishing Limited,
a subsidiary of Third Millennium Information Limited.

2–5 Benjamin Street, London, United Kingdom EC1M 5QL
www.tmiltd.com

ISBN: 978 1 906507 64 0

All rights reserved. No part of this publication may be reproduced or transmitted in any form
or by any means, electronic or mechanical, including photocopying, recording, or any storage
or retrieval system, without permission in writing from the copyright owner concerned.

British Library Cataloguing in Publication Data
A CIP catalogue record for this book is available from the British Library.

Editors	Roger Woodburn, Toby Parker and Catharine Walston
Design	Susan Pugsley and Matthew Wilson
Production	Bonnie Murray
Reprographics	Studio Fasoli, Verona, Italy
Printing	Gorenjski Tisk, Slovenia

THE HOUSE IDENTIFICATIONS

A	= Allenby (as a boys' house)	**Hw**	= Highwood	
Aby	= Allenby (as a girls' house)	**K**	= Kipling	
Alb	= Alban's	**L**	= Lawrence	
B	= Batten	**LeB**	= Le Bas	
BF	= Bartle Frere	**LS**	= Lower School	
C	= Colvin	**M**	= Melvill	
E	= Edmonstone	**RD**	= Russell Dore	
Ha	= Hailey	**Th**	= Thomason	
Hi	= Highfield	**Tr**	= Trevelyan	

The year that appears after a (former) pupil's name is his/her year of entry and the .1, .2, .3 that follows refers respectively to January, April and September of that year. Staff dates are given arriving and leaving. Dates for an individual appear only when they are first mentioned in the book and are not repeated.

CONTENTS

	Foreword	6
1	**On the Origin of Haileybury**	8
2	**The Estate**	32
3	**An Active School**	44
4	**A Creative School**	68
5	**The Common Room**	88
6	**School Life**	104
7	**Service Before Self**	120
8	**Progressive Learning**	148
9	**The Divine Scheme**	170
10	**The Wider World**	182
	Appendix	196
	Explanatory notes on some Haileybury terms	198
	List of Subscribers	200
	Index	204
	Acknowledgements	208

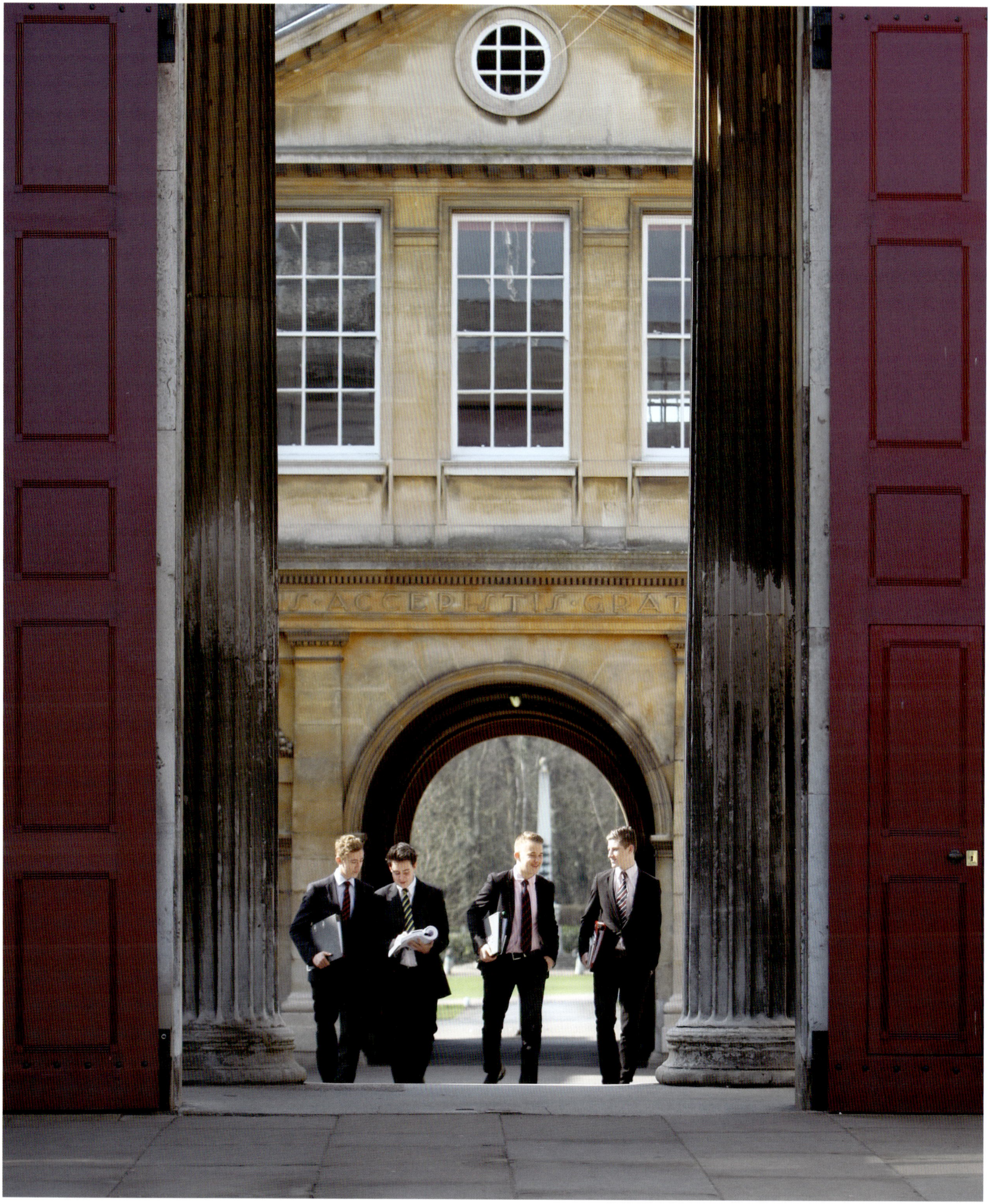
S·ACCEPISTIS·GRAT

FOREWORD

No dry history, this book is a living testimony to an institution, born in the days of empire but which has adapted remarkably to the 'changing scenes of life' over a century and a half in a world now changed beyond recognition. Written entirely by her sons and daughters – some who have devoted their lives to her service and others whose formative years were shaped by her – it brings to life scenes from a distant past as well as more recent events, and recounts the achievements of many of her former pupils, as well as her own influence and activity in the wider world.

At the heart of all this there seems to be a continuous thread – the concept of service to others – that has characterised this great school from its earliest days. In a post-imperial age there is nevertheless reason for pride in what, since the amalgamation in 1942, has been and is still the full formal name of the school – Haileybury and Imperial Service College (and the surviving OISCs will, like any OH, find much to rekindle their memories here). The need and opportunities for selfless service in the modern world are greater than ever before and it is heartening to read here how today's Haileyburians, like their forebears, are responding to them.

Vivat Haileyburia!

Michael Freegard (Bartle Frere 1947.1)
*Past President and former Honorary Secretary of
The Haileybury Society
Member of Council 2000–03*

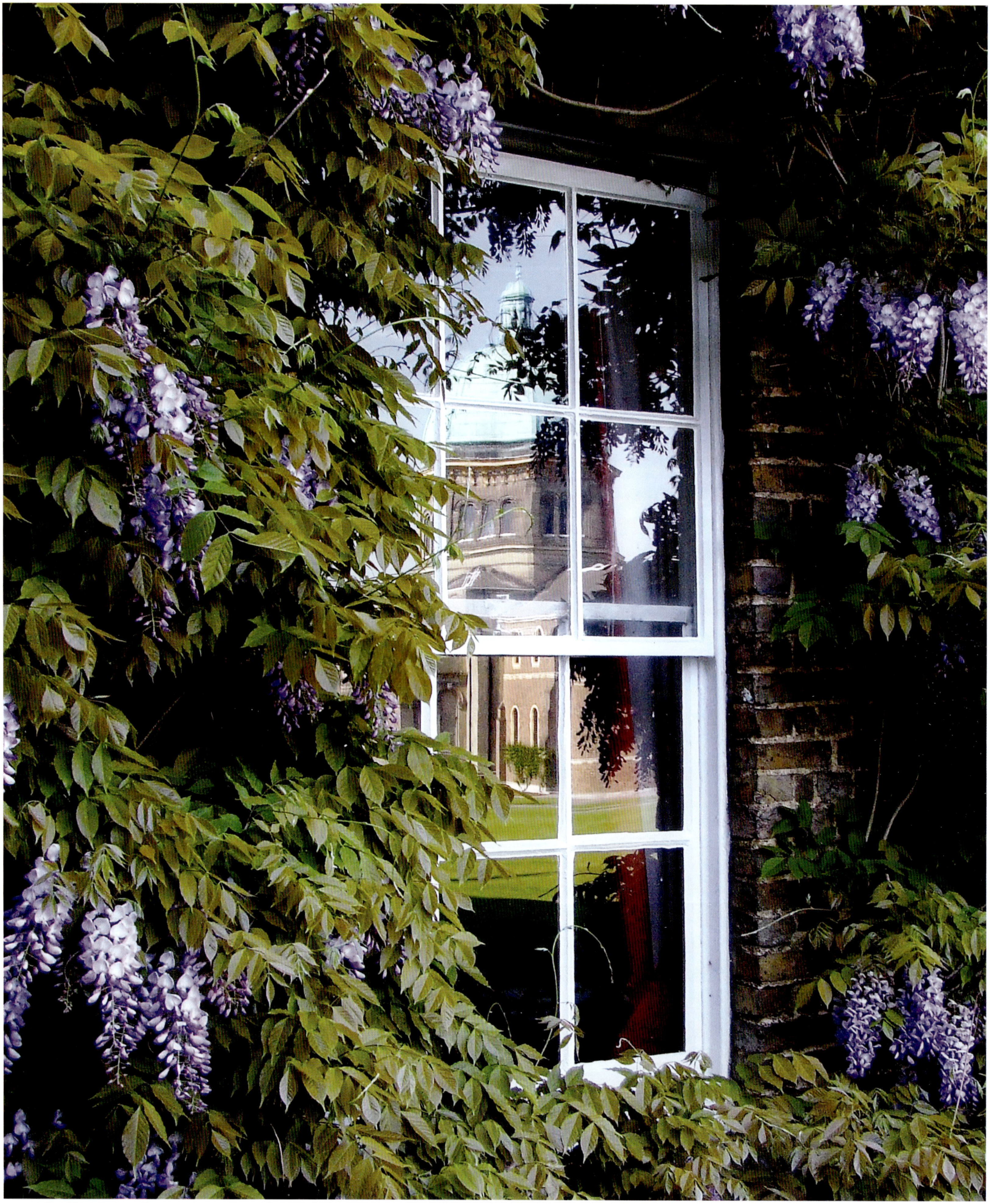

Chapter 1

ON THE ORIGIN OF HAILEYBURY

THE FOUNDATION

The first pupil to join Haileybury when it opened on 23 September 1862 was George Hoste (Tr, Th and C 1862.3), a fact noted with pride in the diary of his father, the Rector of Boyton. After an early breakfast at the Bull Inn at Hoddesdon, the Hostes, father and son, walked to Haileybury on the opening day and met with Arthur Butler, the first Headmaster. The Reverend George Hoste remarked with pleasure on the architecture of the College, but he also noticed that parts of the College (Quadrangle) were unused. The opening of Haileybury College was not met with a fanfare and no dignitaries were invited to add lustre to the event. It was merely the beginning of the school year.

When Haileybury College opened, it was a huge relief for Arthur Butler and the School's governing Council who had twice been forced to write to the parents informing them of the need to push back the opening day. The original opening date was to have been 9 September, but the amount of work needed to get the buildings ready to function as a modern school meant that the Council members had to swallow their pride if the pupils were to be properly catered for.

The founding of a public school was not an easy task. Eton, Winchester and Harrow slowly changed from endowed charitable schools for the poor into bastions of privilege over centuries. Wellington College was founded in 1853 but finally opened its doors to pupils in 1859, while Haileybury was founded and opened in the space of nine months. The speed of the enterprise was breathtaking considering that there was no rich endowment to support the scheme. What Haileybury did have, however, was the support of the Very Reverend George Bowers, Dean of Manchester, who had already played a part in the founding of Marlborough College and Rossall. Bowers understood the pitfalls in establishing a school from nothing and he was instrumental in making sure that Haileybury was a public school rather than a proprietary one.

Right: *The Very Reverend George Bowers, Dean of Manchester, credited with helping to found Marlborough College and Rossall School, he was also a founding member of Haileybury's Council.*

HAILEYBURY — *A 150th Anniversary Portrait*

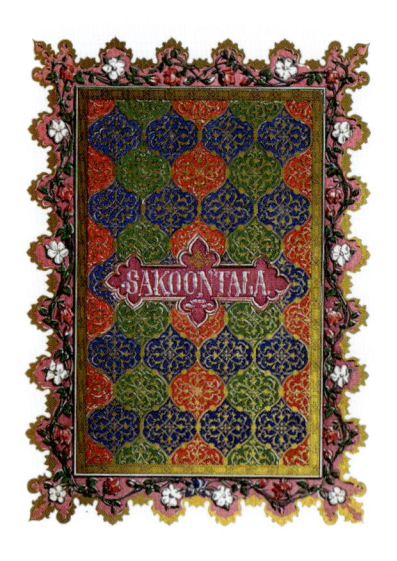

Kalidasa's Sakoontala, translated by Monier Williams (EIC 1840), Professor of Sanskrit at the East India College, and published by Stephen Austin in 1855. Stephen Austin's printing and publishing business was greatly enhanced by its status as official bookseller to the East India College. A number of early meetings were held at his home, Cowbridge House, concerning the founding of Haileybury College.

Below: *Arthur Gray Butler, first Master of Haileybury, by George Richmond, RA.*

From the beginning the School had the support of the Archbishop of Canterbury and the Bishops of London and Rochester, no doubt pleased that a school was being opened for the education of clergymen in the south-east of England. Indeed, in February 1862 it was suggested that the foundation also allow sons of Military and Naval officers at the same rates as the sons of clergy, but it was felt that the financial burden would be too great for such a new school.

At the first meeting of Haileybury's governing Council on 21 March 1862, with Dean Bowers presiding, it was decided that the estate, which had just been purchased from the British Land Company with two huge mortgages, would be placed under the trusteeships of William Baker of Bayfordbury, Robert Smith of Goldings and Robert Dimsdale. Less than a month later the Council elected the Reverend Arthur Gray Butler, an assistant master at Rugby, to be its first Master over 15 other candidates, including the Reverend W.G. Henderson and the Reverend Henry Temple, headmasters of Victoria College, Jersey and Henry VIII School, Coventry, respectively.

Aged only 30, Butler was active in the development of Haileybury from the moment of his appointment and instrumental in the adoption of the hostel or dormitory system rather than separate Houses. The new Master was sure that the hostel system was able to sustain 'much greater facilities for the maintenance of discipline rather than a system of smaller rooms'. Arthur Butler's support for the long dormitories

Chapter 1 — ON THE ORIGIN OF HAILEYBURY

Right: *The first calling over list, 1862.*

Far right: *Report for George Hoste, 1862.*

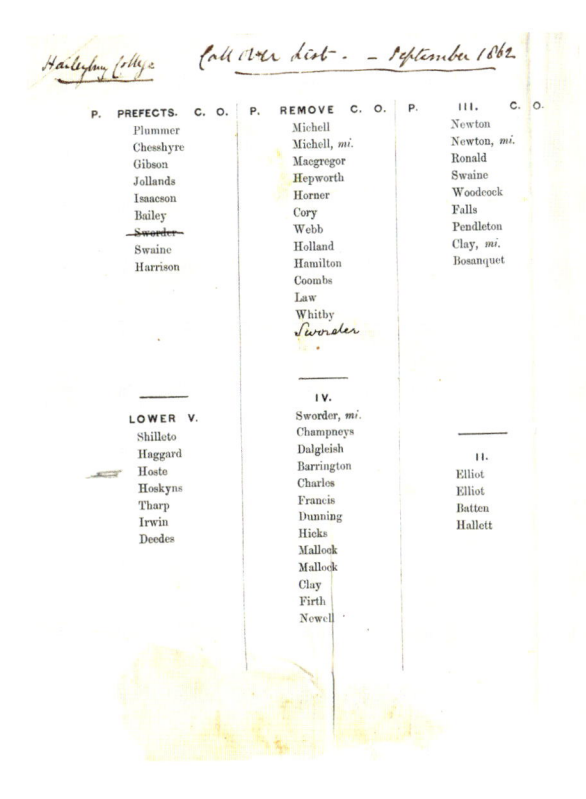

presented his new employers with something of a problem, however: the new plans required a large capital investment. To create dormitories it was necessary to knock through the bedsits designed by William Wilkins and employ architects, builders and other tradesmen. In May, the first College architect, Arthur Blomfield, presented his plans to the Governors, but it was not until August that the work on the dormitories was started.

Meanwhile, details about fee levels, holidays and the number of boys per House were agreed; the authorities at Marlborough and Rossall as well as the Dean of Manchester were helping to deal with the myriad questions that a fledgling school had to ask. At one point Rossall's authorities were forced to write indignantly to Haileybury about the way that their fees were being misrepresented in the new school's publicity; Rossall's fees were cheaper by £5 a term. When Haileybury opened there were only two dormitories, able to sleep a total of 84 pupils, under the care of the first two dormitory servants (known as Tobys or Boots), Thomas Barett and Joseph Taylor.

The original 57 boys who joined Haileybury in its first term were latterly known as 'the Aborigines' and they were proud of their special status in the School's history. On the earliest calling over list, Rowland Plummer (L 1862.3), later vicar of St Paul's, Bow, was positioned as Head of the School, while Edward Hughes Hallet (L and Th 1862.3) took up the lowliest position in the II Form. While there was no Sixth Form in the first year of the School, it is clear that Butler deemed it necessary for pupil discipline to appoint a body of prefects to regulate the rest.

In the Christmas term of 1862 there were only three under/assistant masters – the Reverend Augustus Hensley, the Reverend Charles Walford and the Reverend Henry Reade – each of whom was allotted a form to teach. Lessons were learned, repeated and then examined by the Headmaster. The emphasis was on Classics, although Butler himself provided a rough and ready modern education to pupils in his drawing room outside of the mainstream timetable. Alfred Haggard (Tr and C 1862.3) claimed to have been the first boy punished at Haileybury on 24 September for a minor transgression, leaving him to copy out ten times a line from Ovid:

Martis erat primus mensis, Venerisque secundus:
Haec generis princeps, ipsius ille pater.
Tertius a senibus, Juvenum de nomine quartus.

At the beginning of second term there were 95 pupils but the governing body were already becoming weary of the escalating costs of setting up a school for 300–400 boys. After the first term there was a growing tension between Council and Butler; the Headmaster felt his power limited as the members of Council demanded that almost all day-to-day business of the School be brought before them. Council believed that Arthur Butler did not understand the tricky financial situation that the School found itself in. Butler required that new dormitories be created on the North Range of the Quadrangle, that Hailey House be converted into the preparatory school and that a new school room or Great School be built. To achieve this programme of development Butler demanded that the fees be raised, an idea that the Council members refused to countenance. John Chessyre, the Secretary to Council was finally forced to write a stern letter to Butler informing him that his demands for further investment had upset the members of the Council. Chessyre revealed that, if Butler had wanted 'this' type of institution, Council should perhaps have purchased a site and built a school from scratch. Butler's determination was beginning to be rewarded with increasing pupil numbers but Council continued to put immense pressure on him to rein back his vision for a completed school.

In August 1864 Haileybury was granted its Royal Charter of Incorporation, removing the immense financial burden from the individual members of the governing body and giving them greater powers to regulate the School. The Charter itself was modelled on Marlborough's, as were the byelaws and the formal title of the Headmaster: the Master of Haileybury College. To the horror of his colleagues and pupils Arthur Butler had a breakdown in that year and was unable to return to work until the middle of 1865.

Toby Parker (ATMP) (Staff 2004.1–)

Above: *The Common Room, with Reverend Arthur Butler seated (centre), flanked by the first two Housemasters, Hensley (left) and Walford (right) 1867.*

Chapter 1 — ON THE ORIGIN OF HAILEYBURY

THE COAT OF ARMS

The Arms for Haileybury College were designed by the first Master, Arthur Gray Butler: Azure an open book Argent bound Gules edged and garnished with seven clasps Or and inscribed with the words *Sursum Corda* Sable the initial letter of the third between three hearts Or winged of the second. The unofficial Arms of Haileybury were used from the early days of the College.

The College used these Arms without legal authority until 1 January 1920, when a Grant of Arms was paid for by James Morris as a memorial to his son, George Morris (Ha 1908.2), a Lieutenant in the Royal Flying Corps who was killed in action near Arras in 1917. George Morris had been very interested in heraldry and his father, acting as his son's administrator, used funds from the boy's deferred regimental pay for the purpose.

After the merger with Imperial Service College (ISC) the name of the Corporation of the Governors was changed to Haileybury and Imperial Service College by Royal Charter dated 12 January 1942 and a warrant was issued for an alteration to the Grant of Arms on 18 August 1943. The reconstituted institution was granted the addition of a chief to celebrate the merger with the ISC. The addition to the arms was blazoned thus: on a chief Or an anchor and a Sword the point upwards in saltire of the field. The motto, which is an unofficial element of the Grant of Arms and may be changed at will, was altered in 1943 to 'Fear God Honour the King'.

The celebration of the College's centenary in 1962 led to the Governors of Haileybury and ISC making an application for a grant for the addition of a Crest. The petition to the Earl Marshal was undertaken by Lord Trevethin and Oaksey, then Chairman of the Corporation of the Governors. The Crest that was granted alludes to the East India College's (1806–57) own Crest and can be blazoned: A lion serjant guardant erect crowned with an eastern crown Or and holding between the fore paws a scroll with a seal pendant therefrom proper.

ATMP

HOUSES: THEIR ORIGINS AND EMBLEMS

Trevelyan has the privilege of being the oldest of all of Haileybury's Houses. Originally known as the Reds, Trevelyan moved from the south-east block (the ground floor of the present Lawrence House) on Quadrangle when its Housemaster, Augustus Hensley, married and needed more suitable accommodation. When the second Master, Edward Bradby, decreed that the Houses should be named after famous East Indiamen, Sir Charles Trevelyan was adopted for Mr Hensley's House. Sir Charles was the brother-in-law of Thomas Babington Macaulay and a leading figure in making English the official language of India.

Charles Trevelyan (EIC 1824). As a young civil servant in India, Trevelyan was very active in the promotion of education and the improvement of conditions for native Indians. The brother-in-law of Thomas Babington Macaulay, he seems to have shared his views on the promotion of an English education in India. When recalled to London, he served as an assistant secretary to HM Treasury and was charged with administering relief during the Irish famine. His Malthusian views and lack of sympathy for the Irish have meant that he is a figure of hate in Ireland, rivalled only by Oliver Cromwell. However, the Northcote-Trevelyan Report of 1853, which he co-wrote with Sir Stafford Northcote, is generally credited with the foundation of the professional civil service based on merit rather than patronage. He served as Governor of Madras, 1859–60, where he was popular locally but fell foul of the Legislative Council and was recalled. From 1862–5 he returned to India as Minister of Finance.

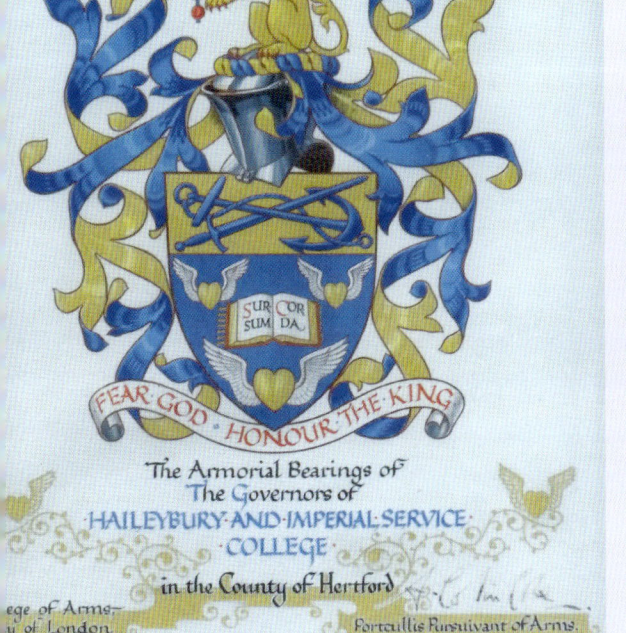

HAILEYBURY — *A 150th Anniversary Portrait*

The badge of Trevelyan is a red cross pattée, not a Maltese cross, a symbol whose origins at Haileybury are lost in time, while the motto 'Time tryeth troth' was adopted from the Trevelyans of Trevelyan, Nettlecombe and Wallington.

Lawrence House has perhaps the most complex history of all the Houses at Haileybury. Lawrence, or the Blues, was opened at the same time as Trevelyan but considered its junior in precedence because the Reverend Charles Walford was appointed Housemaster after Augustus Hensley. The Lawrence dormitory was above Trevelyan's and one of the studies demolished to create the space had belonged to Sir John Lawrence, later Lord Lawrence, sometime Viceroy of India. In 1940 Lawrence was closed, and when Haileybury and ISC amalgamated, 'C' House from Windsor took over the dormitory. 'C' House was also known as Lawrence, although it was named after Sir Henry Lawrence, Sir John's brother. The old Lawrence colours of blue and black were succeeded by the red, white and blue, and the skull and crossbones badge was dropped. The new House badge was the triquetra (symbol of the Trinity), a device that came from the ISC's merger with the Army School, but later the skull and crossbones was adopted again.

Thomason was the third House to be opened, under the care of the Reverend Lewis Prance (Staff 1863.1–68.2). While the Registers of Haileybury have always accorded Bartle Frere third place in precedence, its Housemaster the Reverend Henry Reade had no pupils while Prance had boys from 1863.1. The first Head of House was George Hoste, who was given the short-lived title of Captain of Clock House. Thomason was named after James Thomason, Lieutenant Governor of the North West Province and Governor-elect of Madras, who was the great-great-uncle of Field Marshal the Viscount Montgomery. Thomason was used as a junior House before Hailey became the preparatory department and the pupils originally used a blue cap with a ribbon laid out as a yellow star. The House colours were adapted from Trinity College, Cambridge, Prance's alma mater, while the badge was a griffin's head couped between two wings sable. Thomasonians also went by the name 'Griffins' for House matches as an allusion to their House symbol.

Bartle Frere was named after Sir Henry Bartle Frere, Governor of Bombay and later High Commissioner of the Cape Colony. The 'Frere' was originally a Quad House, a dormitory which included

Right: *Bartle Frere House, photographed in the summer term of 1993. It moved to its current site in January 1994. A comparison is worth making with the photograph on p25.*

Opposite: The East India College at Haileybury *by Thomas Medland, Drawing Master at the East India College, 1810.*

Chapter 1 ~ ON THE ORIGIN OF HAILEYBURY

HAILEYBURY — *A 150th Anniversary Portrait*

A PLAN OF THE LAYOUT OF THE ROOM ALLOCATIONS SHORTLY AFTER THE OPENING OF THE SCHOOL

Plan of the College, prepared by Digby Wyatt in 1861, based on the original design by William Wilkins, showing the location of the first dormitories and other rooms.

A The Lodge

B Mr Couchman's Form-Room

C The Grubber

D Mr Walford's Form-Room

E The Cockpit

F Mr Hensley's Private House

G House (Lower)
Edmonstone 1863.3–64.2
Trevelyan 1864.2

H House (Upper)
Bartle Frere 1863.1

I Matron's Linen Room

J House (Lower)
Thomason 1863.1

K House (Upper)
Colvin 1863.3

L Sick House

M Beaks' Private Rooms and House Rooms

N House (Lower)
Trevelyan 1862.3–64.2
Edmonstone 1864.2

O House (Upper)
Lawrence 1862.3

P Kitchen

Q Dining Hall

R Masters' Common Room

S Great School

T The Chapel

U Master's Lodge

V Mr Reade's Form-Room

W Mr Hensley's Form-Room

X Studies

Chapter 1 ～ ON THE ORIGIN OF HAILEYBURY

17

the site of Sir Henry's study above Trevelyan. Crimson and blue were the colours adopted by the House and, as a badge, a blue moon 'thereupon' a crimson moon. Today Edmonstone and Bartle Frere are paired, contentedly, in a modern building below Allenby.

Edmonstone was opened in the second year of the School's existence, in the north-west block, which it exchanged with Trevelyan in 1864. The Edmonstonians adopted the colours of Trinity College, Oxford, the college of their first Housemaster, Henry Couchman (Staff 1863.2–1900.1). Edmonstone was named after Sir George Edmonstone, Lieutenant Governor of the North West Province and Foreign Secretary to the Government of India during the Mutiny.

Colvin was the last of the Quad Houses and opened in 1864, with the first Housemaster, Cormell Price (Staff 1863.2–74.2), selecting the Brasenose College, Oxford colours of gold and black. A wasp was chosen as the House badge to symbolize 'what foes might expect on close encounter' and they used the motto 'Nitere ut discas'. The Colvin House colours were adopted by Crofts' House at the USC. Colvin became a girls' House in 1999 and moved to a new building by the Master's Pond. For a time a tiger was used as the girls' House symbol but in recent times the wasp has been re-adopted.

Hailey was originally the preparatory department for Haileybury with its own Great School for lessons. During the days of the EIC, it was home to the Reverend Thomas Malthus, Professor of Political Economy, and before that it was the 'mansion house' for the Hailey estate. The first Housemaster, the Reverend Henry Walford, had already run Bartle Frere and he relied on other Houses to provide him with Prefects until the House became part of the College in 1877. The colours, crimson and blue, were brought over from Bartle Frere and a crest used by Walford's family was chosen as the House emblem. When Hailey was converted into a girls' House, the badge was retained but the crimson and blue were changed to pink and dark blue.

Highfield was the only private House at the School, built by the poet and mystic James Rhoades (Staff 1864.2–74.1), the first Housemaster, in 1867. It is likely that the name 'Highfield' was simply a literal description of the position of the house. In Highfield, a boy's parents paid the fees to Rhoades, who then settled an agreed sum with the School for the cost of the tuition. The black eagle displayed, symbol of Highfield, was selected as the major element in the coats of arms used by various families called Rhoades.

Above: *The new Edmonstone building, opened in January 1994.*

Below left: *The Kipling Memorial Plaque, or Jungle Book Relief Panel, by Benno Elkan, which was commissioned by the Kipling Memorial Fund Council and installed on the south front of the Rudyard Kipling Memorial Building built at the ISC, Windsor, in 1939.*

THE REDS AND THE BLUES

When Haileybury opened on 23 September 1862 there were only two Houses for the pupils to be placed in. Arthur Butler had appointed the Reverend Augustus Hensley (Staff 1862.3) and the Reverend Charles Walford (Staff 1862.3) to be Housemasters of dormitories created out of the individual studies of the East India College (EIC), with no name or distinguishing symbols. The tribal nature of pupils and the desire for new tradition led to the adoption of colours for the two Houses: one was to adopt blue as its colour and the other red. Walford's House became known as the Blues and Hensley's dormitory was called the Reds. Later, the Reds became Trevelyan and the Blues became Lawrence, but their new names never quite eclipsed their identification with their colours; the war-like cry 'Red Army' can still be heard at Cock House final on a misty winter's afternoon.

The men from the Blues and Reds competed among themselves for everything and the rivalry was fierce, but there was also a bond which unified them against all others; they were the 'Aborigines' and all other Houses were *arrivistes*, unworthy of any real attention or respect.

For the first year and a half the two Houses lived together on the block that is now completely settled by Lawrence. It was only when Hensley married that Trevelyan moved to its present position in the north-western corner of Quad. Previously this had been the territory of Edmonstone, but the Reverend Henry Couchman (Staff 1863.2–1900.1), swapped dormitories to give the Hensleys accommodation suitable for a family.

By 1865 there were seven Houses at Haileybury, but it was not until 1867 that a Cock House competition allowed any House other than Trevelyan or Lawrence to take part. Bartle Frere, Thomason, Edmonstone and Colvin were 'College' Houses opened only as they were needed and did not share the same history and traditions. At the Lawrence House Entertainment of 1868, for which the Blues' *Metrical Alphabets* were devised, the boys sang 'R is for Red whose victory the Blues will cheer', an allusion to that year's Cock House final when Colvin and Trevelyan met and where a unified front was required against the new Houses. Rather surprisingly, at the beginning of their lives the Blues and Reds are believed to have shared the same badge, the cross pattée, differenced by colour and still used by Trevelyan. It was not until H.G. Harte (Staff 1866.2) became Housemaster of Lawrence that the blue cross was succeeded by a skull and crossbones.

ATMP

Above right: Field Marshal the Viscount Allenby (BF 1875.2).

The House was renamed in 1937.3, in honour of Field Marshal the Viscount Allenby (BF 1875.2), but it retained the House colours, green and black, as well as the eagle displayed. **Allenby** became a girls' House in 1993.3 and altered the House colours to light blue and dark blue.

Batten was opened in 1879, one of three 'outhouses' named after the Principals of the East India College. When the three Houses were built, they were considered so ugly that many Haileyburians thought they resembled workhouses. The Reverend Joseph Batten was the second Principal of the EIC and at least 11 of his descendants attended the school. The crest, an arm grasping a battle axe, used by the Battens of Penzance, was assumed as the House badge, with orange and brown as the colours.

Le Bas was closed in 1940 after only 60 years in existence and unlike Batten and Melvill, it was not reopened. The House was named after the third principal of the EIC, the Reverend Charles Le Bas. The House appropriated the coat of arms of the Hugenot Le Bas family, and light blue and black as its colours (these are now used by the Kipling House Society for its tie).

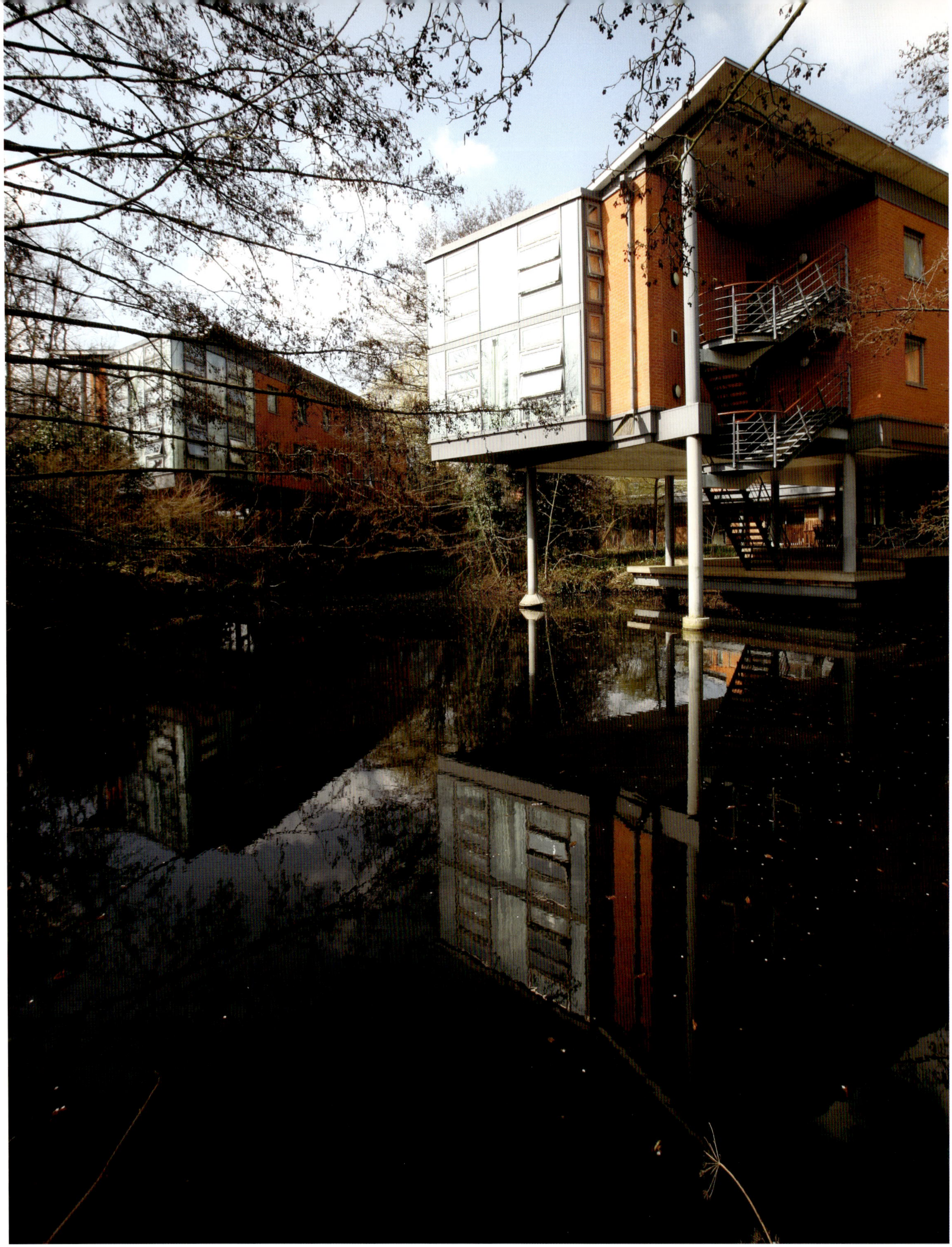

Chapter 1 — ON THE ORIGIN OF HAILEYBURY

Right: *St Mark's Lions in Memorial Quad. These came from the top of the Goodhart Gates at St Marks, the site of ISC. These lions were reproduced from figures in Ripon Cathedral.*

Below: *Pavilion and far right the KBM Block, likened to a workhouse when first opened.*

Opposite: *The new Colvin building opened in 1999 (right) and the new Melvill building opened in 2001.*

Melvill was the final outhouse to be built and was named after the Reverend Henry Melvill, the last Principal of the EIC and one of the finest preachers of his time. Like Joseph Batten, many of Henry Melvill's descendants have attended Haileybury, although Teignmouth Melvill VC, one of his grandsons, who was killed with Nevill Coghill VC (Tr 1865.2) at Isandlwana, was educated at Harrow. In 1940 Melvill was closed and turned into an emergency hospital for the Army and did not reopen until 1945. The House colours were initially pink and black, but because the ribbon on the caps faded, the colour was changed to scarlet. The arms, argent a cross gules, were adopted as their badge, and the motto *Delectando pariterque monendo* was taken from the Melvill family. In 2001 Melvill left the outhouses and became a girls' House situated next to Colvin.

Kipling is a reminder of two of modern Haileybury's ancestors, the United Service College and St Mark's School, Windsor, which merged in 1906. It was named after Rudyard Kipling, who was a pupil at USC, Westward Ho!, and a passionate supporter of his old 'Coll' and its reincarnation, the Imperial Services College. The colours chosen for the new Kipling House in 1942 were green and black, which had been used by 'A' House at the ISC and Stevens' House at the USC at Westward Ho!. The badge selected for Kipling was a St Mark's lion, the symbol used by the Reverend Stephen Hawtrey, who founded St Mark's in 1862.

Russell Dore was opened as a day House in 1982 and was named after one of the School's greatest benefactors, Frank Russell Dore (Ha 1904.3). The colours of the House were navy blue, taupe and light tan. After its closure and re-opening as the Lower School, the latter adopted red and gold as its colours.

The Lower School was opened in 1993 and is in many ways the spiritual successor to the original Hailey House, acting as a preparatory department for the main school, taking pupils from the age of 11. The Lower School boarding House assumed the name Highfield and took girls from 2011.3. Before this, the Lower School girls had been resident in Alban's for a time.

Alban's was the first girls' House, opened in 1977.3 using the buildings of the original Sanatorium, built by Sir Arthur Blomfield in 1867. The House was named Alban's to mark the centenary of the diocese and the badge used by the girls today is a dove.

ATMP

HAILEYBURY — *A 150th Anniversary Portrait*

MASTERS ON MASTERS:
The Reverend A.G. Butler

It seems that setting up new schools is all the rage at present. The Coalition Government is intent on extending its predecessor's commitment to establishing new Academies as a way of reviving the falling educational standards in the state sector. Successful established independent schools are being urged to provide their support in sponsoring these Academies. The Government is keen to get the 'DNA of public schools' into their own system – so says the driving force behind the Academies movement, Lord Adonis. Not content with extending the reach of new schools through Academies, Michael Gove, the Secretary of State for Education wants another type of new school – Free Schools. These are based on the Swedish model where parents who are dissatisfied with local provision can lobby the Department of Education to set up their own schools, free of Local Education Authority influence but funded by the state. In essence it seems the old Victorian public school with a highly distinctive ethos and structure is being asked to provide the blueprint for English Education in the 21st century. I wonder if the government really knows how difficult it is to set up a new school?

This is what Arthur Gray Butler did in September 1862 when he became the first Headmaster of the new Haileybury College. Strangely we have some recent experiences that might help us understand what the Reverend Arthur Butler had to experience back then. In September 2008 and September 2011 Haileybury set up two new schools, both in Kazakhstan; one in Almaty, the other in Astana. The same Headmaster, Andrew Auster was responsible for setting up these new schools, about which he writes more fully, later in this book. I do know, from having spoken to Andrew on numerous occasions, the associated stress. There is chaos; there is panic; there is worry, but once open, there is great joy and excitement. We can only imagine all these aspects in Butler's life because with typical Victorian *sang-froid* there is little that he or his colleagues have written that gives us an idea of the emotional rollercoaster they must have experienced in their early days.

Even before he set up the school, Butler was aware of the strong ethos of the old East India College. One witness, speaking of the East India College at Haileybury, giving evidence to the Committee of the House of Commons in 1853, said 'Our mission in India is to qualify them for governing themselves'. This forward-thinking, service-orientated viewpoint of the College, so influential it seems for Haileybury's future, is confirmed in Philip Woodruff's *The Men who Ruled India – There is about them a consciousness that they have a great task and that they belong to a service. There is also ... a distinctive undernote, an independence of outlook, a readiness to criticise and to state an opinion, however unfavourable to the administration... they were most of them when they reached India on the side of the yeoman rather than the noble.* It is this ethos of service that Butler sensed and it is one on which he built with great success. The East India College closed its doors on 31 January 1858 and until four years later the buildings at Haileybury were virtually deserted. However, as with such ventures, the phoenix of a new school resulted from sustained teamwork. What would happen to the deserted buildings? One suggestion was that they should become a workhouse, another that there should be a lunatic asylum. However clerics and a number of the local gentry saw an opportunity to found a school. The plan was for the education to be *equal to that in all our best Public Schools, qualifying pupils for high positions in universities, for the Army, Navy and the Civil Service Departments; for Engineering, and Commercial pursuits; also for Foreign Service.* The Council stipulated that 'the utmost care will be taken to secure Religious and Moral Training according to the doctrine and formularies of the Church of England'. The man they chose to be Headmaster not only had to be an Oxbridge clergyman but would also be paid 'not exceeding £800 p.a.' It was agreed that he would receive £800 p.a. with free accommodation in the Master's Lodge. Motivational methods were also used

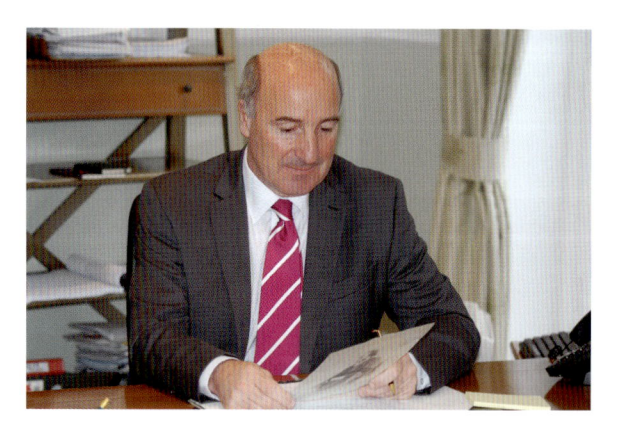

Left: *Joe Davies, Master since 2009, looking at a photograph of his predecessor, Arthur Butler.*

22

Chapter 1 — ON THE ORIGIN OF HAILEYBURY

ROYAL VISITS

In 1912, to celebrate the School's 50th anniversary, Haileybury welcomed Princess Henry of Battenberg, Queen Victoria's youngest daughter, Beatrice. Celebrations centred on 5–7 June, a brilliantly sunny Speech Day weekend featured at length in the national press. A new Big School, costing an estimated £13,500 would replace the 1876 building. the last time in the old building, Reverand F.B. Malim, the Master, welcomed guests from far and wide, including two previous Masters (Lyttelton from Eton and Wynne-Willson from Marlborough) and the widows of two other Masters (Butler and Robertson). Four OH cricket matches, gymnastic and aquatic displays, were followed by a dinner in the Dining Hall (now the Attlee Room). A unique torchlit march by 500 boys completed the day, while crowds lined Hailey Lane, and the Terrace Field, and some watched from the Water Tower (near Red House, demolished in 1933). On Saturday 6 June a private train brought hundreds more guests from London to the Commemoration Service addressed by the Archbishop of Canterbury (the Visitor) before the Princess cemented the Foundation Stone (a plaque in the foyer of Big School marks the spot) behind which was placed a time-capsule with a copy of the July Haileyburian, the Blue and Red Books (the roll of boys and their form-placings) and some current coins. More displays and a final dinner in a marquee on Pavilion ended the day. Of the 128 'new guvnors' in 1912, 30 were to be killed in action in 1917–18.

At the opening of the Memorial Dining Hall in 1932, HRH The Duke of York, later King George VI, unveiled the tablet in Memorial Quad. A few days prior to this Queen Mary, the Duke's mother, paid an unofficial visit to see the Dining Hall while she was staying at nearby Balls Park.

The Centenary, in 1962, was celebrated by a visit from Queen Elizabeth II and The Duke of Edinburgh, who spent the day touring the School. This is the only visit to the School by a reigning monarch, marked by a stone plaque on the House opposite the Pavilion. To mark the opening of the indoor Swimming Pool in 1996 a swimming gala was arranged, with a team from Eton, which included the young Prince William, though with the minimum of protocol.

Andrew Hambling (Staff 1956.3–91.2)

Above: The visit of Princess Henry of Battenberg and the Archbishop of Canterbury in 1912 laying the foundation stone of Big School.

Below: The Master, John Talbot, with HRH The Duchess of York and HRH The Duke of York, accompanied by Mrs Talbot in 1932.

Right: The Queen's visit, 1962, with Robert Scott (Ha 1957.3), Head of School, on her left.

for what the Council thought important. Butler would receive a bonus payment of two guineas for each pupil above 150. When numbers reached 300 he would be paid £1,500. He agreed with the Council that there would be Housemasters with about 40 boys in each House. The appointment was made on 17 April 1862, so Butler had just over four months to get the School some pupils, teachers, support staff and a curriculum. I am sure even Andrew Auster would have found that a challenge.

Butler was remarkably young in our eyes – just 30 on his appointment. He had been educated at Rugby School. He went to Oriel, Oxford, gained a first in Classics, was President of the Union and returned to Rugby as an assistant master having been made a Fellow of Oriel. The all-round ethos was encapsulated in Haileybury's first Master. Not only was Butler a scholar he was also a poet and a sportsman, as we shall see. He was certainly hugely energetic and he threw himself into overseeing the establishment of the fundamentals for the new school. A key decision was to turn the old EIC study bedrooms into the famous long dormitories – so pupils could be 'better supervised'.

There was a furious rush to get things ready. Teaching staff had to be appointed and here Butler showed real talent. He appointed some outstanding schoolmasters, the key, of course, to a successful school.

Even now at Haileybury there is an element of uncertainty over exactly how many pupils will turn up at the start of each year in September; it was worse in 1862. However on 23 September term began. Indeed the first two pupils arrived a day early – from Yorkshire! Now they fly in from all over the world.

So 54 boys began that first term and the usual elements of confusion prevailed. No Bursar had been appointed, so Butler had two roles to fulfil. But the School kept going, no doubt because of his skill and because of the effectiveness of his appointments: a year later there were 173 boys and the next 255. Before long Butler claimed that he was turning away three pupils every day. In these circumstances he kept appointing new staff.

Butler also established the routine of a typical day starting with Chapel at 7am. Afternoons were filled with sport – a real sign of Rugby's influence on Butler – fives and rackets, swimming and rugby. Nothing works so well in schools as when you have an enthusiast in charge and Butler puts us all to shame by the encouragement he gave to the boys to play this new game. He'd appear from his garden, hand his square and gown to the nearest small boy and hurl himself into the fray. More often than not he emerged with the ball in hand, though sometimes his pupils knocked him over into the mud. One pupil describes Butler as 'eventually returning from the fight with great detriment to his clothes but none to his dignity'. What a wonderful man he must have been.

Very quickly Butler had the School up and running and its academic record was impressive. In contrast to some older schools there was both a Modern and Classical Side so Haileybury's tradition of curriculum innovation (the IB Diploma, for example) dates back to Butler. Maths, French, English, geometrical drawing and scientific demonstrations were all part of the academic diet. Indeed Butler's energy had given Haileybury a full list and strong name. Yet all this had tired him and his health began to fail. In November 1867 he sent the Council his letter of resignation. He'd set the School on its legs and it was ready to run. On his death in 1909 one of his successors, Canon Lyttelton wrote 'no more attractively eager personality could be found among the Headmasters of the Century'.

Arthur Butler gave us an ethos that lives on today. Indeed much of what he established – routines, sport, singing – are central features of our current educational diet. In the photograph of Butler working at his desk one can see the seriousness of purpose in his approach. A letter from his daughter to the Master written, amazingly, in 1981, allows us to peel away some of the Victorian formality and see the man a little more clearly. She says of her father *He never ceased to grieve at his enforced resignation* – happily his health did recover as he flourished back at Oriel. She then adds *I well remember his telling me that after morning assembly the whole school filed out before him and he studied each face to see if the owner looked healthy and happy*. It is clear that Arthur Butler gave us, too, an approach to pastoral care that remains central to what we seek to do. His legacy to us is formidable.

Joe Davies (Master, 2009.3–)

HAILEYBURY COLLEGE.
(Late East India College),
NEAR HERTFORD.

HEAD MASTER:
THE REV. ARTHUR GRAY BUTLER, M.A.,
Fellow of Oriel, Ireland University Scholar, and 1st Class in Classics, 1853; and Assistant Master at Rugby.

THIS SCHOOL is intended for the Education of the Sons of the Clergy and Laity, half of each class, and will be conducted on the same principles as the Public Schools of Marlborough and Rossall.

The Education will be equal to that of our best Public Schools, in Classics, Mathematics, and Modern Languages, qualifying Pupils for high positions in the Universities, for the Army, Navy, and Civil Service Departments, for Engineering and Commercial pursuits, and also for Foreign Service.

No Pupil will be admitted under 8 years of age, nor, except with the special sanction of the Head Master, above 14.

Admission, will be obtained either by Nomination or by Annual Payment.

The Payment of £100 constitutes the Subscriber a Life Governor, who shall have the right of having always one Pupil in the School on his Nomination.

Donors paying 25 Guineas have one Nomination only, to be exercised in turn, as vacancies occur.

Pupils, not Nominated, to pay—
    Sons of Laymen, £65 per annum.
    Sons of Clergymen, £55 "

Pupils, Nominated by Life Governors or Donors, to pay—
    Sons of Laymen, £55 per annum.
    Sons of Clergymen, £45 "

The Dormitories will be so arranged that each Pupil will have a separate compartment.

The School will be opened in August next.

All communications are to be addressed to the Honorary Secretaries.

REV. LEWIS DEEDES, Bramfield Rectory, Hertford............... } Honorary
E. D. BOURDILLON, ESQ., Amwell, Ware .... } Secretaries.

Chapter 1 — ON THE ORIGIN OF HAILEYBURY

Right: *The high divisions between compartments of the long dormitories that Butler developed out of the EIC bedsitters. The photograph dates from before 1908, when the divisions were lowered on medical advice.*

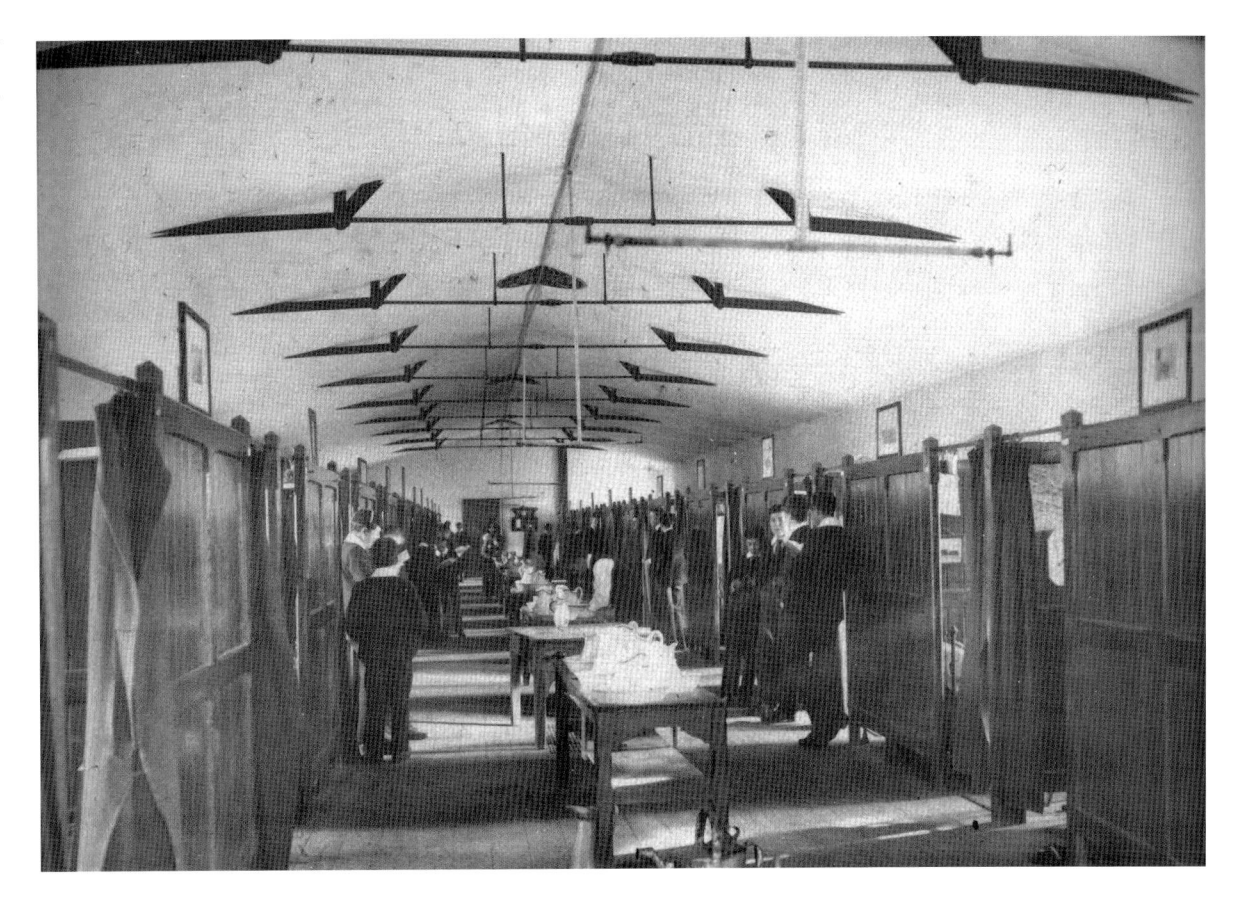

MASTERS ON MASTERS:
The Reverend Dr E.H. Bradby

Dr Bradby's portrait in the Dining Hall shows a balding but heavily bearded man set against a brocade background and massively black-gowned: a fine portrait, but at first glance a rather forbidding representation of Haileybury's second Master. Let us look a little closer to see whether the picture reveals the man and, indeed, the Master.

Edward Henry Bradby (1868.1–83.3) was the son of a Captain Edward Bradby, who died in India before his son was born. Having been a day boy at St Paul's, he was moved to Dr Arnold's Rugby in August 1839 at the age of 11; an only son, and 'rather delicate'. Early letters to his mother are not entirely reassuring: *Put in a study with a boy named Smith who, though he does not work himself, will allow me to do so. I do not wish to make friends with him as I think him very idle … besides which he is accustomed to swear*'; 'The thing I most dislike here is the dinner, when the housekeeper gives you literally lumps of pudding and dabs of fat'; 'I rejoice in the name of 'Swottie' which [he writes, with touching innocence] *means 'hard worker'*. However, Rugby enabled him to gain a scholarship to Balliol and he duly took a First in Classics, one of only two awarded. He became a Fellow and Tutor of the University of Durham and Principal of Hatfield Hall; his honorary DD was granted by Durham when Bradby was Master of Haileybury. From 1858, as an interesting reflection on the significance of major schools in those days, he moved to teach at Harrow, where he became a Housemaster.

A special paper in the School Archives records the voting of Council when it came to appoint the School's second Master at Christmas 1867 on the resignation of Arthur Butler: first the shortlisting, in which Bradby came third of four; then the first vote after the interviews when he came second; and then the final vote, which Bradby 'won' by eight to six against a very highly regarded fellow Harrow master. Very tense, but the Council made a good choice.

The headmaster of an almost new school has a fascinating task: he must consolidate but he must also build. On his election to the Mastership, Bradby reflected to his predecessor: 'I see my place is to be

HAILEYBURY ~ *A 150th Anniversary Portrait*

everywhere and to do everything – I'll do my best.' Butler was to praise Dr Bradby after his death for his *strength, dignity, generosity, wise insight, and transparent honesty ... In a young school, a headmaster has (or thinks he has) to do much which, in an old school, is better diffused and delegated to others. He has to watch over beginnings, to direct movements, and to create traditions.*

One of the more daunting traditions created by Bradby was his composition of the 13 Latin verses of *Carmen Haileyburiense*, but no doubt the School took them in its stride in those days. He founded a Literary Society, a Natural Science Society, an Antiquarian Society and the Agra Mission; the *Haileyburian* first appeared in 1868, and the first Haileybury entry in the Public Schools Rackets Competition was in 1869. A number of new buildings such as the first version of Big School and the Houses of Batten, Le Bas and Melvill were established to cope with increasing numbers. And, of course, he created the new Chapel and dome. It is appropriate that his memorial is a building given his name (though originally referred to, unglamorously, as 'Bradbonesan') for the display of art and as a kind of museum. Reginald Blomfield (E 1869.2), architect of the Bradby Hall, wrote: *Even we boys could see, beneath his grim but kindly humour, a keen appreciation of courage, hardihood, and endurance – qualities which were always the tradition of Haileybury and which no man did more to create and develop than our great Head Master. The more one knew of Dr Bradby, the more one respected and loved him. He was a man of singular indifference to popularity and current reputation.*

It was particular qualities in Bradby which seemed to enable the School to move forward so positively, developing already solid initial foundations. In later tributes one reads again and again of his 'genius' for organisation, his 'absolute justice', his 'real kindness', his 'simplicity of life' and 'devotion to duty', and his fine teaching. His success as Master was *effected solely by quiet steady work of the most genuine and thorough character, without the least attempt to arrive at prominence or notoriety or any short cut ... Dr Bradby was not one of those who worship rapid results, and he had a perfect horror of the system of puff and self-advertisement. At the time some of us used to think he kept both himself and the School too much in the background; but we can see now not only that his course was the wisest policy, but that it was part and parcel of the noble and Christian ideal of a really great man.* How infinitely refreshing.

Left: *Reverend E.H. Bradby, Master 1868–83, by Sir Herbert von Herkomer RA.*

Below: *The ballot paper showing the results of the election of Edward Bradby as Master in 1868.*

Of course, all was not always plain sailing. Dr Bradby had parents to deal with, too. In May 1873 he sent a letter to parents (fathers only in those days): *There is a growing evil here ... It is this: many parents send their sons back to school laden with provisions, and despatch a further copious supply once, or even twice, a term. Cake and ham are becoming, not the rare ornament, but the standing dish for the schoolboy's table. This conduces to luxury, expensive habits, inordinate love of eating, and, in some cases, disease.* And, of course, there followed a defence of School food. But in April 1876, there was a plaintive reference to this message: 'Many parents may not have seen it, and some, if I may say so, must have forgotten it.' There was another letter to parents, in 1870, in which Bradby announced that exeats would be discontinued except for new boys in the first two terms and that holiday tasks would no longer be set. 'They vex far more than they instruct,' he said with perceptive realism, 'and they cannot really be enforced.' Nonetheless, there is a strong hint that younger boys may 'safely be employed on French

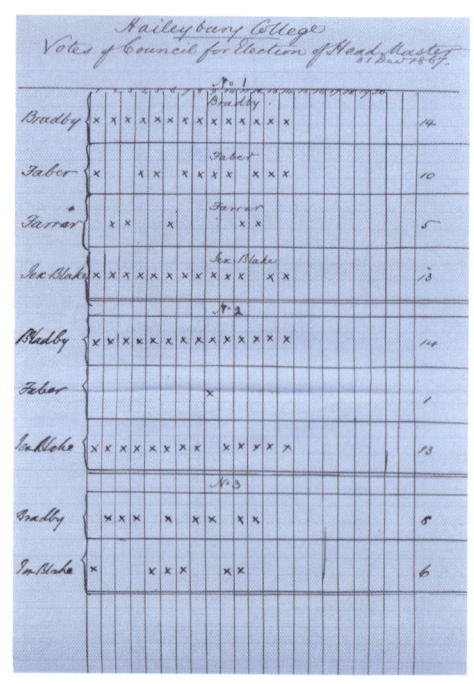

26

Chapter 1 — ON THE ORIGIN OF HAILEYBURY

Above: The building of the Chapel, designed by Arthur Blomfield, c.1877.

Grammar, Modern History, and Geography' – just for fun, of course.

And I like, and admire, Bradby's report to Council in 1873: *There is little of special moment on which to report to you of the past year: but it is with School life as it is with that of individuals; uneventful years may often be the happiest and the most prosperous.* What masterful economy! He was wise enough to comment elsewhere: 'A good staff of masters ... They are the soul of the place.' He kept a Master's Book at Haileybury; meticulous, hand-written notes which appear to be a record of exams and tests which he set to different classes to keep an eye on their quality and progress. The last entry of all ends: *Has the study of the errors of Alcibiades made them prematurely sad and cautious? If so, they attend more to the matter of their work than most boys can be induced to do. Anyhow their answers seemed to die upon their tongues very often as though they feared to commit themselves. They should be encouraged to speak up cheerily and freely, though of course respectfully. The two things are not incompatible.'*

Bradby resigned the Mastership at Christmas 1883. He felt that a younger man with fresh ideas would benefit the School and he was aware that the strain for Mrs Bradby was considerable. He went to live in the East End of London, amongst the poor and working for them. He died on 1 December 1893, aged nearly 67. By all accounts his sermons at Haileybury were quiet and simple, as if thinking aloud (and undoubtedly very long in those days when time seemed to stretch out more comfortably). He preached on the death of a teacher to a text from *Psalm 37*: *Keep innocency, and take heed unto the thing that is right; for that shall bring a man peace at the last.* His own last words were: *Do not think I have the slightest fear of death; I have an absolute trust in the goodness of God.*

David Summerscale (Master 1976.1–86.1)

USC AND ISC

United Services College was founded in 1874 by a group of army officers, headed by General Sir Charles Daubeney with the approval of Field Marshal HRH The Duke of Cambridge. The first Headmaster was Cormell Price, known by the pupils as 'Bates', who had come from Haileybury, and 12 of the first boys were Haileyburians. Situated in Westward Ho!, in Devon, the USC, or 'Coll' as it was more affectionately known, was extremely remote and the facilities that the School offered were very basic.

The USC had been founded in response to a growing discontent amongst officers in the Services about the lack of affordable public schools for their children. Great Victorian foundations such as Marlborough, Cheltenham, Wellington and Haileybury were by then concentrating on providing an education for pupils to enter Oxford and Cambridge, rather than preparing their charges for the military. Wellington came in for particular attack by the *habitués* of the London military clubs. After having been endowed with £250,000 through public subscription to help educate military families,

HAILEYBURY ~ *A 150th Anniversary Portrait*

My family's story embodies the history of the three schools which formed the modern Haileybury: My father, W.G.H. Vickers (later Lieutenant-General, CB, OBE) had the distinction of being the School Captian of USC, Windsor in 1907. The photo right shows him commanding a Guard of Honour, which the College provided for the Kaiser in 1907. He later became a Governor and Council member of Haileybury and ISC and President of the Haileybury Society. Subsequently, my brother, P.J.H. Vickers (D House and Kipling) was the senior ISC boy to move from Windsor to Haileybury on amalgamation as Head of Kipling House. Three of his sons (Andrew, Jeremy and Robin) also went to Kipling. I was Head Boy of the Junior School at the time of the amalgamation, and followed the family tradition to become Head of Kipling and the School at Haileybury. Like my father, I later became a Governor and Council member and President of the Haileybury Society.

Richard Vickers (K 1942.3)

Wellington disappointed many military families by treating preparation for the military academies as of secondary importance, and because of the scale of the fees. Cormell Price believed that the USC existed to provide 'a public school education of the highest class, at as low cost as might be compatible with efficiency, and of the kind especially needed by them'.

The School was made up of a row of houses adapted to the needs of an educational establishment, and the boys were separated into four Houses, known by their Housemasters' names. While the most famous old boy was Rudyard Kipling (USC 1878.1), the USC produced an especially distinguished number of army officers, including Major General Sir Hubert Hamilton (USC 1875.3), who was killed commanding a division in the First World War, and Lieutenant Colonel Gerald Hill (USC 1898.2), who, as well as winning the DSO and two bars, represented Ireland in tennis and running. Sadly, by 1903 the USC was in a terrible financial situation caused by poor administration, competition by reformed public schools such as Wellington, and its remote position. The USC was a proprietary school and funds had vanished, making it impossible to settle the debts accrued each term. The School's shareholders wished to wind it up, but the recently formed Imperial Service College Trust, under the chairmanship of Lord Chelmsford, was determined to secure the School's future. In 1904 the USC left Westward Ho! and took over the buildings of St George's School at Harpenden, but money continued to be an issue. There were only 38 pupils at Harpenden and the School moved again to share the buildings of the Military College, Onslow Hall, at Richmond, during the summer term of 1906. In autumn of that year the USC made its final move, settling into a merger with St Mark's School at Windsor (then having only 60 pupils) under the Reverend C.N. Nagel (Headmaster 1906.3–10.1). Over the next five years pupil numbers increased slowly, with money continually pumped into the School by the Imperial Service College Trust, and in 1910 it was mooted that the USC change its name.

On 21 November 1911 a meeting of the Board of Governors decided to change the name of the 'Old Coll' to that of the Imperial Service College, under the headship of E.G.A. Beckwith (Headmaster 1912.1–35.1), formerly Headmaster of the Army School, which he merged with the ISC.

In the second half of 1941 private conversations took place between Lord Aldenham and H.E. Seebohm, members of the Haileybury Council, and two governors from the Imperial Services College. The ISC authorities were keen to join their School with Haileybury, which would prevent their numbers dropping to levels which would force the School's closure. For the previous two years the Headmasters' Conference had circulated a series of papers on the national fall in public school numbers and possible amalgamation. Canon Edward Bonhote (Master 1934.2–48.2) made no response to the suggestions for amalgamation but informed Council that it might be necessary later. In 1940 Haileybury's

Right: *Rudyard Kipling, aged 16, taken at Bideford on 23 May 1882 before leaving to take up a post as a cub reporter for the* Civil and Military Gazette *in Lahore in October.*

Below right: *Dunsterville, the real Stalky of Rudyard Kipling's* Stalky and Co. *(USC 1876.1). Major General Lionel Charles Dunsterville served on the North-West Frontier, in China and, during the First World War, in France and Flanders before forming Dunsterforce, an elite Allied task force which he commanded in Persia from 1917 and which was tasked with training local forces, countering German propaganda and defending the Baku oilfields from the advancing Turks. In 1927 he became the first President of the Kipling Society.*

numbers had dropped by 140 boys and there was a significant mortgage to be serviced on top of the usual running costs, making the future prospects of the School look bleak.

There was unanimous approval from the Haileybury Council for the amalgamation with the ISC on 9 January 1942. It would bring an endowment worth £2,000 a year, a prep school and enough pupils to make up for the fall in numbers since the outbreak of the war. There was, however, one major impediment to the amalgamation: the Ministry of Health's emergency hospital at Haileybury, which had requisitioned the Sick House, Melvill, Batten and Le Bas, meaning that there was no room for the ISC pupils. After careful negotiations with the Ministry, led by H.E. Seebohm, an agreement was struck, recovering Le Bas and Batten for the School. The name Haileybury and Imperial Service College was agreed without any issue, a supplemental Royal Charter was applied for and Canon Bonhote decided on May as the month for the 'fusion'. On 25 July 1942, two months after the event, Bonhote reported to Council that the 'amalgamation has proved a most happy experiment, and that the organisation has worked very smoothly', but he also recorded the tragic death of an ISC boy, David Beatty (ISC 'B' and K 1939.3), who fell from the Kipling window and died from his injuries on 31 May 1942.

ATMP

THE KIPLING CONNECTION

The connections between Rudyard Kipling and Haileybury have often been called 'distant', 'non-existent' and 'tenuous', but these denials ignore the fact that Haileybury amalgamated with the Imperial Service College, which was the United Services College renamed. In Kipling's short story *An English School*, he wrote about his old school, the USC, and asserted that the 'School considered itself the finest in the world excepting perhaps Haileybury'. The connection was centred on Cormell Price, the former Head of the Modern Side at Haileybury, a man whom Kipling treated as a second father.

Kipling's education at the USC was based on Haileybury's Modern Side and many of the School's traditions, such as Pastimes, came from Price's previous school. Kipling himself took a part in the 1881 Pastimes production of Sheridan's *The Rivals* and he wore the Colvin House colours on his House cap (Crofts'). Kipling had a huge affection for 'Coll' and he continued to support the school even after it became known as the ISC. When Kipling died in 1936, his widow presented to the ISC the manuscript of *Stalky and Co*. That manuscript transferred to the newly amalgamated Haileybury and Imperial Service College, where it resides today.

In 1942, when Haileybury and ISC came together, 68 years after Cormell Price took 12 Haileyburians to the 'Coll', 120 pupils made the journey back to start a new educational chapter.

ATMP

CORMELL PRICE

'Crom' Price was perhaps one of the most important and dynamic masters who ever taught at Haileybury. He was the first Housemaster of Colvin, bestowing on it the yellow and black colours of his old college, Brasenose. Price was the founder and innovator of the Modern Side at Haileybury, and the first Headmaster of the United Services College (USC) in 1874, but his fame stemmed from his role of mentor, friend and headmaster to Rudyard Kipling.

Cormell Price was born in Birmingham into a family of industrialists and educated at King Edward VI's School. While there he made friends with Edward Burne-Jones and Henry MacDonald, whose four sisters went on to marry Lockwood Kipling, Edward Poynter, Edward Burne-Jones and Alfred Baldwin. When Price went up to Oxford, Burne-Jones went with him and he soon became a close friend of the group which became known as the Pre-Raphaelites. Price became a good friend to William Morris and helped him, with others, to paint the ceiling of the Oxford Union.

Price had wanted to become a doctor but after witnessing dissections he realised that he did not have the stomach for the profession. Medicine was then replaced by education and he became a tutor for a princely family, the Davidoffs, in Russia. The Russian experience greatly affected him and the poverty and massive inequality of the empire strengthened his already liberal political stance.

In 1862, shortly after the School opened, Arthur Butler identified Price as the man to set up the Modern Side and offer a wider educational experience at Haileybury. Butler was proved right in his assessment of Price and they became lifelong friends. As Head of the Modern Side and Housemaster of Colvin, Price supported his pupils with a level of care and devotion that few Haileyburians ever forgot. His innovations on the Modern Side allowed boys to pass directly into Woolwich and Sandhurst, instead of spending vast sums of parental money supporting them through military crammers. The huge amount of correspondence from old pupils that Crom Price

Left: *Cormell Price, first Housemaster of Colvin, Head of the Modern Side and founding Headmaster of the United Services College at Westward Ho!.*

Left: *The USC at Westward Ho!.*

Chapter 1 — ON THE ORIGIN OF HAILEYBURY

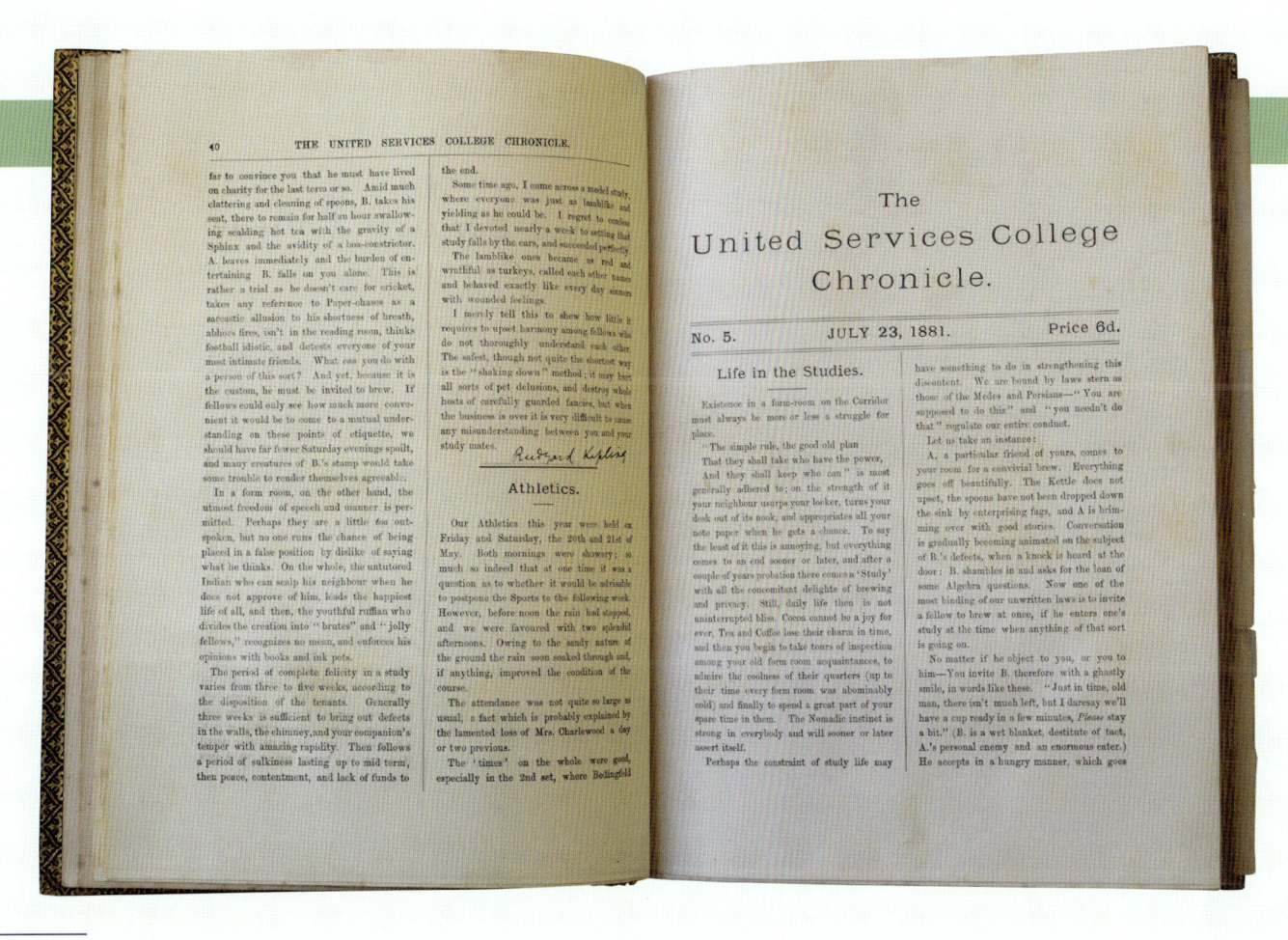

Above: *Rudyard Kipling's own copy of the* USC Chronicle.

kept up with was a testament to their love for him, and vice versa. It is strange to think that Crom Price, educator of hundreds of doughty defenders of the Empire, slipped away from the spartan regime of Haileybury to enjoy boat parties with William Morris, helping to sober up Algernon Swinburn after a bender, and coming across a 'red-haired stunner' in his railway carriage. Price was certainly not a dusty 'Mr Chips' figure.

In 1874 Price was offered a headmastership, something he did not expect, not having been ordained. The appointment was to set up the United Services College at Westward Ho! and he took with him 12 boys from Haileybury. His new school did not have a Classical Side and it offered a different style of education compared with the public schools at that time. The young Rudyard Kipling was put into Price's care in 1878 and so began a relationship that was to last until Price's death. It was Koji, as Kipling's family called Price, who set Rudyard on his career path as a journalist and writer. Price made Kipling editor of the *USC Chronicle* between 1881 and 1882 and allowed him to go to Bideford to learn how to set type with the printers.

The first 15 of the 20 years that Price was Headmaster of the USC were exciting and successful; the school became justly famous for turning difficult young men into pillars of the empire. However, it was the educational success that he enjoyed that was ultimately to be the cause of his school's decline. Other public schools such as Haileybury and Wellington looked at Price's approach to preparing boys for the Army and copied his ideas. The restructuring of the Haileybury Modern Side and similar changes in other public schools meant that parents were able to send their children to mainstream institutions again rather than to remote Westward Ho!. By 1890 Price was left with falling pupil numbers and too many debts to settle and in 1894 he retired, his health damaged and in terrible financial straits. He died 16 years later, still beloved by his boys, feted for his connections with the Pre-Raphaelites and remembered by both Haileybury and USC as a great schoolmaster.

ATMP

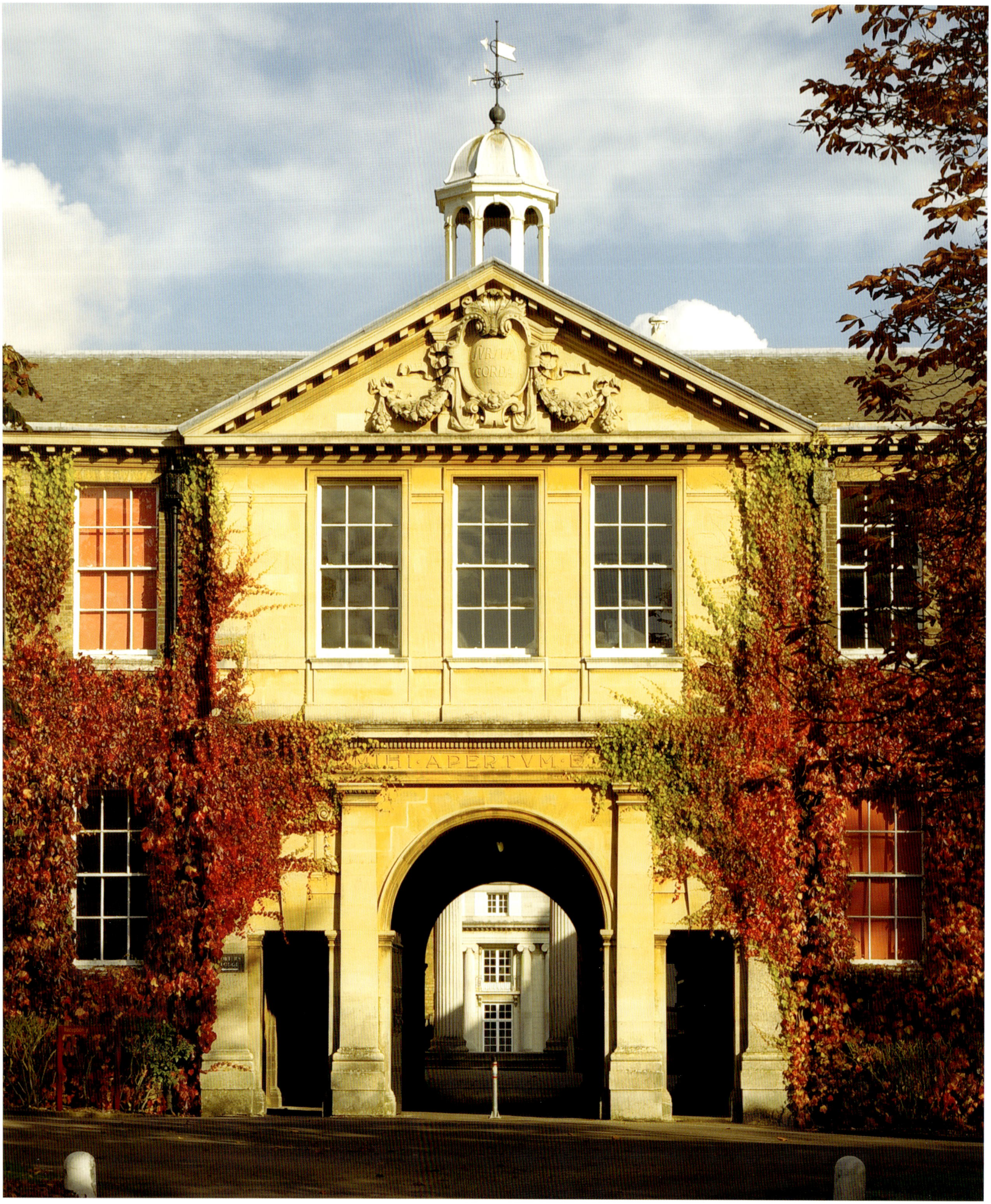

Chapter 2

THE ESTATE

Opposite: *The Form Room Block, 1908, by Maxwell Ayrton and John Simpson with its inscription from Corinthians 16:8: Ostium mihi apertum est magnum (There is a real opportunity here for great and important work).*

Below: Hailey House *by E.J. Burrow. The original estate, Hailey Bury, was bought at auction in 1805 by the East India Company as the site on which to build their new college.*

THE HAILEYBURY ESTATE

The Haileybury estate lies between two thoroughfares of major historical importance. Less than a mile to the west runs the old Roman road, Ermine Street, which connected London to York and along which, in 1066, King Harold's army marched north to defeat the Danes at Stamford Bridge, returning rapidly to face defeat by the Normans at Hastings. Drop eastwards down Hailey Lane and you are in the Lea Valley, near the confluence of the rivers Ash, Stort and Lea, which was the site of King Alfred's defeat of the Danes in 895AD, and the river that for centuries was a major artery for agricultural produce bound for London.

The estate, as it now exists, is the culmination of a long series of sales and acquisitions over many centuries, full details of which are given in the late Molly Matthews' book *Haileybury since Roman Times* (1959, revised 2000). The hamlet of Hailey appears in the Domesday Book of 1086 as land owned by Geoffrey de Bec and reckoned of very little value (£1 10s), probably due to the damage caused by the Norman army, and with a population of about 50. The focus of Hailey was then Hailey Hall, at the bottom of Hailey Lane, and the lane itself was a track leading up to the heath where domestic animals would have been grazed. Going up Hailey Lane on the right was a large meadow, Hailey Bushes, which has become the site of the College. 1560 is the earliest reference to buildings at Hailey Bushes, but the site of the oldest part of the College – that is, the Housemistress's side of Hailey House – was not built on until the late 1690s. The elegant building that we now see dates from around 1720, although much has changed, including Matthew Wyatt's monstrous addition of the pupils' accommodation on the west side, which occurred in 1865.

Hailey Bushes, as the house was known, passed through a series of owners, mostly associated with the Dimsdale family, until by 1786 it was in the hands of a Dr William Walker, who had served with the East India Company. By this time the name had been changed to Haileybury or Hailey Bury, it being a more distinguished sounding name. The term 'bury' was used locally to denote the principal house in a village. Dr Walker added to the 30 acres of the original purchase by acquiring Brambles Grove, where the tennis courts are now, on the south side of Hailey Lane, and Quitchells, which Haileyburians know as XX Acre. XX Acre, a pasture since the 14th century, was owned in the mid-17th century by a local Quaker brewer by the name of Henry Stout, who grew barley on it, and it is almost certain that the term 'stout' in relation to brewing can be traced back to this time and place.

On 23 October 1805, 'Hailey Bury House near Hertford' was sold by auction at Garraway's coffee house in London to the Directors of the East India Company for the site of their proposed college. The price was £5,900. Apart from the construction of the buildings under Wilkins' direction and landscaping under Humphrey Repton's, Hailey Lane itself was moved southwards, creating more space in front of the 'neo-classical' frontage and the familiar sharp bend in the road by what is now called the White Gate entrance. The total cost of the building and landscaping was a little short of £60,000.

Above: *Plaque still attached to the Quitchell's Oak, once a parish boundary marker.*

Left: *The Dumb-bell Oak at the south end of Terrace.*

Below: *Lightning Oak, which was struck by lightning in 1898.*

During the 50 years that the East India College existed, the estate was not extended. By contrast, from the foundation of the School in 1862 there was steady acquisition of land and buildings. Included in the many purchases were the two woods to the north of XX Acre, Goldingtons and Quitchells (the two

Chapter 2 — THE ESTATE

Right: *The Grounds' and Gardens' staff, 2012.*

Below right: *The dormouse, which has been the subject of a conservation project in Hailey Wood in collaboration with Herts and Middlesex Wildlife Trust since 1973. Like jackdaws, dormice were once a common pet amongst pupils at Haileybury.*

being known as Goldings,) and to the south Hailey Wood, and Dell's Wood on the far side of Hailey Lane. The woods are interesting because of the mix of tree species and the management methods used in the past. One notable feature is the dominance of over-mature coppiced hornbeam throughout much of Goldings. Hornbeam is a characteristically hot burning wood and would probably have provided fuel for much of the local community, as well as fence posts. In recent years work has been carried out to diversify the habitats by opening up rides and restoring ponds.

The formal gardens contain a wide variety of native and non-native species. Of the former, four oak trees are worthy of special mention. The iconic Lightning Oak, still vigorous after being struck in 1898, the Quitchells Oak, located on the corner of College Road opposite Batten House, which was of sufficient size to be a parish boundary marker in 1634, the unusually shaped Dumb-bell Oak at the southern end of the Terrace Field, and the relatively young Attlee Oak between Pavilion and the Armoury. The arboretum below the Master's Garden contains many commemorative plantings of fine specimens of unusual trees. Elsewhere there are ginkgos on Pavilion, a deciduous redwood in Trevelyan Garden, the Avenue flanked by horse chestnuts and a drive of flowering cherries from the main gates to the new Bartle Frere. An enormous amount of effort goes into the management of the estate, with at least one eye on the environment for future Haileyburians.

Three editions of the *Fauna and Flora of Haileybury* have been published and another is long overdue as a project for a resurrected Natural History Society. The estate has also been the site of a number of conservation projects, most notable perhaps being attempts to reintroduce the once common dormouse to Hailey Wood.

There can be no doubt that Haileybury is blessed to be situated in such a spectacular setting – a veritable oasis amidst nearby urban sprawl.

Roger Woodburn (PRW) (Staff 1978.3–)

PINDARS

> BY Commander James Wallace Maulden, Officer of the Most Excellent Order of the British Empire, Royal Navy, Bursar and Secretary to the Governors of Haileybury and Imperial Service College, Hertford
> TO Francis William Manning, Esquire, Allenby House, Hertford Heath   BY VIRTUE OF the powers vested in me by the Governors of Haileybury and Imperial Service College as Lords of the Manor of Great Amwell and Goldingtons
> I HEREBY LICENSE you to graze two horses on the Wastes of the Manor of Great Amwell and Goldingtons for a period of twelve calendar months from 1st April 1959
> SUBJECT TO payment at my Office between the hours of 9.0 a.m. and 5.0 p.m. within fourteen days of receipt by you of this licence of the sum of One Shilling.
>
> THIS LICENCE is subject to revocation at any time at the pleasure of the Lords of the Manor. If this should occur a proportional part of the payment made by you will be refunded.
>
> GIVEN UNDER MY HAND this Ninth day of April in the Year One thousand nine hundred and fifty nine

The office of the pindar, also known as the pounder, was one of the stranger jobs at Haileybury. After the School had purchased the manorial rights of Great Amwell in 1901, it became responsible for common land that surrounded the School's estate. The appointment of a pindar was vital if the common land was not to be taken advantage of. A pindar's job was to make sure only people with a licence grazed their animals on it. Other duties were to look after all the cattle and horses turned out on the heath and to protect the turf, minerals, gravel and timber, as well as generally to defend the rights of the lord of the manor.

In 1901 the pindar was paid £2 2s, while in the 1930s he was paid £20 for his troubles, but the job was not an easy one. Animals that strayed onto the manorial waste were impounded by the pindar and he had to fine the owner, which naturally did not go down well with certain villagers. There were, in fact, only eight commoners in the village with rights to graze animals in 1908, but as late as 1959 the Bursar was still issuing licences for grazing.

ATMP

AN ARCHITECTURAL MISCELLANY: BUILDINGS ADDED SINCE 1862

The Master Bill Stewart (1963.3–75.1), brought the mercurial Jack Hindmarsh (Staff 1966.3–89.2) to Haileybury as Director of Music in 1966, but it was not until 1979 that the purpose-built Music School was opened. Connecting the new building to Bradby on the second floor necessitated removing one section of the monumental relief of Latin verse composed by the Master, James Robertson (1884.1–90.1): *GRATA FAVENTIBUS / ALMA COLENTIBUS / HAEC PIA SEDES / NON SINE NOMINE / GAUDEAT OMINE / PALLADIS AEDES / DIGNA PRIORIBUS / EXSTET HONORIBUS / INCLUTA PLENIS / CONSCIA NUMINIS / HOSPITA LUMINIS / APTA CAMENIS* (Pleasing to those who please you, beloved by those who love you, hallowed hall, not without name, take pleasure in the prospect of becoming the shrine of Wisdom, worthy of your predecessors, excel in esteem by your numerous distinctions, partners of inspiration, home of illumination, fit for the Muses.) Fortunately, the section removed – *APTA CAMENIS* (fit for the Muses) – can stand alone and still make some sense.

The old Sanatorium, now Alban's girls' House, was opened in 1867, and the 'new Houses' (Batten, Le Bas and Melvill) in 1878. The Bradby was the next major

Left: *A grazing licence for the common land of the manor of Great Amwell.*

Below: *The Music School Relief, after it was relocated in 1979 to make room for the connecting bridge between the new music building and the Bradby. Known as the 'Bursar's pissoir', it is flanked by the Director of Music, Jack Hindmarsh and Roger Bass.*

Chapter 2 — THE ESTATE

Above: *Bradby Hall architectural drawings by Sir Reginald Blomfield, RA.*

Above right: Interior of Bradby, *etching by E.J. Burrow.*

building specifically designed to serve the School and not part of the EIC legacy. Soon after the great Dr Bradby retired after 15 years as Master, an appeal was launched for funds to raise a worthy reminder of him. The School's first Master, A.G. Butler, Dr Bradby and the building's architect Reginald Blomfield (E 1869.2) attended the formal opening of the new hall. *The Haileyburian* (June 1888) recorded the event, which coincided with the School's Silver Jubilee year and Queen Victoria's Golden Jubilee, which is commemorated in a further inscription over the principal doorway.

For nearly a year we have watched, with an interest and admiration which grew as the structure grew, the erection of the fine block of buildings on the south side of the Pavilion Field. Quite recently, the scaffolding which concealed some of their outline, and the line of workmen's sheds which hid their base, were rapidly removed, and the exterior of the Bradby Hall, with the science-rooms which support it, the Carpenters' Shop and the Gymnasium which flank it, stood clear to view. Seen from anywhere on the Pavilion or the Terrace Field, the rich red-brick walls, lightened by the white-framed windows and by the horizontal pale-brown band round which runs the inscription, and the lofty tiled roof, with gable and lantern complete, stand in harmonious contrast of colour with the fresh green turf below, and with the varied foliage of elm and lime and oak around and across the building.

The style of the main structure, sometimes described as Victorian Tudor or Jacobean – neither term does it justice – is eclectic; the building is like an overturned ark, with a smooth hull, and full of strange effects, not least of which is the inscription. Art Master Wilfrid Blunt (Staff 1923.3–38.1), who worked in it and inveighed against the lack of light inside, described the Bradby Hall as 'a white elephant'.

37

HAILEYBURY ~ A 150th Anniversary Portrait

However, with modern electric lighting, the interior is a gem – as a concert hall – but let's not get ahead of ourselves here. The first historian of the School, L.S. Milford (L 1867.2, Staff 1879.3–1919.1), writing about 20 years after the opening of Bradby, observed: *Every week the School societies meet there; concerts and lectures for which the Big School is too large are held there from time to time. For any receptions at School functions, or teas on match days in winter or wet weather it is invaluable, for it is at once spacious, comfortable, and good to look at.* Milford goes on to describe some of the art works deposited in the Bradby: *Mr Robertson gave casts of five slabs of the frieze of the Parthenon ... Upstairs there are bronze statuettes and vases; exact replicas of originals at Naples; a very fine series of permanent photographs of Old Masters in eight cleverly designed showcases, and in the opposite gallery similar frames for sculpture and architectural photographs.*

Where has it all gone? And when did it go?

In 1965 art teaching moved to the new Art School, formally opened by Earl Attlee (L 1896.2), allowing the whole of the upper level of the Bradby to be used for music, and in 1979 the new music 'teaching and practice block' was formally opened by John Manduell (BF 1942.1), Principal of the Royal Northern College of Music, following a 'spirited and vital' orchestral and choral performance of Vivaldi's *Gloria* in the Bradby, directed by Jack Hindmarsh. Of the new Music School, Graham Rogers (Staff 1976.1–85.1) affectionately wrote in *The Haileyburian* (March 1980): *Mother Bradby's offspring is deceptively small and most are surprised at the wealth of facilities it contains. The five teaching-rooms are more than adequate in size and the 18 practice-rooms are acoustically excellent, light and fresh, and not at all like the 'prison cells' one has often seen in similar establishments. That they are used is testimony enough. Even now, from the almost too warm staff-room a distant trombone can be heard, and somewhere a violin plays: a singer dabbles in uncertain chromatics and moves on somewhat thankfully to Mozart. And from the window, double-glazed and sun-dimmed, the Fifteen can be seen practising on Terrace in the autumn sunshine.*

The opening of the new building freed the old Music School at the bottom of the Avenue to be converted into bedsitters for Oxbridge candidates (1981), and subsequently into somewhat eccentric staff accommodation.

Wilfrid Blunt had not been back to visit Haileybury since before the Art School was built, an admission by him that prompted the Haileybury Librarian to invite him over. On the occasion of his visit in 1982, Blunt described the Art School as 'architecturally the most exciting thing that has happened at Haileybury since the Second World War'. That may sound like high praise from the author of *The Buildings of Haileybury*

Above: William Denny (Staff 1966.3–70.2) instructing a pupil in throwing in the Art School, opened in 1965.

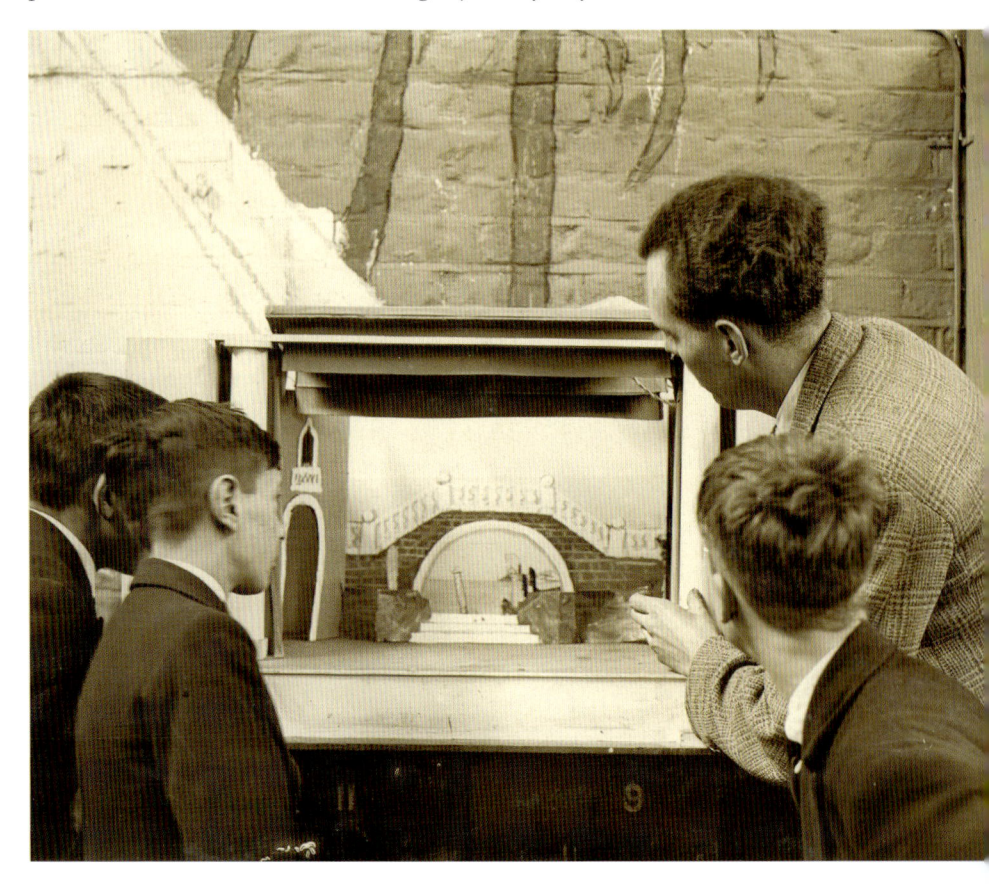

Opposite: *Wilfrid Blunt in the old Art School working on the design of a set for a production of The Gondoliers, the Pastimes performance for 1931 in which Blunt played Luiz. He served as Art Master from 1923–38 and after teaching at Eton went on to be Curator of the Watts Gallery, Surrey.*

– and indeed it was intended as such – but for the 20 years between the war and the construction of the Art School, there were few architectural alterations to the School, aside from the removal of the Lawrence arch, the unblocking of the loggia adjacent to the Master's Lodge, and the demolition of the White City, a lavatory complex, due south of Big School, virtually indescribable to anyone who had no first-hand experience of it. (Of course, the elimination of the White City could not be achieved without the addition of lavatory facilities to the boarding Houses, and these annexes, which still survive, especially the KBM Annexe, are among the ugliest blots on the Haileybury architectural landscape.)

Bob Butler, Head of Art (Staff 1957.3–85.2), described the new Art School in loving detail in *The Haileyburian* (October 1965). The architects were L.A. Porri, who served as Haileybury's architects for 20 years, and Dr Foyle, Professor of Architecture at the University of London. But it was Bob Butler, with the warm support of Master Bill Stewart (1963.3–75.1), who was responsible for the striking beauty (and no doubt expense) of the materials used. *They have made the most of the semi-isolated position and their design is excitingly modern and yet fits happily into the surroundings. A very dark brick has been used and it contrasts well with the natural concrete on the first storey; on the ground floor the concrete has been covered with a dark granite facing. The window units are white.*

Butler's description is too detailed to quote here in full, but it attests to the loving care with which this fine building was designed and executed. One further brief extract: *Between the pottery and the form-rooms is the entrance hall with stairs to the art studio at the north end. These are wide and flooded with light from the tall windows. A showcase for the pottery exhibitions is set in the Columbian pine-panelling at the turn of the stairs half-way up. Both the floor of the hall and the stairs is of grey Terrazzo tiling.*

For the first few years of the new building half of the ground floor was occupied by English or history teachers, but ceramics took over the whole ground floor shortly after the arrival of the inspirational Martin Hughes (Staff 1974.3–84.3). Under Bob Butler's successor as Head of Art, John Higgins (Staff 1985.3–98.2), especially with the addition of a popular and academically successful art history course, the Art Department burst its bounds and had to accommodate the overflow in a temporary classroom behind the main building. *Ars longa, vita brevis* springs to mind – and in a sense the *ars* in the quotation from Hippocrates, referring to *techne* or method, is almost appropriate to today's world, as anyone who visits the annual art exhibition at Haileybury can aver.

With the completion of construction of the sports hall in 1986, the old Gymnasium, part of the Bradby complex, became redundant and in 1987–8 was converted into an intimate and versatile theatre, with excellent acoustics. It was the the brainchild of Haileybury's doyen of drama (chairman of the Entertainments Committee), Jack Thomas (Staff 1954.2–88.2), and opened by – and named for – Alan Ayckbourn (Tr 1952.3).

By 1990 it was increasingly apparent that 47-bed dormitories, whatever their strengths, were not the way ahead with 'modern' parents looking for decent boarding facilities for their children. The first step in solving the problem required two Houses to leave Quad and relocate in what by Haileybury standards were radically different facilities, where all aspects of a House's life were under one roof. Bartle Frere and Edmonstone moved into their current accommodation in January 1994. The building had been designed by Andrzej Kuszell and incorporated in part some of the Whatton Studies (1979). The same design team produced the imaginative new buildings for Colvin (1999) and Melvill (2001), which were integral to the School's switch to full co-education, as well as the award-winning Swimming Pool (1997) and Technology Centre (1999).

David Wright (Staff 1973.3–2006.2)

THE AYCKBOURN THEATRE

BEHIND THE GREEN BAIZE DOOR

I cannot pretend it was all glorious. Living above the shop created a hectic environment, which inevitably affected daily family life, with my father, David Hunt (Staff 1974.3–94.3), ensconced in his housemasterly duties as well as general teaching duties, and a timetable to rival any top-level businessman. There seemed a constant flow of comings and goings through the Trevelyan green baize door – from duty prefects, boys wanting to see 'Sir', homesick 'New Guvs' whom mum would normally attend to, punishment duties being served in our garden, anxious parents invited in to see the Housemaster on urgent matters. So my sanctuary was my bedroom, the old Victorian maid's room half-way up our elegant staircase, in striking distance of the daily rituals of school lessons and Chapel Bell, my panoramic view of the Quad and Chapel from my bedroom window allowing a beady-eye to be kept on proceedings. It was this closeness to daily Haileybury life that fuelled my ambition to one day become one of those many smart, tweed-jacketed boys – 'a New Guv' below that window of mine. Alas, prep-school boarding beckoned before this dream might become a reality.

Historically, it was an interesting time to be at the School, as the late 1970s and early 1980s saw a spate of new builds. I'll never forget arriving home from a day at School to witness the felling of an old oak and an orchard of apple and plum trees in what was then the Trevelyan vegetable garden – consisting too of a wealth of gooseberry and raspberry bushes and proud vegetable beds that had been lovingly nurtured over the years. It was to become the Whatton Studies, and it left a sour taste in my mouth. On the plus side, I was able to gather some of the builders' timber to create a tree house in Trevelyan garden.

And who could forget that wonderful Olympic-sized pool, which used to be a magnet for families and picnics during the long, hot summer holidays? Diving from those lofty boards into icy waters – the pool I learned to swim in – then lying down to warm oneself up on the slate-slabbed surround. Now, alas, it has been filled in and used as a car park – what a loss.

Chapel, too, struck me early on in school life as a vital part of the morning routine, the wealth of sermons to grab a boy's imagination, the lode and passionate delivery of such familiar hymns, anthems sublimely arranged for the choir (of which I was to become a keen member), and the majestic way these all seemed to resonate up into Arthur Blomfield's dome.

Sport was ever present through my five years – squash, rackets, cross-country and athletics gave me some really treasured memories and opportunities. There was plenty of encouragement in Kipling, too; our Housemaster even used the dormitory in winter for 100m hurdles training for Steve Hawkins (K 1980.3) who would go on to compete at the XIV Commonwealth Games in Aukland, New Zealand.

Justin Hunt (K 1982.1)

Above: View of Quad by Justin Hunt. One of a series commissioned for the School's 150th anniversary.

Below: Big School, opened in 1914, by architects Maxwell Ayrton and John Simpson.

Chapter 2 — THE ESTATE

THE MOUSEMAN OF KILBURN

There must be many in the School who have been intrigued by the small mice carved on all the furniture in the Dining Hall. They were the advertising inspiration of a Yorkshire furniture maker, Mr Robert Thompson, who claimed never to have advertised in his life. Born in Kilburn in 1876, the son of the village wheelwright, he devoted ten hard years to practice and study, especially of the 15th- and 16th-century woodwork in cathedrals, before receiving his first major commission to make a chair and table for the Head of Ampleforth. Working entirely in matured English oak, Thompson adopted the signature of the church mouse as a symbol of hard work in quiet places. He was commissioned to provide the furniture in the Dining Hall for its opening in 1932, and all the tables and benches feature a mouse and are in his trade-mark simple monastic style. Thompson's mouse has also made an appearance in Westminster Abbey and Workington Priory and cathedrals such as Peterborough and York.

Below: *Jack Howe, who was employed by the School from March 1865 to just before his death in 1883. He was almost blinded by a cricket ball in 1881.*

HAILEYBURY AND THE VILLAGE BOYS

Although I knew of Haileybury and had heard stories of it, I was nine or ten before I realised how much the village depended on the College and how many of its members worked there in the dormitories, the Dining Hall, the Laundry, the sports fields and the gardens.

I suppose one of the first things I remember was going through the Heath to watch the building of the Dining Hall, which was opened in 1932 by HRH The Duke of York. Many of the local housewives took in laundry from the College and I'm told that this was laid out to dry next to the pond on the green. My grandmother was not one of these good ladies, but she did a similar job for Christ's Hospital (The Blue Coat School) at Hertford, and I did see the wooden mangle, flat irons and stoves that she used.

I understand that quarter day (pay day) was an amusing sight and left the local inn-keepers rubbing their hands.

The 'dorm' men had many long-servers in their midst who would tell us amusing stories about what went on. The end of summer term was of particular interest to us as 'leavers' sold off bicycles, sports gear and even household items such as shoe polish, brushes, etc. to their 'man' who, in turn, passed them on to us to get some beer money (I still have a rather battered 'Roy Kilner' bat).

PORTERS

George Dorset, the last Porter of the East India College, became the first person to hold the post in the newly founded school. Dorset was the son of one of the waiters at the East India College. It has been alleged that Dorset coined the term 'New Guv'nor' after seeing small children swarm through the Great Gate rather than confident men in their late teens, but the claim is likely to be untrue. The second Master, Edward Bradby, went so far as to immortalise George Dorset in the *Carmen Haileyburiense* as the 'custos benignus', and when he eventually retired, his cottage in the village became a place of pilgrimage for early Haileyburians. Dorset was succeeded by Sergeant George 'William' Campbell, grandson of the first East India College Purveyor. Campbell, known to the pupils as 'The Sergeant', began the tradition of military men holding the post of Head Porter. One of the duties of the Porter was to attend floggings, a punishment that could be administered only by the Master; Stone, 'The Sergeant's' successor, famously attended the 'Ladysmith Incident' and was depicted in a cartoon by Cyril King (L 1895.1) standing behind Edward Lyttelton (Master, 1890.2–1905.2) with a bundle of canes arranged to look like a fasces, a ceremonial axe used by the Roman lictors as a symbol of their office – a visual pun on the slang 'to lick' meaning to beat. The fourth holder of the post was the immense Sergeant William Blyth of the 21st Lancers, who weighed more than 20 stone. Blyth was a powerful figure and clearly a man who could endear himself to the pupils as well as intimidate the staff. There exists a wonderful cartoon of Blyth, towering over five nervous members of staff who are humbly petitioning him to stop winking at the pupils when he enters the Form-Rooms. When Blyth lay dying in 1928, he begged Dr Lempriere to keep him in the sound of the College Clock, a true servant of Haileybury.

The Head Porter is still a military man, Donald Walsh, who served 12 years in the Royal Navy as a Leading Signalman. The Lodge may have moved to the other side of the Great Gate, but some of the original tasks that George Dorset performed 150 years ago remain the same: the Lists Bell pulled every Monday is the same bell that Dorset pulled to call the School to Chapel.

ATMP

Above: *Cartoon of Blyth, the fourth incumbent of the Head Porter's post.*

Far left: *Barry Osman, College Porter, ringing the Lists bell.*

Below left: *The Ladysmith Plaque by Cyril King who went on to become a professional artist and was a leading figure in the development of the 'Dazzle' camouflage for the Royal Navy.*

Right: *Bill Camp (centre), groundsman, with players during Haileybury Cricket Week in 1959.*

Below: *Bert Wensley, commentating. He came to Haileybury in 1937 as a professional coach after playing for Sussex from 1922–36. He retired in 1963.*

The first boys' club I remember in the village was organised by a Mr Atherton (ex Haileybury), who lived down the Roundings and put his garage at our disposal every Wednesday evening. In 1935 the village hall was completed thanks to the great efforts of many people both from the village and the College. Our club then moved into these new, plush surroundings. As youngsters we were fortunate enough to be able to enjoy the amenities of the College. Summer saw us practising in the nets, often under the expert guidance of Jim Seabrook (LeB 1913.2, Staff 1931.1–32.1 and 1933.2–58.2) and Bert Wensley. In those days boxing was popular – Haileybury, Dulwich, Bedford and Eton would participate in the Four Schools Tournament. Two cups, Shaw and Stafford, provided House competition. Here again we learned the ropes from Sergeant Major Copeland. I watched many inter-school cricket matches, but one of my greatest pleasures was the annual OH Week, when three two-day matches were played and I helped to run up scores on the scoreboard. I well remember a match in August 1936 when Test players Percy Fender and Freddie Brown played for A.T. Barber's XI.

Our summer Sunday afternoons saw us either hiding in the thicket holding long hazel sticks with which we would try to flick off the boaters worn by the pupils as they walked along the coke path through the Heath. Or we would meet a small group, by arrangement, down in the woods where we would sit listening to gramophone records and devouring tuck-shop goodies while the 'home side' puffed away at cigarettes which we had obtained from a machine outside the shop in Downfield Road, then known as The Street. Incidentally, the 'cigs' cost 2d for ten. Carolling and 'guying' were not forgotten. Well wrapped up and equipped with jam jars containing a lighted candle we would try to sing beneath the dormitory windows, with the boys tossing 'hot coins' down from above. Happy days!

Cecil Hudson
(Grandfather of Edward Wright Tr 1999.3)

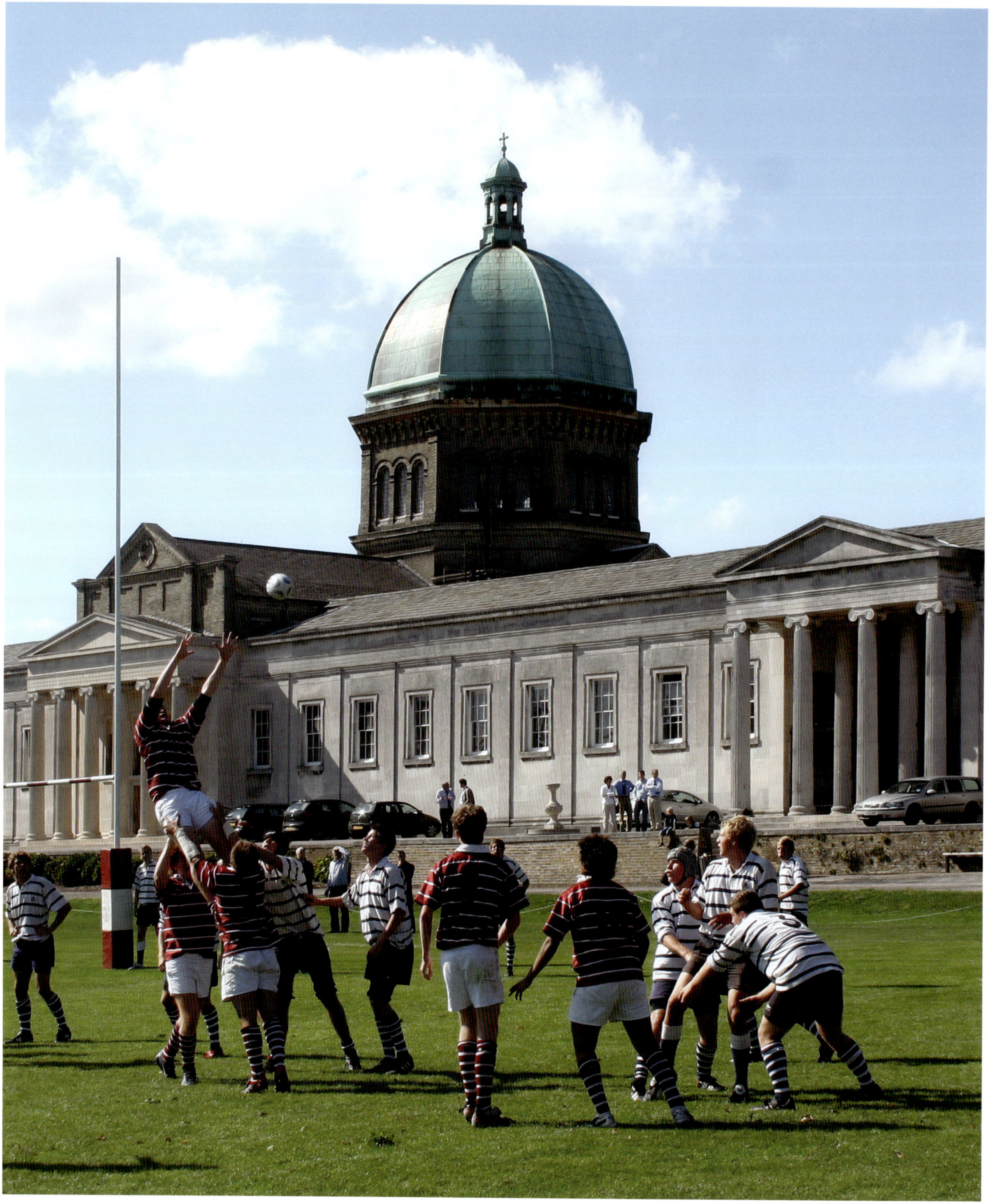

Chapter 3

AN ACTIVE SCHOOL

Opposite: *The XV playing Sevenoaks on Terrace, September 2006.*

Below: *One of the trophy cabinets which hangs in the Dining Hall. The silver rugby ball, awarded to Cock House, is shown on the middle shelf to the right. It was presented to the College by a group of OHs in 1885, among them Charles Gurdon.*

RUGBY PAST

If Lightning Oak could speak it would tell of stirring battles, of triumphs and disasters, thrills and spills, and echo the shouts and cheers of thousands on Terrace over more than 150 years, much longer than on 'Billy's cabbage patch', which became Twickenham in 1907. In 1840, in East India College days, the Harrow game was played, mostly a kicking and catching game, with no running with the ball. The Rugby game was played after 1850 until the College closed in 1858 and then again from 1862 under the Mastership of Arthur Butler.

Rugby reflected all the Victorian manly virtues – leadership, courage, team spirit – in which Butler believed, and he made it compulsory in 1864, as it has remained more or less ever since. Butler himself, and most of the other masters, joined in the games, even in the 'foreign matches' which came to be played; House matches created intense rivalry. Teams of XX, 15 forwards and five outsides, were official after 1868, while XV became the norm in 1877. Results depended on kicking a goal and a touch-down entitled the player to attempt a kick. Often, in the muddy conditions with a heavy leather ball, no goal was kicked and games were adjourned for another day and could continue for hours. A points system was introduced in 1887, modified many times since, and games were restricted in time. Before then there were no referees or whistles to stop play, and captains settled disputes as the game progressed. Laws were developing, but it was a game of shoving, mauling, running, passing, tripping, even hacking, though there was a rule banning 'the wearing of projecting nails or iron spikes on the soles or heels of boots'. Tackling ('collaring') was legal, but not below the hips to avert the danger of broken collar bones. XX Acre was bought in 1890 and the division of age groups and skills established a pattern of Firsts, Seconds, Thirds and 'Hoips', which lasted many years.

House matches were familiar from the start and in 1885 the OHs subscribed to a large silver rugby ball to be awarded to the winner of the final. For some time Eton had called their winner 'cock of the walk' and 'Cock House' stuck, bringing enormous kudos to the House. Between 1886 and 1990 Lawrence played in 25 finals and won 14, with Hailey and Thomason close behind. Recently the format has changed greatly, though the enthusiasm has not diminished. However, headmasters of public schools were reluctant to permit inter-school games until 1890, the year Haileybury played Bedford (lost 21-0), followed closely by Dulwich and Tonbridge. The first wins were against Sherborne and Dulwich in 1894. The first really successful XV was in 1917, winning all five school matches and losing only to the Royal Naval Division and the Machine Gun Corps.

Fortunes fluctuated between the wars, with many good players, but with one controversial match against Uppingham in 1930. The two as yet unbeaten XVs met at Uppingham. Haileybury closed down the game from the start, denying their free-running opponents any opportunities and possibly stretching the off-side laws. Haileybury won 6-0 and were accused of unfair tactics, an accusation that was taken up by the respective Masters and fully covered by the national press. The two schools did not play one another again until 1960, though they enjoyed many an amicable game of cricket. The vacant slot was filled by Oundle, who proved doughty opponents for many years. The 1958 XV, captained by A.R. Godfrey (Ha 1954.3), won all of its ten school matches, as did the 1971 XV, captained by G.R. Stitcher (L 1967.3). The 1972 XV lost only to Dulwich, 6-3.

From the start the Masters were enthusiastic rugby coaches: Lionel Milford and Reverend William Fenning (Staff 1875.3–1910.3), Robert Ashcroft (Staff 1919.3–57.2), who resigned after the Uppingham Incident, and Colin Cobb (Staff 1940.3–84.3), Peter Cole (Staff 1974.3–78.2) and Dan Hearn (Staff 1965.3–2000.2), who coached from his wheelchair after a crippling rugby accident; Bass and Ian George (Staff 1988.3–), Peter Johns (Staff 1989.3–) and Julian Brammer (Staff 2005.3–) in turn inspired their XVs. In the early days, many boys left for Oxbridge and a significant number earned Blues, some captaining the team. C. Gurdon (Tr 1869.1) played for Cambridge in 1877 and rowed in the Cambridge boat for four years. Blues are rare now, just three in the last 20 years. The public schools were the backbone of early internationals, the first against Scotland in 1871. E.C. Cheston (BF 1863.3) won the first of his five English caps in 1873 and was the first OH international; J.G.G. Birkett (C 1898.3) won 21 caps between 1906 and 1912 and is the most capped OH for England. The Gurdon brothers, E.T. and C. (Tr 1868.1 and 1869.1 respectively), won 30 caps between them, often together. The most recent internationals, P.J. Warfield (Ha 1964.3) and D.H. Cooke (Tr 1969.3) for England and C.T. Wyles (Tr 1997.3) for the USA, are the only three OH internationals since the war. Undoubtedly the finest OH player was G.V. Stephenson (BF 1916.3), who won 42 caps for Ireland, 13 as captain, between 1920 and 1930, a period when only three matches were played by home countries, a record which seems unlikely to be broken.

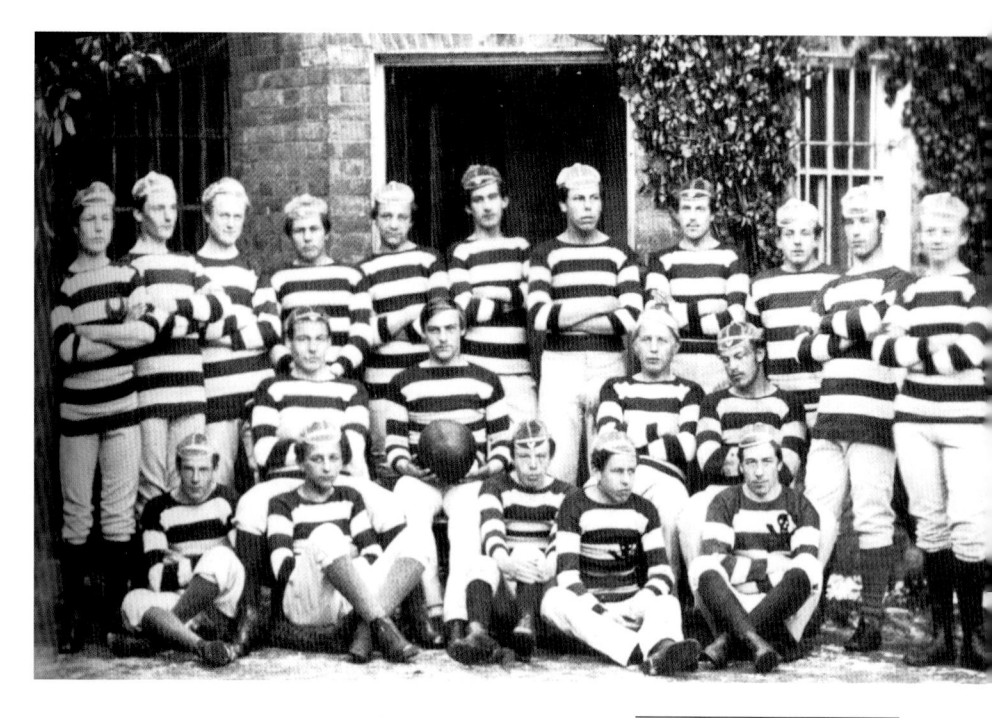

Over the years the game has changed, facilities improved, velvet-tasselled caps have gone, the old leather ball so difficult to kick has been replaced by an aero-dynamic plastic ball moulded to be passed and thrown with one hand. Butler and his successors believed that the morale of the School reflected the success of the XV. A parent in the 21st century wrote in *The Haileyburian*: *You have missed something if you have never struggled inconspicuously for the sake of the side, or had your shins kicked, or never known the shame of fumbling a pass in front of the goal line. These things cut a man down to size. They help a young man to know himself, and this is the beginning of wisdom.*

Lightning Oak could tell it all.

Andrew Hambling (Staff 1956.3–91.2)

Above: The XX, 1871. Edward Gurdon is sitting on the ground, second from the left. His brother, Charles, is standing fifth from the left, against the door frame. Haileybury played a variation on the Rugby game, called simply 'Our game'.

Chapter 3 — AN ACTIVE SCHOOL

AN EARLY SPORTING HERO

A flavour of a different era is captured in George Coldham's (BF 1863.3) letter to L.S. Milford, the first to compile a history of Haileybury: *We lived in very different times from the present; for instance, no one ever thought of 'changing for games' except on very grand occasions. In 1863 practically none of us had football jerseys, and I remember, when playing for the Sixth against the Modern School, getting a try which I converted into a goal because Isaacson was too much of a gentleman to hold on to my clothes, which gave way when he tried to collar me. I am afraid I did not realise what a mean advantage I had taken of him.*

House matches were more gruelling than in the 20th and 21st centuries – unless either side scored two goals on the first day, the game had to go on for two or, if necessary, three days. It was not until 1882 that play was limited to one day, yet many people thought the innovation was disastrous.

Perhaps the most distinguished of all the talented rugby players who have had their native skills honed at Haileybury was Edward Temple Gurdon, whose portrait hangs in the Common Room dining room. He played through the period when the game changed most significantly in terms of both numbers per side and the skills required. *The Public School Magazine* wrote: *Gurdon captained Cambridge and played altogether 16 times for England [1878–86, Captain 1883–6], a record which no other Englishman has equalled. His brother Charles approaches nearest to him, having worn the red rose on 14 occasions. Perhaps the most marked characteristic of the brothers was the ability with which they adapted themselves to, and were among the best exponents of, each successive change in the style of play. In the old pushing matches of 20-a-side they pushed better than their contemporaries. When on the reduction to 15 players, dribbling and open play came more into use, they excelled at both. Later, when passing came more into fashion, they were among its most proficient. Reliability was another of their great gifts. Crack players nearly always have off days, but the Gurdons – and to this the writer can testify from having played with and against them for many years – never indulged in off-days. Whether in club games, international or trial matches, they always played up to form.*

E.T. Gurdon became President of the English Rugby Union in 1890.

By 1910 Haileybury had gone on to produce ten international players, eight for England and one each for Scotland and Ireland.

PRW

Below: *E.T. Gurdon by 'Stuff' from* Vanity Fair, *January 1892.*

Below right: *The Ball, the Cock House trophy.*

RUGBY PRESENT

The 21st century has seen a change to the traditional fixture list and, whilst a fully co-educational Haileybury could no longer compete across the board against the larger boys' schools, the quality of the rugby on Terrace remains high, and at times, outstanding.

The teams of 2001, led by Chris Wyles and 2002 led by Tom George (B 2001.3) were hugely successful and played some of the best rugby seen by Haileybury XVs for many years. David Gregory's (LS and BF 2000.3) XV of 2005 had an outstanding season, recognised by being awarded the Rugby World Team of the Month for September. These teams all had similar qualities which one has come to expect of Haileybury XVs: they worked extremely hard in practice, played with passion and high levels of skill, whilst always giving of their best.

The recent XVs have all enjoyed a good deal of success and a number of individuals went on to achieve International Schoolboy honours. Ben Thomas (BF 2004.3) played for the England Under 20 squad that lost to New Zealand in the final of the Junior World Championship in Wales in 2008. Jamie George (LS and BF 2002.3) played for England at Under 16, Under 18 and Under 20 level, and captained the Under 20 team against France in Argentina in 2010, whilst Nicholas Fraser (L 2007.3) and Matthew Hankin (L 2009.3) both played for the England Under 18 XV in 2008 and 2011 respectively.

Ian George (Staff 1988.3–)

19TH-CENTURY SPORT

The renaissance of sport in the 19th century served a practical purpose for a small country that had a lot of the world to administer. Games were a way of quickly and enjoyably working out leadership material, extolling and teaching all those things that the administrative class admired so much. Games, in particular team games, fostered clannish bonding and hierarchy worship – all of which was held as a good thing when dealing with lesser people. If you had to find a district commissioner, a police chief or a civil servant to run some lost corner of the Empire, then a games captain or a boy with House colours was as good a bet as any.

The quote is from A.A Gill's book *The Angry Island* and summarises quite elegantly the reason why games became such a part of public school life.

Left: *The silver winged heart badge awarded to Colours in the XV. The badge was worn in the side caps and the Colour caps.*

Below: *The High Jump, one of the events in the Sports that took place in the Easter Term of 1895 on the Terrace Field.*

Although the Reverend A.G. Butler, Haileybury's first Master, didn't necessarily like sport *per se*, he was from Rugby. Rugby's greatest Headmaster, Dr Arnold, was hugely influential in the world of 19th-century educational thought and his ideas of how the Christian gentleman should behave were adopted by many of the Rugby schoolmasters who went on to be headmasters elsewhere. Games were at the heart of the vision and Butler, when appointed at Haileybury, brought 'football' with him. It was considered the most important sport at Haileybury in the early years.

Butler (and Bradby after him) actively encouraged the 20-a-side version they knew from Rugby School and it was compulsory for boys in the autumn term.

Chapter 3 — AN ACTIVE SCHOOL

Inter-school matches were difficult in the early days, however, as the major schools all had their own rules. Most matches were against Old Boys, or were played internally. Big Side (an elected group of 40–50 boys) would play Little Side, comprised of everybody else. Tripping was legal, which allowed smaller boys parity in this full-contact sport. Other matches reported include Prefects vs School and This side of Chapel against That side of Chapel. Almost any combination could be found. An early edition of *The Haileyburian* notes that the sport wasn't always the most popular on wet pitches in the middle of winter. All matches were organised by the boys, with little input from the Masters; in fact, a rule book from the 1860s notes that House captains should be assigned as umpires. Colours in the XX and latterly the XV were rewarded with a silver winged heart worn in the dormitory cap.

Cricket was firmly established by the time Haileybury came into being and had the advantage of consistent rules, meaning inter-school matches were possible, but at a school like Haileybury, obsessed with rugby football, cricket was seen as the poor relation. It was not considered a compulsory sport in the 1860s and even seemingly trivial things like membership of the Natural History Society could get a boy out of a cricket match. There was no coaching and the only recognition a first XI player would get was a ribbon for his boater: no silver badge here. Haileybury was playing matches against Wellington from 1866 and Uppingham in 1868. That first Uppingham match, over two days, is lovingly recorded in *The Haileyburian*, with comment made on the breakfast quality and the nine-hour journey there. The telegram sent back after Haileybury's victory arrived before the team got home.

Cricket had to wait for a cricket-loving Master before things improved. That man was Canon Edward Lyttelton (Master 1890.2–1905.2). Under his guidance, cricket came on in leaps and bounds and by 1897 it was played to a very high standard indeed, with many boys going on to play for Oxford or Cambridge and some playing first-class cricket for the counties.

Above: *Antonio Infantino (LS and Tr 2002.3), English Schools sprinting champion, who set the School 100m record of 10.6s in 2008.*

The Pavilion was built in 1887 and the annual Lord's fixture against Cheltenham started in 1894.

Paper Chases

These have long since died out at Haileybury, although Harrow still run a similar ten-mile event, called the Long Ducker, from Harrow to Marble Arch. A paper chase required a couple of 'hares' who set off on a pre-defined route, dropping paper to allow the 'hounds' to try to catch them before they got to the finish, or back to Haileybury. Not a well-documented sport, although popular, it seems that the catching and paper-dropping parts soon became less relevant as the routes became well known. The most notorious route was the enormous 12½-mile Berkhamsted, which ended in exhaustion for some of the competitors. The winners of the Berkhamsted were given the paper chase 'blue riband' for the year.

Sports (Athletics)

Even in athletics it is impossible to make a true comparison between performances then and now. Distances were in yards, not metres, and tracks, where they even existed, did not conform to any standard measurements. High jump would have been into a sand pit, not onto a huge sponge mat – a Fosbury Flop would have killed you. The first modern Olympics were not until 1896 and that track, which you can visit to this day, was simply an elongated C shape. Athletics was performed on Terrace in the 19th century, with an oval track where the rugby pitch is now and a straight sprint track near to where Chapel is. Events in the early years were not necessarily House events; the glory was in the individual performance. Some matches were divided in novel ways. *The Haileyburian* reports a match where boys were divided into those taller than 5ft 4in and those below this magic height.

With a rough conversion from imperial to metric, a brief and not definitive comparison of some early records is possible: H. Jupp's (Le B 1892.3) 1897 100yd time of 10.2 seconds would be approximately 11 seconds for 100m, which remains pretty good, whereas C.H. Dickinson's (Tr 1890.2) 2 mins 6.2 seconds for the half mile is fairly average (current School record 1 minute 56 seconds). N.S.A. Harrison's (Th 1893.1) 'broad jump' of 1894 of 6.32m would still be considered 'county standard' in 2012.

49

HAILEYBURY — *A 150th Anniversary Portrait*

Fives and Rackets

Fives is often seen as the precursor of most modern indoor racket sports. Haileybury had fives courts even in the days of the East India College. Originally the College preferred bat fives, which indeed used small wooden bats rather than the 'bunch of fives' one imagines. Fives competitions were very popular in the 19th century and there are reports of courts being 'bagged' in the afternoons to allow play. The more common Eton fives was only introduced in 1895, a case of the sport devolving, as bat fives had superseded the original fives in the 1700s. The new courts were modelled on the originals around the chapel at Eton. At Haileybury, versions of the game were played outside the Library. Fives can no longer be played at Haileybury as the Rugby Fives courts adjacent to the Rackets Court have been converted to Changing Rooms.

'Racquets' evolved out of various ballgames played in the debtors' prisons in the 18th century. Harrow School popularised the sport in the public schools and courts soon spread around the country. Butler improved the first racquets court at Haileybury around 1865 and the sport became very popular. Haileybury then began entering schools racquets competitions, as it still does. A better court was provided in 1908. The sport is now known as rackets and is played almost exclusively by the public schools. Squash, also very popular with current Haileyburians, developed at Harrow and unsurprisingly evolved from rackets. Sport has and always will be a major part of life at Haileybury. Long may it continue, and long may it continue to evolve.

Ray Dexter (Staff 2001.3–2010.2)

Above: *Eton fives, with the familiar left wall buttress, being played in 1895. These courts now serve as garages for groundsmens' equipment. Fives players at Haileybury in the 19th century were known as 'Backwallers'.*

Left: *Rackets players 1869. L–r: Edward Ash (Staff 1865.3–1902.3), Jeremy Pollock (L 1866.3), Edwin Hoskyns (Tr 1865.1) and William Brooke (BF, Th and C 1864.1). Hoskyns and Brooke were the earliest Haileybury pair to compete at Prince's (later Queen's) in 1869. Pairs have reached the finals of the Public School Championship 11 times, triumphing on four occasions in a sport traditionally dominated by Eton and Harrow. In 2011, the first girls' championship was staged at Queen's, with Jessica Billings (LS and C 2006.3) losing out in the final of the Under 16 title.*

Opposite: *Charlie Carr (BF 2007.3) who, with Will Stanyard (BF 2010.3), made up the 1st Racket Pair in 2011/12.*

Chapter 3 — AN ACTIVE SCHOOL

COCK HOUSE AND KILLER COOK

Douglas Cook (Staff ISC 1928.3–42.1, Haileybury and ISC 1942.2–65.2) was known as 'Killer' not only to the boys in Hailey, where he was Housemaster, but throughout the College and, I suspect, among his colleagues in Common Room. He had risen to the rank of Colonel in the war and he ran his House with military discipline. There were constant inspections when we had to stand by our lockers with the door open so that Cook could examine the contents. If there was something he didn't like the look of, he would pull it out on to the floor and say: 'Get rid of it, get rid of it.' If you argued about why you valued the object in question he would turn to the prefects who were escorting him and say: 'I see we have a barrack-room lawyer here; keep an eye on him – he's a trouble-maker.'

Cook believed in the principles espoused by Dr Arnold, and foremost among these were loyalty to your House and team spirit. Rugby seemed to him the ideal way to inculcate both and no one on the rugby field was allowed to be injured. You had to get up and carry on until the referee spotted that you had broken your arm or had concussion and sent you off. Once when a loose scrum broke up and the mud-covered players picked themselves up, one player was left face down in the mud and motionless. Cook strode on to the pitch and prodded him with his stick: 'Is he dead; is he dead?' was all he said.

Winning the Cock House Rugby Cup was of huge importance to him and the House scrum would practise on the private lawn in his garden where the walls surrounding them meant that no spies from other Houses could observe their tactics. Certain phrases had coded meanings for the scrum. For instance, 'Very low, Hailey' meant that we were going for a shove-over try. Other phrases meant that we would wheel to the right or to the left or hold the ball in the back row of the scrum before suddenly releasing it when the opposition was in disarray. The only time I ever saw any emotion from Cook was when we had just become Cock House. He returned to Hailey from Terrace twirling his hat on the end of his walking stick above his head.

Cricket was also considered a team game, although it seemed to me an opportunity for a few individuals to have all the fun while the vast majority stood around in the field becoming increasingly bored. I had some ability at tennis and played in the School VI for three years. Tennis, according to Cook, was an individual game and therefore encouraged selfishness. So I was required to play cricket, at which I had no ability, for four afternoons a week. My partner in the School team was also in Hailey and, although we won the inter-House competition for several years in a row, we received no acknowledgement or congratulations from Cook.

Above: *Douglas Cook, Housemaster of 'A' House, ISC, and Hailey.*

Chapter 3 — AN ACTIVE SCHOOL

LACROSSE

Lacrosse was one of the first sports to be introduced for girls and the Haileybury programme has grown out of the Small Schools League in recent years, with teams regularly competing in the National Schools Lacrosse Championships:

Without any established female sports, I was particularly keen to form a lacrosse team and we had just enough lacrosse players. To provide an opposing team for practice, we enjoyed some hilarious games periods teaching chaps lacrosse and frightening them to death in the process! One of our first fixtures was against my former grammar school, St George's, whom we managed to beat. We were aware of concerns expressed that girls might play lacrosse on the sacrosanct rugby pitches, but we were determined to have our own team sports. In lieu of dancing, Ken Bartlett (Staff 1973.3–91.3) kindly allowed me to join in his PE lessons as the only girl. We could also play squash in rather antiquated courts as well as swim in the summer term.

Jennifer Parsons (née Van Horne) (B 1974.3)

Above: *Adriana Zurita (M 2008.3).*

Other House trophies were pursued relentlessly. Cook spotted that anyone who entered the boxing competition was automatically awarded a point. Most Houses entered one or two boys who fancied themselves as boxers and who, if successful, might build up a score of about 40 points, which would be enough to win the Boxing Cup. Cook, without asking us or indeed telling us, entered the whole House for the competition. There were 55 boys in Hailey so we had won the Cup before the competition had even started. One by one off we went to the slaughter, but could console ourselves that we had earned a point for the House.

The House Singing Competition received the same treatment. Instead of those boys who had good voices getting together a song or two, perhaps with some accompaniment, to represent their House, Cook insisted that the whole House would sing. The 'Agincourt Song' was chosen and we were told to look the judges in the eye, open our mouths wide and sing loudly. Those judging the competition were, I think, terrified by the mass of boys in front of them, all with mouths wide open, and by the volume of noise (the only word to describe it) that we made, and duly awarded the cup to Hailey.

Cook would have dearly loved to win the Army Bugle. Many of us, however, hated being in the Corps and were determined to sabotage the practice sessions. There was always some person in the House who had risen to the rank of Sergeant and who enjoyed issuing marching orders in a manly voice while the squad were marched up and down the hard parade ground. The boy in command would let us get as far away as possible before issuing his command of 'About turn!' in a stentorian bellow. I would

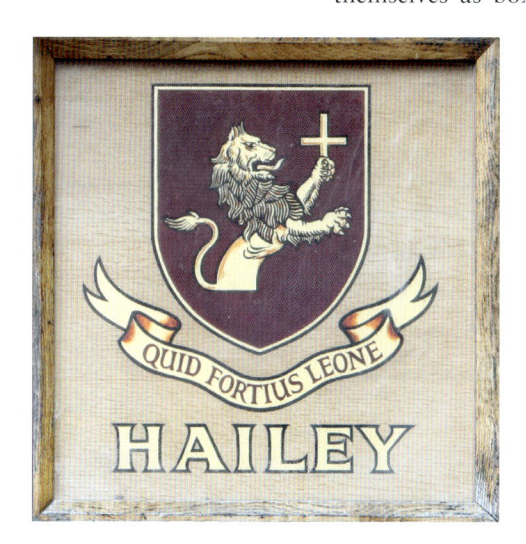

Above: Hailey House, 1956, with its hoard of 16 trophies. Top row (l to r): McLellan, Gilbert, Hoare, Pringle, Greer-Walker, Havers, Walker; 2nd row: Fawcett, Millar, Hughes, Hart, Ballam, Shaw, Rider, Shapeero, Scorer, Harris, Dobbie, Churcher, Godfrey, Duff, Zagalsky; 3rd row: Chuter, Drury, Bond, Steadman, Ware, Richardson, Fowkes, Wilkins, Sheasby, Innes, Moore, Roberts, Golding, Lofting, Caswell, Hubback, Khalidi, Groves, Mitchell, Jolliffe; seated: Pankhurst, Anslow-Wilson, Mr Thomas, Hardcastle, Mrs Cook, Cooper, Mr Cook, Parrish, Albright, Miss Fairlie, Coates, Gray, Waring; seated (on ground): Smith, Glover, Goatcher, Dawn Cook, Bushell, Wallace, Fitzgibbon, Sleight.

encourage those around me to pretend we had not heard the words of command and so, while the squad executed an about turn, we would march blithely on until we reached the perimeter of the parade ground where we would tumble over the fence one on top of another with enormous glee. This had the effect of deflating the overblown ego of the boy in command as well as alleviating the boredom of square-bashing. The Army Bugle was one trophy that Hailey never won in my time.

Hate would be too strong a word, but I certainly disliked Cook for my first four years in Hailey. In my last year I became a House Prefect and then Head of House. Only then did I occasionally get a glimpse behind the iron mask and, to my utter astonishment, observe that there was a twinkle in his eye. Gradually over that last year I began to appreciate all that Cook had done for me and I grew to love the man and to feel proud that he was my Housemaster. He had drilled self-discipline into me, which, over more than 50 subsequent years, including 18 as a headmaster, has stood me in very good stead.

Malcolm Innes (Ha 1953.1)

Dancing cheek to cheek with your Housemaster

That summer it was agreed that there would be a dance with Queenswood involving senior members of the two schools. It soon became clear that none of us boys had much of a clue about dancing. I was in Hailey, whose Housemaster, Douglas 'Killer' Cook, had been a prop forward for Lancashire in his younger days, so our minds boggled when he announced he would give his Hailey dancers lessons in the waltz, quickstep and foxtrot – *de rigueur* dances in those days.

Below: Rugby House Captains, 2009.3.

Chapter 3 — AN ACTIVE SCHOOL

HOCKEY, HELSINKI 1952

The final 16 to travel to Finland were selected at the end of May and included Steve Theobald (E 1937.3), a Scottish International who had played in the Hockey XI 1940–1. We arrived in Helsinki in cold weather in a country more associated with ice hockey but the facilities were excellent. Our match for the Bronze Medal against a well-drilled Pakistan was a thrilling encounter. We scored goals either side of half time but Pakistan fought back and scored with a few minutes to go. A great defence effort by all the team was needed in the remaining time, I remember a shot flying past my ear and hitting the goal post when defending a corner! However, we survived to win 2-1. Radio commentary on the game was provided by Max Robertson (E 1929.1). The Medal Ceremony had a long delayed codicil, for at that time only 11 medals were awarded: those who played in all games received a medal whilst others drew lots; 58 years later in 2010, the unlucky players finally received medals in a ceremony in Nottingham.

Tony Nunn (Ha 1941.2)

NUNN...never beaten

Right: Master, Canon Edward Lyttelton, first president of OHRFC. He later became Headmaster of Eton.

I shall never forget trooping over to Bradby Hall to find 'Killer' winding up an old gramophone, putting on a '78' record and grabbing hold of me. I found myself clasped in the arms of my dreaded Housemaster doing a 'one, two, three; one, two, three; one, two, three' to the scratchy strains of 'The Blue Danube' waltz. He was very light on his feet and I found out later that our Lancashire forward had won prizes at ballroom dancing competitions.

The great evening came and the superbly coached Hailey dancers joined battle on the floor with the dainty dishes of Queenswood. It was a great success and for many of us our first close encounter with the fair sex. We never looked back!

Mike Bolsover (Ha 1947.3)

THE OLD HAILEYBURIANS RUGBY FOOTBALL CLUB

The Old Haileyburians Rugby Football Club (OHRFC) has a long and glorious heritage. The Club was founded in 1875 as the Old Haileyburians' Cricket and Football Club, adopting the colours of magenta and white.

The OHRFC in its current form owes its conception to two students, L.J. Morson (Th 1897.3) and G.A.P. Thomas (Th 1898.3), when they found themselves confined to the School Sanatorium in 1901. The inaugural meeting was held in January 1902, with Canon Lyttelton, then Master of Haileybury, in the chair.

The Canon agreed to become the first President of the Club and since then the office has always been held by the Master. It was decided that the Club should be called the Haileybury Wanderers and up until 1907 they really were wanderers, playing games at various grounds around Hertfordshire. The Club quickly established itself as a force to be reckoned with and even boasted a rare victory over its near-neighbours Saracens in December 1926. The Club's present ground in Ewell, Surrey, was purchased thanks to the generosity of Club members and the OH Society in 1934.

The OHRFC lost an incredible 48 of its 85 playing members during the Great War, but those who survived refused to let the Club die and in April 1922 the OHRFC was invited by the French Rugby Union to tour France – the first old boys' rugby club to do so, according to contemporary press cuttings. The Club survived the loss of 30 more playing members in the

Second World War but went on to celebrate not only its jubilee in 1978 but also, more recently, its centenary.

The Club grounds boast two rugby pitches, two cricket squares and a lovely club house. OHRFC is open to OHs and honorary members alike and fields two sides in the Surrey leagues. The Club has managed to strike a balance between high-quality, committed rugby and a reputation as one of the most successful 'social' sides in old boys' rugby.

The Club is financially independent as a result of a substantial income from both a sports centre and a telephone mast situated on its grounds at Ruxley Lane in Ewell. As a result, OHRFC has in recent years been able to support talented rugby players at the School through a bursary arrangement.

Tom Huckin (B 1965.3)

THE HONOURABLE SCHOOLBOY

For the most part I was a pretty law-abiding citizen and was never beaten. Perhaps my most serious crime was carried out on the orders of the head of the DC and was to steal some logs for firewood from the store under Clock House. As luck would have it I was spotted from his study window by the Head of School, later to become Lieutenant General Sir Richard Vickers, who awarded me X10 dates. I thought (misguidedly I expect) it was incumbent upon me to take my punishment without revealing that I had been acting under orders.

On reflection I suppose I did break the rules rather more seriously and consistently by sneaking off on several Saturday afternoons, without permission, to watch Tottenham Hotspur play at White Hart Lane. In those days soccer was a dirty word at Haileybury, but my father, who had grown up in North London, was a keen Spurs supporter and before I came to Haileybury he had taken me there from time to time. This had instilled in me what became a lifelong emotional attachment to the 'Lilywhites', who at that time were playing some undistinguished football in the second division. I found several fellow soccer supporters among my classmates in the Fifths and upwards. None of this detracted from my growing love of rugby, but it is gratifying that today soccer holds an honoured place alongside rugby in the School's sporting calendar.

Michael Freegard (BF 1947.1)

SOCCER (ASSOCIATION FOOTBALL)

I introduced organised soccer to Haileybury in 1967 for the first time. Soccer playing was frowned upon. Excluded from XX Acre and all other playing pitches, I was allocated a water-logged, frozen meadow down Hailey Lane to play on. It was covered in cow pats. The few soccer-playing pioneers spent the first weeks measuring out a pitch, making and erecting goal posts and corner flags in woodwork class, removing the solid cow pats and stones, spiking the pitch with forks to drain it and finally rolling it to make it playable. Tracksuits were played in as protection from cuts and infections from stones and animal dung. We persisted against the odds and from that acorn, soccer grew.

C.D.A. Cochran (Staff 1964.3–67.2)

If the decisions of the Editor of *The Haileyburian* can be considered a measure of the significance of soccer or the regard in which it has been held, then it is instructive that no mention of the game appeared in 1968; a single photograph of action from a match against Felsted with not so much as a line of text to go with it appeared in 1969. By 1970 two photographs and about 300 words by Nigel Robbins (Staff 1969.3–73.2) appear, so its star was rising despite some individuals turning in their graves. The game's coming of age at Haileybury might well have been the Easter term of 1981 and, in particular, a game against Charterhouse. Nick Medd (C 1976.1), Captain of Soccer, recalls:

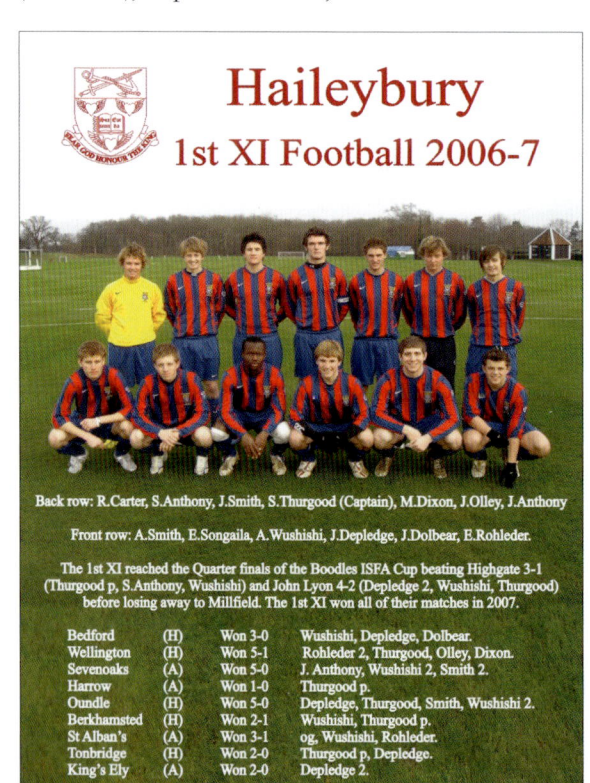

Left: Haileybury's unbeaten 1st XI football team, 2006–7.

Chapter 3 — AN ACTIVE SCHOOL

MOTOR RACING

Stirling Moss (L 1943.3) *(left)* is indeed our F1 hero but Haileybury produced two other F1 drivers, namely Mike Parkes (Ferrari) and myself (Cooper), albeit briefly. I also competed as a driver in the two- and four-man bobsleigh teams at the Winter Olympics in 1964 and 1968.

Robin Widdows (L 1955.3)

Another Haileyburian who made a career in motor sports was Tommy Weber (M 1952.2), a colourful character, friend of The Rolling Stones and adventurer. He is better known for his affair with Charlotte Rampling and his society marriage than for his driving.

Nigel Prentki (Staff 1973.3–88.2) had been fighting hard internally and externally to establish soccer at School, and aware of quite a strong year coming through, had started arranging progressively more ambitious fixtures against the top soccer schools. These schools often took some persuading due to our reputation as a rugby school and our bumpy rugby pitches. That year, 1981, we had played and beaten various strong sides. The Brentwood team, which included Stuart Robson – a future Arsenal player, who didn't know what had hit him when Nigel asked James Bretherton (A 1977.1) to man mark him – and others were put to the sword.

Finally, to NMP's great excitement, he managed to arrange a match against Charterhouse, which with four ISFA Cups and an FA Cup is probably the strongest independent school in the country. NP had built this up as a huge fixture and as we walked down to the bottom of XX Acre on a wet and windy day we were expecting a fierce battle and maybe a lesson. To our surprise the conditions 'and the long walk across country' unsettled them more than us and on one of those freak days when everything goes like a dream we kept scoring and their team spirit rapidly disappeared. One was left with a picture of Nigel's smoking ever more Gauloises, the referee, John Baugh (Staff 1980.3–86.3), looking anxiously to the sideline wondering if he was missing

something, and David Summerscale, the then Master who had been a Housemaster at Charterhouse, getting airborne as another goal was scored. The match finished 9-0 and I understand their goalie never played again.

The magic of the day was epitomised by Nick Brimelow (C 1979.3) scoring four goals on the day in the only School match his father ever watched. The match is still talked about at Charterhouse as an example of what can happen when a team is over-confident.

Since that time soccer has become a major feature of the games programme and enjoyed considerable further success against other schools. The high standard has now continued through to the OHAFC, who in 2011 won promotion to the Arthurian League Premier Division.

PRW

It's a Man's Game?

During the late 1990s, soccer was derogatorily known as 'Kevball' at Haileybury and in some other private schools, too. The animosity towards the sport – and its culture – reached extremes where some pupils received detention or 'hard labour' (administered by some of the older, more anti-soccer staff) for being caught using a football during their free time in cricket and rugby seasons. I was determined to help change this.

HAILEYBURY ~ A 150th Anniversary Portrait

With the backing of then Captain Scott O'Donoghue (LS and E 1990.3), I was brought into the soccer 1st XI at a young age (in the Fifths) alongside my friend and classmate, Adrien Mann (Ha 1994.3). We both knew that soccer wasn't a priority at the School. Later, as Captain, I worked closely alongside the soccer coach, Bert Robinson (Staff 1996.3–2006.2), to create a great side (we continued to utilize the strategy of occasionally calling up talented younger players), almost creating a mini-youth system at School. Due to successful seasons, and an entertaining brand of soccer, with numerous exciting goals scored by talented players, the soccer team slowly gained the School's respect. It was rewarding to see some of the rugby masters showing up at the 1st XI soccer games, too, and investing heavily in the team's success, even bringing it up in class time, when chit-chat was previously reserved for rugby and cricket. In fact, soccer slowly began to be spoken about by rugby- and cricket-loving Masters around Quad, in House, or in the Dining Hall. As the years passed, this was evident to see – and deeply rewarding.

We moved away from playing our 1st XI matches on Quitchells to playing them on Terrace. The groundsmen began taking better care of the surface, closely cropping the grass – normally kept long for rugby – to allow us to play an attractive passing style.

Towards the end of my time at Haileybury, we went a step further and for the first time Bert Robinson brought in Malcolm Blackmore, a charming man and an ex-Tottenham scout, to do some part-time coaching. As a diehard Arsenal fan, I initially had reservations about this. However, to see how full-circle those reservations went, Malcolm ended up pushing me for a trial at Tottenham.

I was determined to get soccer accepted into the social norms of the School, and, as it transitioned to full co-education, to involve the girls, too. So I set up an evening five-aside league, which, by the time I left, had most of the School watching the games in the evening on the astro-turf. Loads of teams entered and I refereed many of them. At one stage it was obvious the social-league games were attracting more pupils

Left: *Josie Kau (C 2005.3) and Mary Bird (LS and Aby 2002.3) in action for the Girls Soccer XI, 2010.*

SAILING

Rhiannon Massey (Aby 2008.1) **(right)**, one of Haileybury's most successful sailors, 2011. Sailing has been a popular sport since its inception in 1939, with some notable successes:

In summer I assisted in organising and coaching sailing on the gravel pits at Broxbourne. That small group was very talented, beating most other schools in fixtures and winning the Public Schools National Championships at Itchenor in 1967. That led to the generous fitting-out of a new fleet of Firefly racing dinghies by the Haileybury Society to add to the dinghy the team won as first prize.

C.D.A. Cochran

Chapter 3 — AN ACTIVE SCHOOL

BUMPS, BOXING AND CONSOLATION

Above: *Three Little Maids*, The Mikado *tour, 1964.*

I won the Best Losers Cup for boxing, a sad little trophy, battered and dented, as I had been by a boy called Shute, a tough boxer who had me on the ropes and gave me a clobbering. I think the fight may have been stopped. It happened only once. The Cup, of which I was quite proud in the circumstances, stood a little sadly on a shelf at the end of the House 'dorm' and had to be cleaned. Fortunately, as it had been shared, it went off somewhere else to be reflected on by the other best loser. No one likes losing, but to be rewarded for it was better than a poke in the eye with a sharp stick. I wonder if he remembers who he was. Captain of Boxing then was Ali (not Muhammad), as I recall. He asked me to join the School Team. A Master, Jonathan Harvey (Staff 1962.2–70.2), supported us.

My first fight was, I think, either at Dulwich or St Paul's. My opponent had an unpronounceable name ending in 'vich'. Our coach, a splendid man called Joe Somerville (a southpaw who'd been a sparring partner to Bunny Sterling), who was as tough as old boots and a fine trainer and mentor, was our second. He helped me win (on a split decision) by telling me, between rounds, what point-scoring opportunities there were. The straight left jab and a good guard stood me in good stead, but I didn't develop much of a right hand at all, unlike Malcolm McVittie (E 1960.3), who was lightning fast and used to knock his opponents down or out. I think I recall him having his foot trodden on by his opponent at one of the Four Schools fights and the boy stopped boxing for a few seconds, stood back, said something like, 'I say, I'm so sorry' and McVittie knocked him down! I suppressed a laugh.

I won my 2nd String and then 1st String colours and was allowed to wear a 'Minor Sports' tie on a Saturday. I think, at that time, I had a broken thumb, from cricket, which has never healed properly. It used to get 'rather sore' even with strapping inside the 16oz gloves we wore. The Murdoch twins (Ian and Peter, Tr 1964.1) would be physically sick before their fights, but usually did quite well. My friend and study mate David Ford (E 1962.3) became well-deserved Captain of Boxing. We often had to fight each other and though he was better than me, he boxed and didn't try to knock me out. It was the same with John Spears (B 1962.3) (McVittie's cousin).

I was boxing while also rehearsing singing in *The Mikado* (in the chorus of girls). I must have been 14 and still a treble. On dress rehearsal night in front of the School, supported by, amongst others, some of those boys in my House who wore tabbed collars, knitted ties and Chelsea boots and played in bands, etc., with a shiner, made up to look oriental and camouflaged with a black wig, I may have consoled myself yet again by not taking myself too seriously. I sang my heart out: *Three Little Maids*. It must have been bizarre. We took *The Mikado* all over Scandinavia (and an LP was made, which I've lost) and I later invited a pretty blonde girl called Viveca from Sweden back to School to show her off to my trendier peers. I'd learned to say 'Jag älskar dig'.

Charles Stuart-Hunt (E 1962.3)

in attendance than the 1st team sports games. It was at that point that word got around, and teachers began to show up to see what all the fuss was about. I wanted to break new ground and included a girls' team in the league. It was the first time girls were included in soccer games against the boys. The only previous male–female sports interaction at Haileybury was the annual semi-serious indoor netball and lacrosse games between the rugby XV and the girls' netball team.

I'm glad to have helped do my part at Haileybury in the promotion and advancement of opportunities for girls to play sport and increased respect for sportswomen amongst the boys. While the soccer know-how was lacking amongst the girls, the determination most certainly was not, and watching a 50–50 tackle between a Haileybury girl and boy was well worth the effort of showing up on a chilly evening to shout some support. The league should be eternally remembered for the first boys-versus-girls game that took place. I refereed the game, and while the girls endured all the expected 'It's a man's game' shouts from the boisterous crowd of classmates on the sidelines, nothing could compare to the entire crowd of watching pupils loudly, passionately chanting, 'The referee's a muffler!' over and over. Perhaps one day we'll see a Haileyburian female player play for England.

Since I left Haileybury in 1999 I've occasionally returned to represent the Old Haileyburians Association Football team, during which time we won the Arthur Dunn (Junior League) Cup beating Eton 4-1 in the final. Still to this day I get teasing from teammates claiming one of my goals (a lob) wasn't intentional! I thoroughly recommend people to go and represent or support the OHs.

Oliver Petersen (Ha 1994.3)

150 YEARS OF CRICKET AT HAILEYBURY

Pavilion was the first pitch upon which cricket was played at the School, even if ground conditions were challenging at the outset: *I hit a ball to square-leg for which we ran six, and then 'lost ball' was called, and we all went off and helped to find it* (G.J. Coldham). The first proper inter-school match was in 1866 against Wellington; fixtures against Uppingham started in 1868 and continue to the present day. David Rimmer's (Th 1976.2–) *Haileybury Cricket 1863–1992* gives copious details of results and fine performances. Twelve Haileyburians have gained Blues, more than 70 have played first-class cricket in England, and approximately 50 have played for minor counties. In this latter regard, Andrew Lewis (L 1989.3), who captained Hertfordshire, was awarded the Wilfred Rhodes Trophy for the 2007 season by the Minor Counties Cricket Association.

The levelling of the Terrace ground in the 1880s provided enlarged facilities for the game, even if overcrowding meant that fielders in one game were

Left: *F.J. Seabrook, Master in Charge of Cricket from 1931 to 1950, who captained Gloucestershire against the Australian tourists in 1930.*

Below left: *A silk scorecard from the Cheltenham vs Haileybury cricket match at Lord's, 1912. The fixture was last played at Lord's in July 1968. The 2012 match at Cheltenham resulted in a draw.*

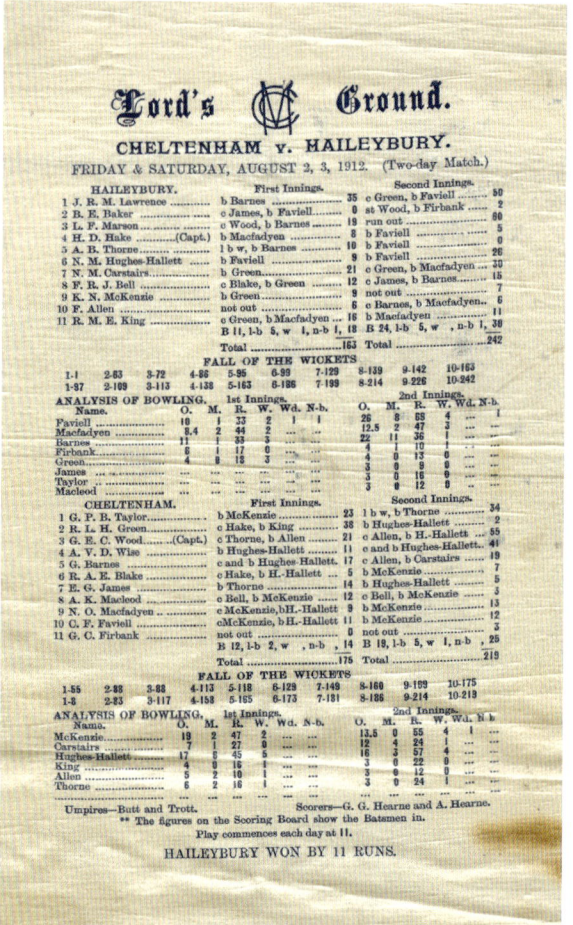

Chapter 3 — AN ACTIVE SCHOOL

inclined to get involved in the adjacent games, to the dismay of the batsmen as they were given out. The Master Edward Lyttelton had won four Cambridge cricket Blues and his arrival in 1890 helped to raise the profile of the game. The introduction of Colts Cricket at his instigation in 1895 developed strength in depth. The strong 1901 side included S.M. Toyne (E 1895.2, Staff 1906.3–13.2 and 1941.3–45.2), who later played for Hampshire, returned to teach at Haileybury and was instrumental in starting the Cricket Week which ran for 82 years from 1910. Another who returned to School as a member of staff and ran the cricket was H.D. Hake (E 1909.1, Staff 1921.3–38.3), who was lauded in the 1915 edition of *Wisden* for, among other things, making 91* and 109* against Wellington. The 1934 side was undefeated in School matches, beating Wellington by an innings and 150 runs, Uppingham by 10 wickets and Cheltenham by 8 wickets. The Cheltenham fixture was played at Lord's for most of its history; the final game there was in 1968. R.J.O. Meyer (B 1918.3) was arguably the best games player that the School produced in the inter-war period. A triple Cambridge Blue, he captained Somerset and even took Bradman's wicket at Lord's when bowling for the Gentleman of England vs Australians in 1938.

PRW

The story is picked up by David Rimmer (Th 1976.3), the author of *Haileybury Cricket 1863–1992* in his view from the boundary:

Group Captain Peter Townsend (L 1928.1) will be most remembered not for his impressive war record but as the man Princess Margaret was not allowed to marry. The Old Haileyburian was a divorcé and his courtship of the Queen's younger sister was doomed to failure. His book *Time and Chance* covered that period of his life and his subsequent trip across the US to blot out the painful memory.

However, earlier in the tome, his love of cricket and his frustration at not being able to bowl spin to the

Right: *Telegram sent to Cornelius Thorne (B 1905.2) to inform him of the result of the Haileybury vs Cheltenham cricket match at Lords in 1912. Cornelius was awarded the Military Cross in 1915 for retrieving his brother, Marlborough's (B 1908.3) body, under fire, near Fricourt, on 28 September. Cornelius, a former Head of House, Captain of Rugby, Cambridge Blue and Harlequin player, was killed in action while leading a bombing attack on 30 September 1916, one of 589 OHs killed in the First World War.*

level where recognition for school teams would follow are recorded. It is a feeling many Haileyburians have probably shared down the years as they have been confined to the ranks of House rather than School teams, unable to master their chosen skill. Yet there is a love of the game that has been passed down the ages, despite not being easy to foster now as it was 100 years ago, when cricket was the dominant summer sport. There are more distractions today, and looking in from the outside, cricket, like any other summer sport, is hit by exam pressure. Whatever the limitations imposed, Haileybury can reflect on a rich cricketing history.

It has not produced as many Test players as the likes of Radley or Tonbridge. In fact, Haileybury's one recorded England Test cricketer is A.G. Archer (B 1885.1), playing in 1898–9 against South Africa at a time when circumstance rather than merit could influence selection. Other notable players include: A.G. Wennink (M 1922.3, Staff 1935.3–69.2) who was in the XI for five years during the 1920s and later became a Master at the school; N.S. Harrison (Hi 1932.3) was a fine batsman of the 1930s, while Alan Fairbairn (E 1937.1), Captain of the XI in 1941, went on to score 100 in his first game for Middlesex; R.F.B. Letts (Ha 1941.3) was a fine leg spinner who took 57 wickets in 1947 and selection for the Public Schools XI followed. England captain Wally Hammond was not impressed by the position of Letts' head in the delivery stride and Gloucestershire advancement was denied him.

The 1945 Haileybury captain, Bill Tyrwhitt-Drake (BF 1940.3), was a considerable batsman and later big run scorer and Captain of Hertfordshire. In later years he was Honorary Secretary of the Haileybury Society, its President, a member of Council and Editor of the 1994 *Register*. All these cricketers played when the annual two-day game against Cheltenham took place at Lord's, and they were given fine instruction by the School's professional and former Sussex all-rounder, Bert Wensley. Wensley was at Haileybury in 1963 and when he retired was succeeded by Peter Ellis, who had been on the Lord's ground staff. Ellis was a fine coach who had a metronomic approach to bowling in the nets and a mordant wit to boot. A particulraly powerful coaching combination was formed when Peter Ellis teamed up with Mark Seymour (Staff 1979.3–2002.2) to produce some outstanding sides in the 1980s and 1990s, retiring eventually in 1995. His son Richard (L 1974.1) had an excellent all-round record in four years in the XI (1976–9), later skippering Oxford University and was in Middlesex's championship-winning side in 1982.

Andrew Miller (E 1976.3) also played for Oxford and Middlesex and was good enough to score 1,000 runs during the 1986 season. Nick Walker (B 1997.3), who played professionally for Leicestershire and Derbyshire, has proved to be a match winner with his quick bowling and explosive hitting in the Cricketer Cup, the competition for public school old boys' sides, in which Haileybury Hermits once reached the final – in 1983 – only to lose to Repton Pilgrims by seven wickets.

Chris Thompson (B 1975.3) was also a fine servant in this competition, being the only OH to take 50 or more wickets in it, as was Nick Gandon (M 1969.3) with his astute captaincy and doughty batting. The late John Lofting (Ha 1953.1) and Sandy Ross (C 1961.3) were not only good players but invaluable workers behind the scenes, while ex-scorer Neil Vyner (L 1960.1) and Hermits Chairman and player Mark Baker-White (Tr 1974.1) contributed markedly. In this century we have been lucky to have had the services of Geoff Howarth, who captained New Zealand, as coach, and our most recent success has been Sam Billings (BF 2004.3), who played for England U19 in 2011.

Many others, such as Roger Kent (E 1965.3) and Basil Hollington (A 1963.2), deserve to be mentioned more fully but space does not allow.

David Rimmer

Below: *The Cheltenham vs Haileybury match at Lord's, second day, 30 July 1960. S.J.B. Newson (E 1957.3) drives a ball from Evill of Cheltenham.*

Chapter 3 — AN ACTIVE SCHOOL

Above: *Sam Billings (right) and Rhodri Dawes (L 2008.3) on Pavillion in 2009.*

A LONG WAY TO SWIM

Before the redevelopment of the Sports Hall complex, the Swimming Pool was located outside beyond the Armoury and was much longer than the new one and extremely cold. If my memory serves me correctly it was 58m long, which as a young lad is a long way to swim, especially when you are in front of the whole School, trying your hardest not to be the last to finish. At that time boys were not allowed in to watch the girls' races, although the girls were allowed to watch the boys, which just added to the nerves. The one particular time that springs to mind is when Bartle Frere nominated one of my friends to do the butterfly. He was not the strongest of swimmers, least of all in the butterfly. Quite predictably he came last, not by a small margin however, but by about five minutes. At least there were a lot of people cheering him on!

Edward Banks (BF 1994.3)

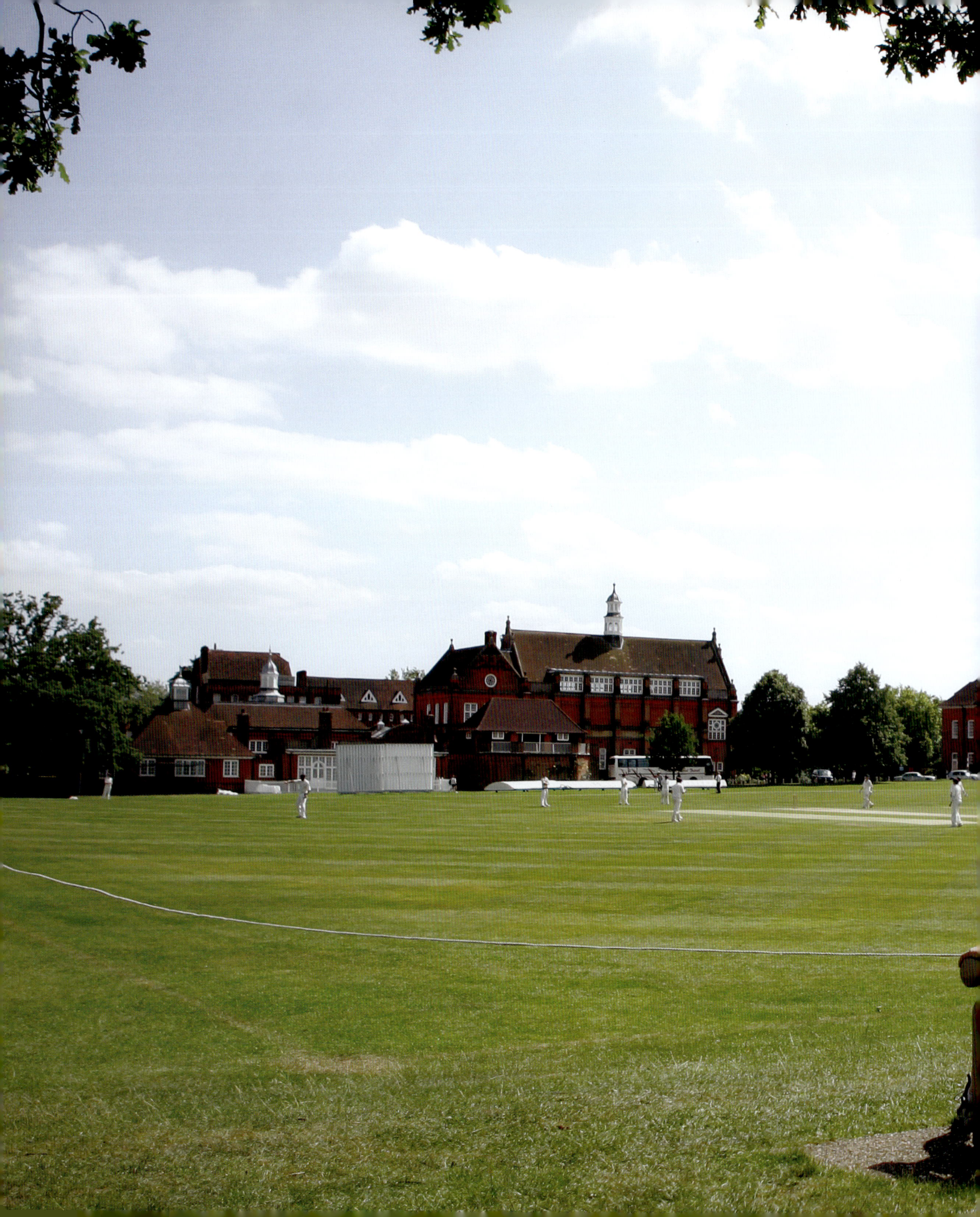

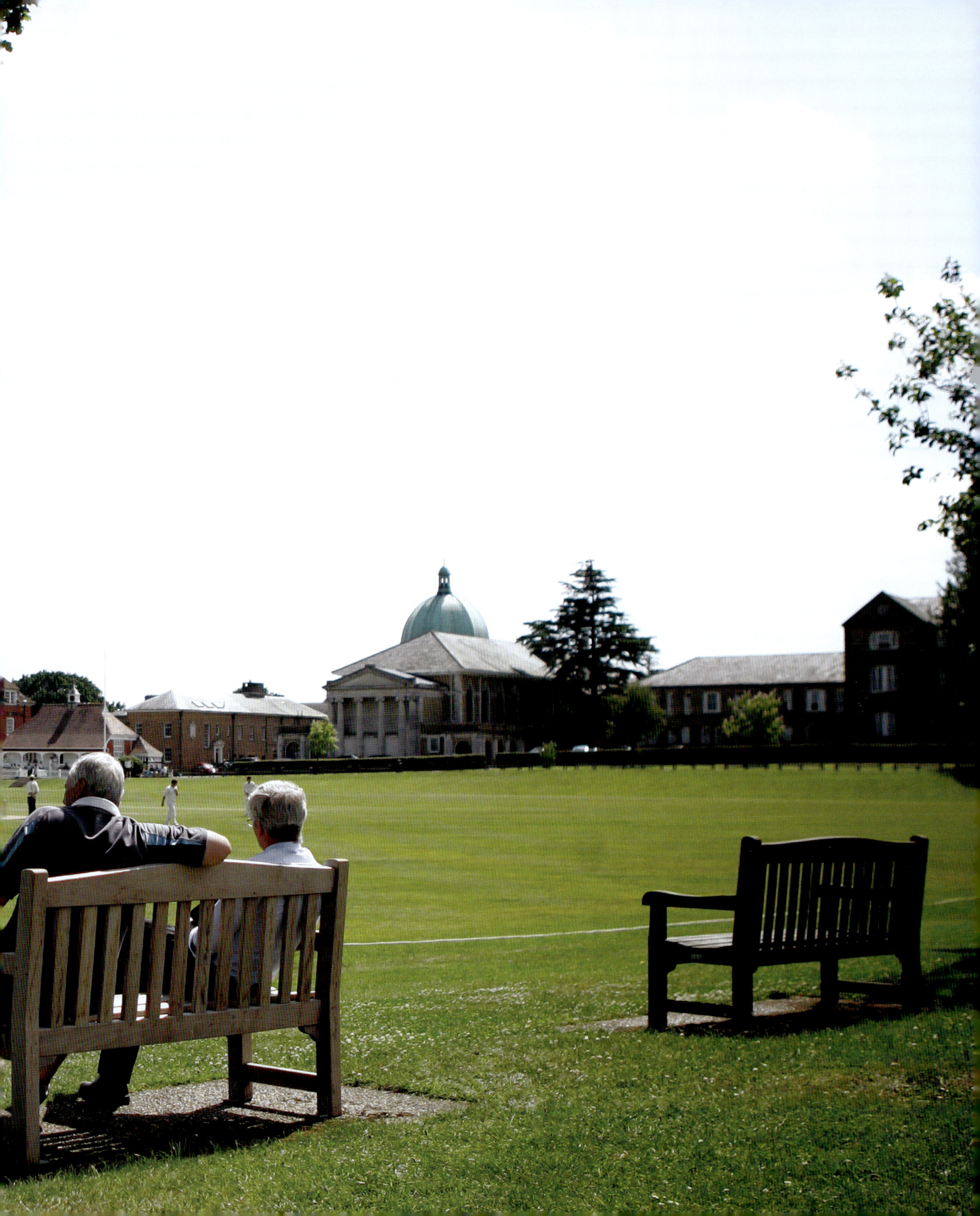

THE DUKE OF EDINBURGH'S AWARD AT HAILEYBURY

The Duke of Edinburgh's (DofE) Award scheme started in 1980, instituted by Hilary Thornburn (Staff 1979.1–83.2), with the first Gold Award awarded, as I recall, to Alex N. McL. Williams (B 1977.3). The practice expedition took place in the Aylesbury area of the Chilterns, with the qualifying expedition in the Lake District in 1982. In the 30 years since, expeditions have continued almost without interruption every October Half-term (three days' Gold Practice) and every July (five days' Gold Qualifier). The October venue has usually been the Brecon Beacons and in July the Lake District has been the place of choice, with occasional forays to Northumberland. These trips have been supplemented every year by two Field Weekends to Derbyshire in October and March. One of the Field Weekends was in fact to the Brecons and one was cancelled because of foot-and-mouth, but otherwise they have not missed a beat in all that time.

In the early years, before the CCF abolished the adventurous training section, all the Field Weekends were joint CCF/DofE trips to mutual benefit. In those days we had a longer Easter holiday so there were quite a number of adventurous trips to the Lakes, Snowdonia, Northumberland and Skye. One year saw several pupils participate in the British Schools Exploring Society's annual trip to the Arctic, which has not been repeated since.

Initially only Sixth Formers were offered Gold and Silver. Big School Reading was the fate of those Middles and Fifth Formers who did not sign up for the CCF. When there was a move to kill off that less-than-challenging activity, a range of alternatives was put forward, including forestry and grounds work, and DofE Bronze. The others lasted only a year but Bronze kept going. The policy that both CCF and DofE were voluntary but that it was a requirement to volunteer for one or the other has never sat terribly easily and has often caused headaches. With full co-education in 1998 came an increase in the Bronze numbers, which have been maintained ever since. That fed through to a greater number taking Gold and in recent years the Lower Sixth intake has often been above 30. Of course, many drop by the wayside and fail to complete the Awards, but the Duke of Edinburgh's attitude has always been that it is not the winning but the taking part that is important and if doing the Award has introduced a participant to an activity which they found enjoyable and/or useful later in life, then it has served its purpose. That said, our completion rate has been quite good, with the number of Golds per year often reaching double figures.

During the period when the School had a number of Malaysian Government scholars, Silver was quite popular among them and produced good participation, if not completion. I still recall the delight of the Malaysians one year on discovering that the map of Brecon had strange un-English names on

Above: *Neil Athey, longstanding expedition leader and organiser for the Duke of Edinburgh Awards.*

Left: *D of E preparation at School, 2012.*

Chapter 3 — AN ACTIVE SCHOOL

it. That generated a discussion on linguistics that put many of our native English speakers to shame. It was also amazing to see how both boys and girls coped with the rain and cold of South Wales in October, something which was quite alien to their native land. Unfortunately that cohort ceased when the Malaysian Government stopped the various scholarship schemes and there is now no market for the Silver Award.

The weather in Wales is nothing if not variable. Certainly, if pupils can cope with the worst that Brecon throws at them, the Lakes expedition in July is a piece of cake, although not without its thunderstorms and cold moments.

There have been many highlights – and low points – over the years, some of which might have Prince Philip asking questions. One boy turned up in Chelsea boots with smooth soles – 'the kit list said "boots", sir, which they are'. A CCF boy (fortunately not DofE) turned up for an overnight trip in Derbyshire in a Crombie and trainers – the sight of snow caking his shoulders in the early hours of the morning on the top of Margery Hill was something to behold. The joint CCF/DofE overnight trips were quite an undertaking and one cannot forget the group who forgot to pick their tent poles out of the minibus when they were dropped off and had not got around to putting up their tents or discovering the lack of poles when checked on by staff that evening. They subsequently got quite wet in the night, so they put their sleeping bags to dry in the campsite commercial-size tumble driers. It was the flake tobacco and, even more importantly, the gas lighter that I observed also rotating in the drum that caused me to switch the drier off instantly.

Then there was the girl who rang me just as I was settling to sleep at the Brecon base camp to say that there was a horse outside her tent in the farmer's field ten miles away from me. Luckily I had a good relationship with the farmer and was able to ring him up and ask him to deal with it. And then there were the girls who were quite surprised to find that their campsite toilet was a bucket in a caravan. At that time, quite a while ago, the scheme did not allow expedition campsites (as opposed to the initial base camps) to be too plush with fancy amenities such as showers. However, the march of progress is such that rare now is the campsite that does not have showers. I recall the lone boy in a girls' group who forgot to pack food so stocked up on peanut butter and bread at motorway services. Not only did he survive but he managed to disguise from the assessor that he was not having the obligatory cooked meal each evening. He is now enjoying a successful army career. I should add that the girls in that group reported that they sang to keep up their spirits whilst he found that their constant singing had the opposite effect on him.

Another group, forced back from their intended route by high winds, driving rain and thick mist, showed great determination in carrying on from an alternative campsite. And so often there were dashes by minibus to catch a train at the end of an expedition.

The Bronze overseas girl, entranced by the beauty of the Peak District, the proud pupils, and their equally proud parents, meeting Prince Philip or Prince Edward at St James's Palace to receive their Gold Awards; those are the moments I will treasure.

Neil Athey (1981.3–)

Below: *Duke of Edinburgh training expedition in the Peak District.*

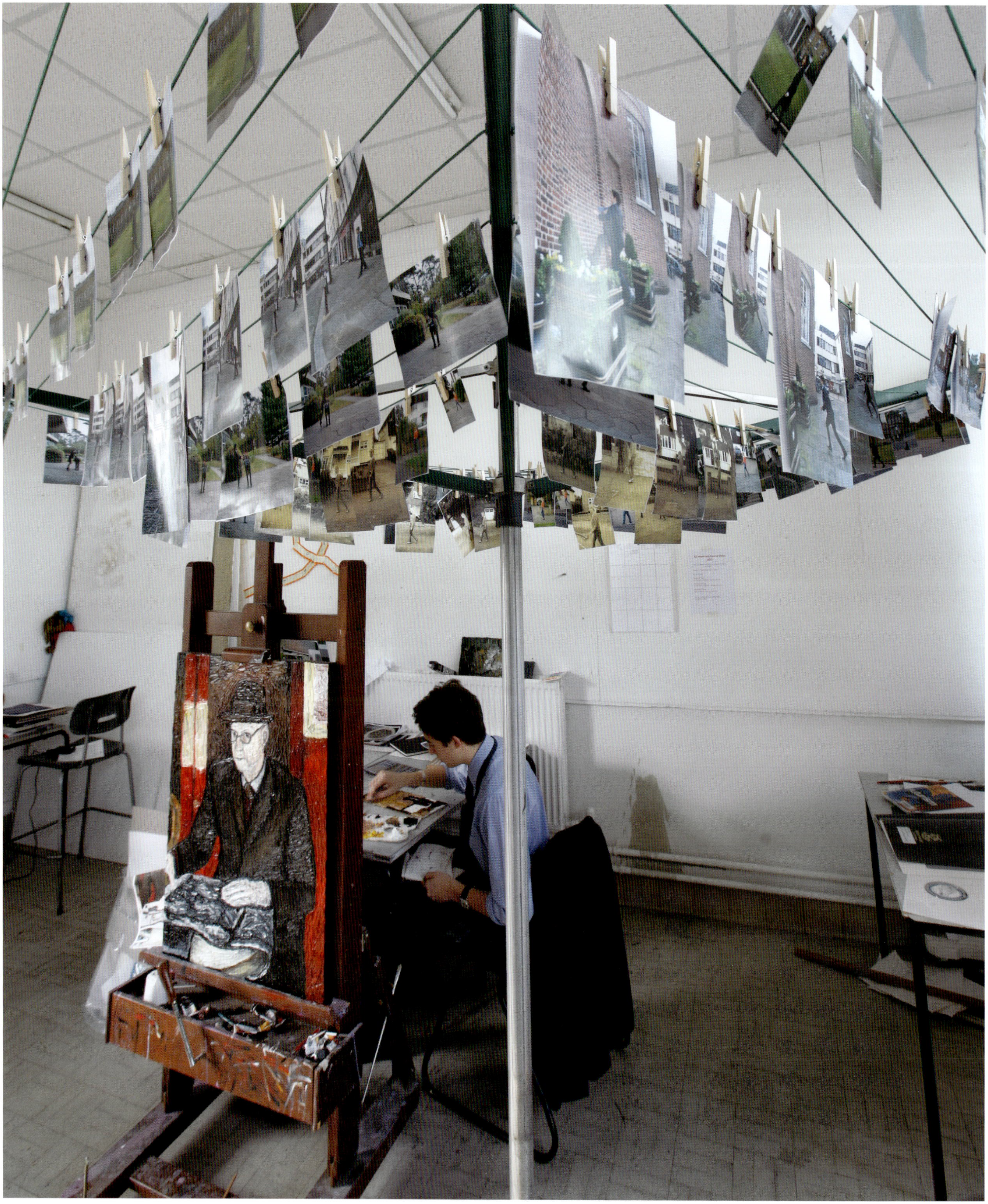

Chapter 4

A CREATIVE SCHOOL

Opposite: *Sixth Form studio space in the Art School.*

Right: *Diana of the Uplands, 1904, by Charles Wellington Furse ARA (Tate Britain). When exhibited at the Royal Academy in 1904, it was described as 'as fine a piece of open-air portraiture as England ever produced.'*

HAILEYBURY ARTISTS
C.W. Furse: A Talent Cut Short

Charles Wellington Furse (BF 1880.2) is a name which has been mentioned in earlier histories of Haileybury, but little has been said about his powers as an artist. He was sent to Haileybury and placed in the care of the Reverend George Jeans (Staff 1874.1–87.1), a family friend. In the 1880s Haileybury employed, under the title 'Geometrical drawing master', Ebenezer Burchett (Staff 1863.3–90.3), and it was he who instructed Furse in draughtsmanship and painting. Furse was not the first boy to have been prepared for art school at Haileybury; George Gascoyne (C 1876.1) had done so already. Furse's time at Haileybury was undistinguished academically, and he never made the Sixth Form, but the education was good enough for him, later in life, to have been very thankful to his Masters.

When Furse was caught slacking in the Form Room, the usual imposition of Dates was put to one side and he was instead set drawing tasks. The Reverend Julian Dove (Staff 1880.2–98.3) set him the task of executing 50 ponies in ink before dinner time the following day and to Dove's delight the ponies came in the form of skeletons running in a steeplechase.

When Furse left Haileybury, he was ready for a new challenge, although he had fond memories of playing in the 2nd XI and the Fives Team. He moved from Haileybury to the Slade effortlessly and at the end of the first year, aged 17, there he was awarded three of the Art School's major prizes. When Furse left the Slade in 1887 he travelled to L'Academie, an atelier in Paris, and there developed a particular skill in portraiture which was to inform his future role as an artist. On returning to England, a firm friend of William Rothenstein, Furse entered the studio of Fred Brown and at the age of 20 entered his first painting, *Cain*, at the Royal Academy,.

From 1889 his reputation took off and he secured commissions to paint important society, political and military figures. He was even given the commission to paint Lord Aberdeen, the outgoing Lord Lieutenant of Ireland, on the recommendation of William Gladstone. Ten years after Furse had left Haileybury he had made his name as one of the most important portrait painters in the country.

From the age of seven Furse had suffered a weakness of the lungs and in 1895 he travelled to South Africa to recover his health, a move which did not cure him. Although two years later he was diagnosed with tuberculosis, his grave news did nothing to temper his output. In 1904 Furse was admitted as an Associate of the Royal Academy. This was also the year he produced his most confident paintings, including *The Timber Haulers*, *Diana of the Uplands* and *Cubbing with the York and Ainsty*. Furse's work was not just valued by the Victorian and Edwardian establishment but James McNeill Whistler, Walter Sickert and John Singer Sargent all praised him for his skill and bravura. He died on 17 October 1904, aged only 36.

ATMP

An Appreciation of the Late Work of Rex Whistler

Rex Whistler's (Hi 1919.2) paintings from the late 1930s until he was killed in Normandy in 1944 are perhaps his most powerful and insightful images. The late paintings have a maturity and delicacy which are all too often obscured by his playful, decorative work and reputation as a member of the 'bright young things', which is unfortunate because they deserve greater attention, especially if one wishes to understand the artist.

Sergeant Isaacs of the Welsh Guards, or *The Master Cook*, c.1941, is a tour-de-force portrait in its composition, lighting and sensitivity. The Sergeant's bulk and meaty thighs spread apart, encased in voluminous white trousers, confront the viewer and it is only after looking upwards, past a groin which never seems to end, that we are greeted with the sitter's kind face. In the background, the mundane domestic tasks of the kitchen continue, composed with the care of a Dutch Old Master. *The Master Cook* gives the viewer a tantalising glimpse of the way Whistler's painting was progressing before his untimely death. The realism and use of natural light seem to be the key developments in Whistler's late work, many miles away from the luxuriant conversation pieces of the early 1930s in

Above: Sergeant Isaacs of the Welsh Guards, *or* The Master Cook, *by Rex Whistler, c.1941.*

which excess and fashion dominated but nature was clipped, trained and ornamented.

Whilst in the Army Whistler executed two other exquisite, eye-catching oils, both capturing moments of solitude and boredom. *The Officers' Mess Tent, Colchester* (1942) and *Portrait Group at Colchester* (1940) remind one of the canvases by Gustave Caillebotte, their clarity and desire to capture the essence of the scene with an intense realism, making them highly desirable. It is as though the theatrical element of his early work is no longer needed, the war is drama enough. As a painter in oils, Whistler was only just beginning to gain his own voice in that medium. This advance, coupled with the masterly way he composed his work, provides the viewer with a small window into which they can gaze on the mature work of a truly exceptional artist.

Rex Whistler has never been treated as a mainstream artist by the arts establishment, but perhaps it is time for a detailed reassessment of his place in 20th-century British art rather than labelling him as simply a decorative artist and bright young thing. Six years ago Andrew Graham Dixon asked what Whistler would have painted after the war and the resulting period of austerity if he had lived. Life and light is probably the answer.

ATMP

A Hidden Haileyburian

Bryan Wynter (Ha 1929.3) is a Haileyburian artist who has hitherto been ignored yet should be acknowledged as one of our most important figures in the Arts. Wynter was a member of the second generation of St Ives artists and led the way in abstract art in the 1950s. After a fairly undistinguished career at Haileybury, he was forced into working in the family business, the Times Laundry Co Ltd, instead of studying art. At the age of 23 he was finally able to persuade his father to allow him to attend an art school and, like his predecessors, Rex Whistler and Charles Furse, he entered the Slade.

Wynter cut a dash among the other students at the Slade – he had money, a fast car, an even faster wardrobe and a flat off Gower Street – but he started his artistic education at a comparatively older age. The Second World War soon put an end to his time at the Slade and he registered as a conscientious objector. The Ministry of Labour posted him to the laboratories of Sir Solly Zuckerman and it may have been there that he learned about the care needed in drugs procedures which helped him in his own mescaline experiments in the 1950s.

From 1943 Wynter's work showed a strong affinity with the Surrealists, but by the end of the decade there was also a clear reference in his work to the Neo-Romantic landscapes of Paul Nash and Graham Sutherland. At the end of the war he moved down to Zennor, just outside St Ives, and it was there that he produced some of his most powerful work and established lasting friendships with artists Patrick Heron, Peter Lanyon and Terry Frost.

In 1951, having been featured in Herbert Read's publication *Contemporary British Art*, Wynter was commissioned to paint a canvas for the Festival of Britain, which was possibly the first large-scale painting he had undertaken. In 1953 he was being exhibited alongside Neo-Romantic artists such as Michael Ayrton, but his work was already starting to take on a strong abstract quality. In 1958, Patrick Heron wrote that Wynter was one of the most important painters working in Britain. His reputation soared for the remainder of the decade and into the 1960s, but British appetite for Abstract Expressionism soon waned and Haileybury's most important modern painter started to lose ground to

Below: *Bryan Wynter in his studio, c.1960. Other more recent Haileyburian artists include Aris Raissis (C 1976.3), Alasdair Rennie (K 1986.3), Christopher Insoll (E 1969.3), Atul Vohora (Th 1993.2) and Maria Lintoff (Alb and M 1998.3).*

younger artists. In the 1960s Wynter moved towards Kinetic Art, producing what he called IMOOS, mobiles which explored physical movement in art and were very popular with collectors. After the publication of Theodor Schwenk's book *Sensitive Chaos*, he explored the possibilities of linking his ideas with science. His work in the 1970s had an expressive freedom and was stopped only by the massive heart attack that killed him in 1975.

When Wynter died, his work went out of favour, but today it is highly desirable again and is held in many major national and international collections. He is certainly a Haileyburian to be proud of and should join Charles Furse and Rex Whistler to form a trinity of great Haileybury artists.

ATMP

TRAVERS OTWAY: A THEATRICAL ENIGMA

Edgar Matthews (Staff 1922.3–55.2) was my first Housemaster. He gave me, alone, a sex talk. I had, he explained, emerged from my mother and she had endured great pains. He asked whether I knew what my testicles were. I, ever the eager show-off, replied, 'Oh yes Sir, they are the things that go round and round inside your stomach.' He rather lost his way after this and the talk petered out.

He was, of course, a pillar of Haileybury drama and, year by year, took a group to the Continent, touring a Shakespeare production. Anyone could apply to be involved and auditions were held during the Easter term. The year I applied the play was *The Merchant of Venice* and I delivered at my audition what was, I felt sure, a hilarious rendering of the Launcelot Gobbo soliloquy 'Gobbo … good Gobbo … use your legs, take the start, run away'. I was not picked, not even as a stage hand, and I was in Batten, Edgar Matthews' House. It was that bad. But, as a result, I have always had an especial sympathy for the 'resting' actor.

Alan Ayckbourn (Tr 1952.3) (one of my contemporaries) was involved with drama at Haileybury and many accounts of his astoundingly successful and prolific career as a playwright mention Haileybury and Edgar Matthews. In fact, in his time there were two pillars of Haileybury drama, Matthews and E.J. Miller (Staff 1943.2–62.3). Their intense rivalry doubtless helped to give Haileybury drama its exceptional vibrancy. Miller was, and remains, a mystery figure. He lived alone in a Red House flat and taught in the Bradby. He was

Far left: *Poster for the Arts Society, 1921 by Rex Whistler.*

Below: *Edgar Matthews playing Macbeth on the 1951 tour of Norway and Sweden with Brende Fullagar as Lady Macbeth.*

Chapter 4 — A CREATIVE SCHOOL

ALAN AYCKBOURN

Ayckbourn has written no fewer than 76 full-length plays, as well as revues and plays for children. This would be impressive enough even if the majority of these plays were now out of print, gathering dust on shelves or occasionally produced by amateur companies in village halls, but the wonderful reality is that they continue to be performed at the highest level, drawing audiences to the West End and to Broadway and ensuring that Ayckbourn is one of the most celebrated playwrights of our age. The challenges are often the nature of the plays themselves. One of Ayckbourn's main themes is the interconnectedness of lives and the ways in which differing perspectives on characters and events can be offered by juxtaposing scenes. One of the most audacious examples of this is *House/Garden*, two plays presenting the events of a garden party and designed to be performed simultaneously in linked theatres, with the actors moving between stages as if they are moving between the house and the garden, so that an exit from one play becomes an entrance into the other. Such ingenuity and playfulness is only part of what attracts audiences to Ayckbourn, however. Principally it is the comic truthfulness of his dialogue and action, pinpointing deeply recognisable characters at heightened moments of confusion and crisis.

It should be noted that almost all of Ayckbourn's plays are actually conceived for performance in the round. This leads us to Ayckbourn's directing career, which deserves special mention. Not only has he directed the initial productions of all his plays since 1967 but he has also directed key productions of the works of other major playwrights, the most notable perhaps being Arthur Miller's *A View From the Bridge*, staged at the Royal National Theatre in 1987 with Michael Gambon as Eddie Carbone. Miller himself considered this the definitive production of a play that will be very familiar to many Haileyburians.

Nigel Parkin (Staff 2006.3–)

Above: *Alan Ayckbourn, cartoon by Clive Francis.*

nicknamed 'Müller' because he had a marked central European accent. Nobody seemed to know where he came from. He was eccentric. He was invariably late for lessons and, because he knew he would be late, he regularly prescribed sections of verse to be learned and declaimed to him when he eventually turned up. He prescribed Milton's great lament on blindness in *Samson Agonistes* 'O dark, dark, dark, amid the blaze of noon, irrecoverably dark …' etc. so frequently that it is fixed in my memory for ever. He was an inspirational teacher, with a wonderful feel for language and rhythm, and introduced us not just to Milton's heroic verse and Browning's dramatic monologues but also to minor poets such as William Morris. The *Haileybury Register* tells us nothing about him: his entry (all of a piece with the mystery) is spare in the extreme. But it shows that alone of all Canon Bonhote's appointments, he was without any degree or qualification.

In my time (1952–7) it was strongly rumoured that he was the playwright (*nom de plume* Travers Otway) who had written *The Hidden Years*, produced at London's Fortune Theatre in 1948 and very favourably reviewed. The play was published by Faber & Faber with a dust cover that proclaimed: 'Its theme is one of those passionate friendships between an older and a younger boy which the public school system at once stimulates and abominates.' Miller was the Master in Charge of the Reading Room (now the Attlee Room) and it can be imagined with what relish boys would repeatedly pen in the suggestion book, 'May we please have the collected works of Travers Otway'. Whether Miller inspired Ayckbourn in any way I do not know, but his one play has been somewhat eclipsed by Ayckbourn's 75 (or so). Ayckbourn's first play was almost certainly written at Haileybury. I have had the good fortune to be involved with the National Theatre and a revival of his *Season's Greetings* had its first night there in December 2010. I was invited and I took as my guest Hugh Mead (Tr 1952.3), an exact contemporary of Ayckbourn's in Trevelyan and his only close friend at Haileybury. Mead became godfather to Ayckbourn's first child, but they had rather lost touch over more recent years. After the show they met and reminisced. Ayckbourn, they were both sure, had written his first play for the Trevelyan House Society when he was 16 or 17. It has not survived.

Edward Walker-Arnott (B 1952.3)

HAILEYBURY ~ *A 150th Anniversary Portrait*

Above: *A screen-printed ceramic transfer on glazed earthenware by Cristina Martinez (Alb 2010.3).*

Opposite: *A hand-embroidered Obi by Dalia Frontini (C 2010.3).*

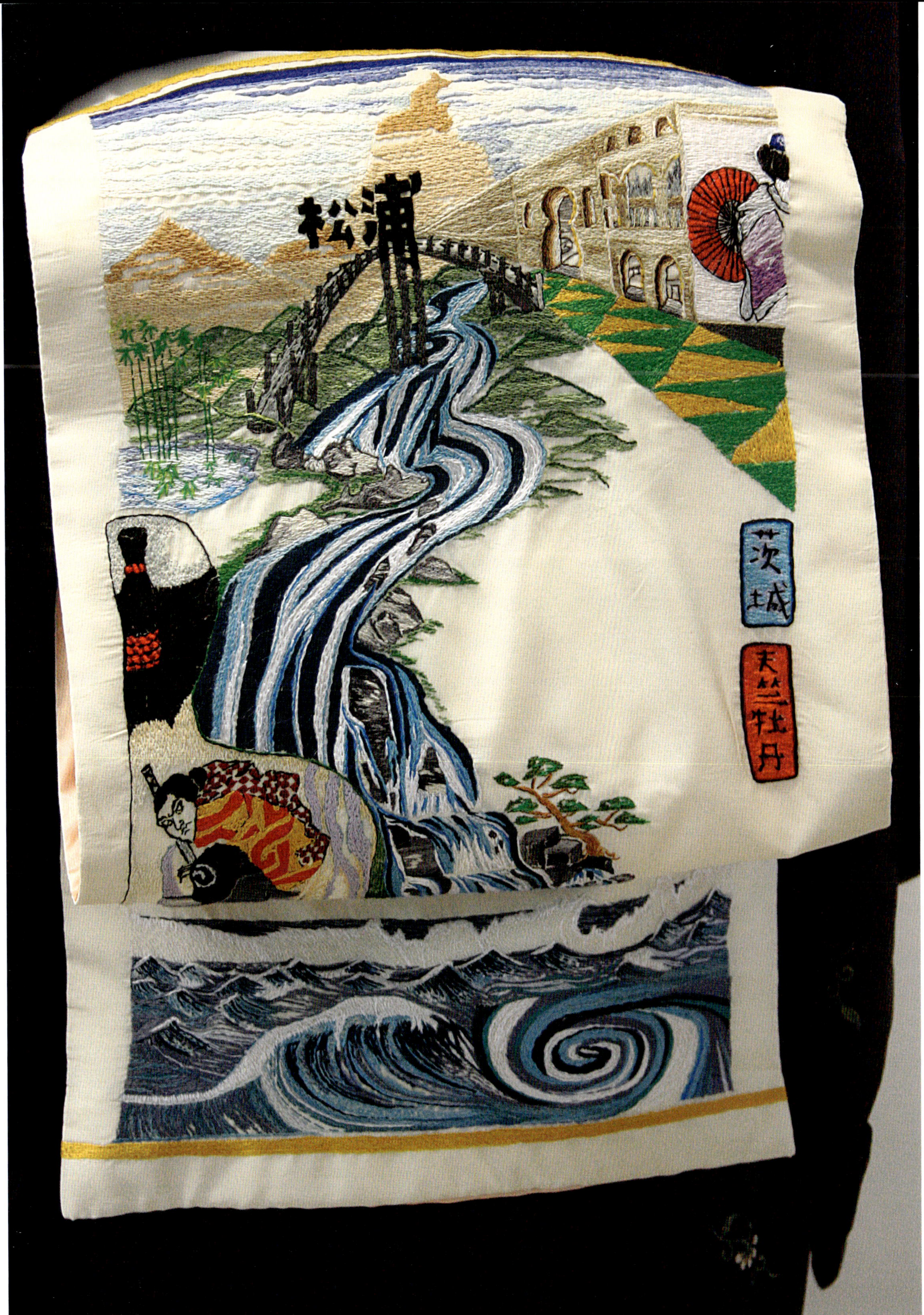

松浦
茨城
天竺牡丹

HAILEYBURY — *A 150th Anniversary Portrait*

RECOLLECTIONS OF DRAMA AND MUSIC IN THE 1960S

Haileybury in my time was blessed with two inspirational English beaks. J.B.W. Thomas – Jack T – put across his enthusiasm for the novels of Thomas Hardy with forensic skill. I can't remember being taught formally by E.B.A. Edwards (Staff 1955.3–72.3) – Basil – but his influence was equal to Jack's. Both were brilliant theatre directors. I have a dim memory of Basil's *Coriolanus*, and clearer recollections of *Murder in the Cathedral* (1960) in Chapel, the *Agamemnon* in Memorial Quad, and a knock-out production of *King Lear* (1962) in Big School, starring Bob Scott (Ha 1957.3).

Basil's successes included a Pastimes production of *The Importance of being Earnest* – who could forget E.F. Williams (Staff ISC 1936.3–42.1, Haileybury and ISC 1942.2–72.2), Housemaster of Lawrence and Second Master, as the suavest of butlers? – in which Jack Thomas played John Worthing. In 1962, Jack both directed and appeared in a delightful Pastimes *She Stoops to Conquer*. One wonders how he found time to prepare his lessons. The following term, Easter 1963, he directed *Henry V*, memorable for its avowedly Olivier-inspired central performance by Anthony 'Reg' Purnell (Tr 1958.2).

This production was then taken on tour to Holland, Jack continuing the tradition begun by his father-in-law, E.C. Matthews. The year before saw the beginning of a new tradition, though a sadly short-lived one: touring not with Shakespeare but with Gilbert and Sullivan. This was the brainchild of E.H.F. Sawbridge (BF 1945.3, Staff 1960.3–91.2), who had arrived as Assistant Director of Music in 1960. We took *The Yeomen of the Guard* (1962) to Denmark and *The Mikado* (1964) to Sweden. Hugh Sawbridge directed the productions, organised the tours, and played the double bass in the orchestra. There were some excellent performances on stage: in *The Yeomen*, Nick Kennedy Scott (A 1958.2) touched the heart as Jack Point, the jester, and Bob Scott was hilarious as the jailer. Their partnership was equalled in *The Mikado* by Tony O'Brien (Tr 1960.3) and Harold Chaplin (BF 1961.1) as Ko-Ko and Pooh-Bah.

All three tours were hugely enjoyable. There was a great camaraderie – singing rude songs on the coach, the naughty pleasure of being able to drink and smoke, and the eye-opening opportunity of staying in private houses and being confronted by alien customs (I never took to meat and vegetables served consecutively). Being allocated your family in a kind of cattle market could be nerve-wracking – some hosts were less agreeable than others – but I still exchange Christmas cards with the former daughter of the house in Sønderborg.

If the stage performances were excellent, the orchestra in *The Yeomen* was not, although the extras drafted in from elsewhere made a big difference in *The Mikado*. The music beaks were first-rate, of course: David Thompson, the leader, who went on to Covent Garden; Nancy Neild, the visiting cello teacher, who had a cigarette permanently clamped to her lips during rehearsal; and Tony Casimir (Staff 1954.1–72.3), a fine clarinettist.

The conductor was W.L. Snowdon (Staff 1946.1–66.2), the Director of Music. Bill Snowdon was a great musician: organ scholar at Pembroke College, Cambridge, he came to Haileybury from Stowe. Did he tell me that he had once conducted a production of *Boris Godunov*? His greatest achievement in my time was a performance of the Verdi *Requiem* (1964) in Big School, where we were joined by the choir from Queenswood. I owe much to Bill Snowdon, and I am glad to be able to salute his memory.

Richard Lawrence (L 1960.1)

Being almost entirely unathletic, I disliked the unchallenged 'ruggarocracy' that prevailed and have to admit that I was hugely amused when the ex-Twickenham rugby posts on Big Side were sawn down by one of my musical colleagues just before the Cock House match. Despite my non-athleticism, I enjoyed squash and my weekly cycle rides to the sailing club in the Lee Valley.

Jack Hindmarsh (Staff 1966.3–89.2), Director of Music was an inspiration to all of us musicians. He

Above: The Yeomen of the Guards *Tour, 1962.*

Chapter 4 — A CREATIVE SCHOOL

built on my prep school choral training and eventually put me into the small Chapel Choir, the Glee Club and the Madrigal Society. On Sunday mornings I used to conduct the Full Choir for the versicles and responses. His colleague, Anthony Casimir, introduced me to the French horn, on which I progressed very quickly, becoming leader of the CCF band. As a reward for this, and my services to singing, I was awarded a Music Scholarship.

William Miller (Ha 1965.1)

CHOIRS AND GOOD COMPANY

'Since singing is so good a thing, I wish all men would learne (sic) to sing.' So wrote the great English composer William Byrd in the preface to *Psalmes, Sonnets and Songs* (1588). Jack Hindmarsh, my first Director of Music, laid great store by this dictum and encouraged all members of the School to sing. Congregational practice on Saturday morning was definitely one of the highlights of the week. Jack effectively ran three choirs: the Full Choir, which welcomed everyone; a slightly smaller, auditioned Chapel Choir; and a select 'mini-choir'. The Chapel Choir performed an anthem every Sunday morning and the mini-choir would regularly sing evensong. A challenge every year was to accommodate the Full Choir in the balcony for the carol services, such was the popularity of these services. Highlights of choral singing during Jack's time included a live broadcast of the 1978 Remembrance Day service on ITV.

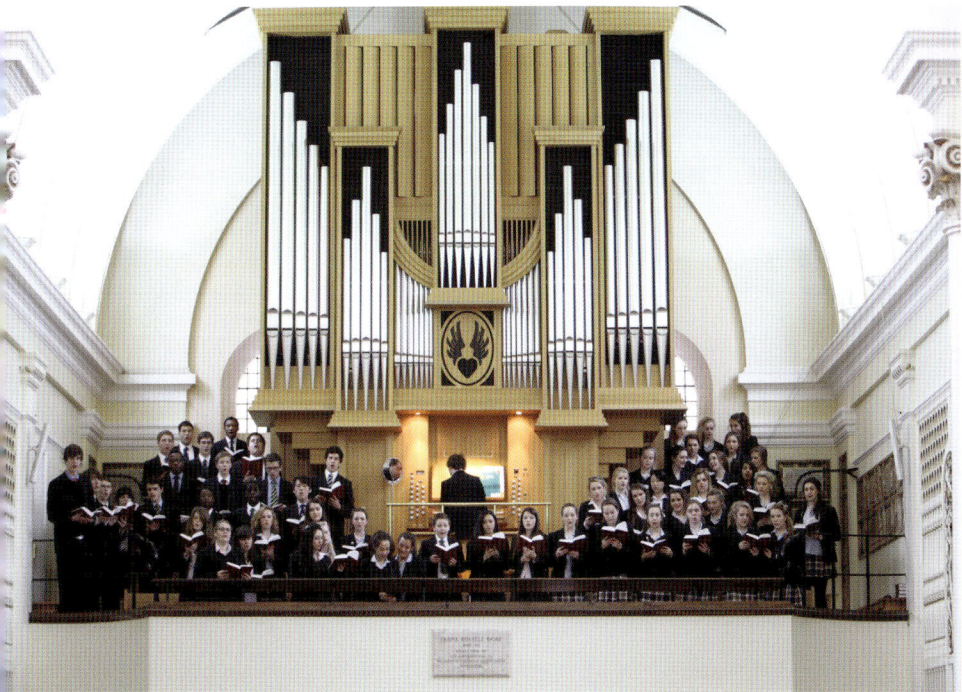

Right: *W.L. (Bill) Snowdon, Director of Music from 1946 to 1966.*

Below: *The Choir singing 'Lift up your hearts', 2012.*

Below right: *Jack Hindmarsh, Director of Music, by Susan Ryder, 1988.*

Away from Haileybury there was a tour to Geneva and regular performances at Sadler's Wells Theatre and the Royal Naval College, Greenwich, as well as mini-choir lunchtime recitals at St Lawrence Jewry and a concert attended by the whole School to celebrate the 125th anniversary of Haileybury at Westminster Abbey. Alec Anderson (Staff 1989.3–2000.2) succeeded Jack. As the format of the Haileybury weekend evolved, there were fewer Sunday services and performances away from Haileybury took on a greater significance. The favoured venue in London was St Martin-in-the-Fields and there were tours to Austria, Belgium, Italy, Spain and the US.

In 2000 Peter Davis (Staff 2000.3–2005.2) succeeded as Director of Music. In terms of repertoire, Peter immediately challenged the Choir to rise to greater heights. There were performances of Britten's *Rejoice in the Lamb* at St Martin-in-the-Fields, Parry's *Blest Pair of Sirens* at St John's, Smith Square and Copland's *In the Beginning* in West Road Concert Hall, Cambridge and Bernstein's *Chichester Psalms* at Haileybury. The Choir made two CD recordings on the *Regent* label, including works by Parry and Leighton and *The Making of the Drum* by Chilcott. The second CD featured Fauré's *Requiem* paired with Langlais' *Messe Solennelle* and *Motets* by Duruflé. Alongside these activities there were tours to Berlin and Leipzig, performing in the Thomaskirche where J.S. Bach had been *Kapelmeister*, Tuscany with performances in the cathedrals of Florence and Pisa, and a tour to

Above: *The School Chamber Choir, 2009.*

Below left: *Alison Stephens.*

ALISON STEPHENS (1970–2010)

Alison Stephens (Aby and Ha 1986.3) won a music scholarship to Haileybury in 1986, having played the mandolin from the age of 11. Her career as a soloist began even before she had left school when, still only 17, she played her first concerto at the Barbican. She went on to become the first person ever to graduate from Trinity College of Music in mandolin and was immediately appointed to teach it. As well as teaching and tutoring students from all over the world, she toured and gave recitals, also working with leading opera and ballet companies. She was invited to play on numerous film scores, most notably *Captain Corelli's Mandolin*, adapted from the novel by Louis de Bernières, which also provided the material for a highly successful stage show with actor Mike Maran. In recent years she began to compose for the mandolin, whilst continuing to broadcast and perform all over the world. She raised large sums for cancer research through concerts and royalties from sales of her recordings before tragically succumbing to cancer herself in 2010. She is credited with both popularising the mandolin and lending it serious credibility for the first time as a classical instrument.

HAILEYBURY MADRIGALS

The evening for my first performance of *Madrigals* at Great Amwell in 1978 it rained, so we performed in the church and I never saw the magical setting of the island. Subsequently, in the 32 years I was involved with *Madrigals*, rain-affected performances could be counted on the fingers of one hand. One of my memories of those early years was singing in the garden under the bedroom window to Mrs Cecily Toyne (Betty Sewell's mother, and daughter of Carmichael Young (L 1863.2), second Bursar of the College, and wife of S.M. Toyne). As Betty Sewell herself approached her 100th year we were to repeat the performance for her. It was a privilege to be a part of *Madrigals*, a tradition that began in the dark days of the Second World War and continues to this day. To begin with, I sang in the choir, conducted first by Jack Hindmarsh and then Alec Anderson. However, after a couple of years Alec handed over the conducting to me and I continued the tradition until 2009. It was always a special evening performing on a floodlit island, with swans drifting by as we sang *The Silver Swan* and then drifting back with the choir into Betty's garden for strawberries and cream. It is a quintessentially English event and a tradition I trust will continue for years to come.

Derek Longman

Above: Derek Longman conducts Madrigals *in Betty Sewell's garden. Betty can be seen at the open window.*

Prague, including singing for the Sunday morning mass in Prague Cathedral. In the UK the Choir sang a memorable evensong at St Paul's Cathedral, London. The service was particularly memorable for me as organist. I managed to cause half of the organ to fail just before the service began. Consequently, I played for the service not really knowing what sounds were going to come forth from the organ. Fortunately, none in the congregation was any the wiser.

In 2003/4 a slightly reduced choir entered the BBC *Songs of Praise* School Choir of the Year. The Choir progressed to the final and was one of the three senior choirs to appear in the broadcast programme from Symphony Hall, Birmingham. The following year the Choir performed even better and was voted School Choir of the Year. This gave rise to further appearances in *Songs of Praise* (from the Sage Gateshead and the Royal Albert Hall) and a broadcast on BBC Radio.

Quentin Thomas (Staff 2005.3–) followed Peter Davis as Director of Music in 2005. Choral activities continued apace, with another CD recording on Regent, tours to Spain and Prague, and concerts in London at St John's, Smith Square and the Barbican. As a reflection of the enjoyment while singing as pupils at Haileybury, Quentin Thomas successfully formed an OH choir in 2010. The first performance was a concert to commemorate the life and service to the School of Jack Hindmarsh. In 2012 the OH choir formed part of a larger choral society brought together by Quentin to perform the Verdi *Requiem* as part of the 150th anniversary celebrations.

Derek Longman (Staff 1978.1–2010.2)

What if…?

As a learner on the trumpet I used to play in the School Orchestra. On one occasion we gave the first public performance of a piece written by Michael Heming (L 1934.1), who had been killed in the Western Desert in 1942. It was entitled *Threnody for a Soldier Killed in Action*. I was too young to appreciate the musical quality of the composition, but I have wondered since what potential was lost with his death. Towards the end of the war 'things' were getting so tight that I remember my brother and I not only copying out orchestral parts for *Le Bourgeois Gentilhomme* but also building music stands in Shops for the performance.

John Nichols (BF 1940.3)

HAILEYBURY — A 150th Anniversary Portrait

An Embarrassment of Riches

I joined the big and small choirs in my first term and remember singing the St Matthew's Passion with Queenswood and in April 1967 was in *The Pirates of Penzance* tour of Sweden. I joined the Madrigal Society, and was a bugler/drummer in the CCF Corps band. Then there were the School Subscription Concerts, which attracted some big names, such as Dennis Brain, Julian Bream, Vladimir Ashkenazy and Humphrey Lyttelton, and I also think I remember seeing Johnny Dankworth and Cleo Lane. I would like to thank fellow Allenby House member Nigel Purdy (A 1964.3), who taught me how to play the guitar. Allenby House carol singing was always great fun and we sang our way around the College, The Roundings and parts of Hertford Heath, before being given sherry by Basil Edwards and ending up at Jack Hindmarsh's house where we quenched our thirst with a good many bottles of cider.

Peter Rye (A 1965.1)

KIPLING AND ME

I first came across Rudyard Kipling in the same way that all young did in my day – by being read the *Just So Stories* and then *The Jungle Book*. These were probably the two most universally distributed children's books of the day. The illustrations in the *Just So Stories* were also very well known and made such an impression on all my contemporaries. Moving on beyond these young children's books was a slower process. *Kim* took a bit more careful reading, and you probably had to be a teenager to appreciate it. Similarly, *Stalky and Co*, although linked to Kipling's time at school, was not so relevant to life at the end of the Second World War.

However, when I was in the Junior School of the Imperial Service College in 1940, I discovered that the reason I went there (or perhaps 'was sent there') was because my grandmother had been a keen Kipling fan all her life and had been one of the original members of the Kipling Society when it was founded in 1927. Their first President was Dunsterville, the real Stalky of *Stalky and Co*. I was also told that when I was four years old I had been at a British Academy event at which Kipling was present. My real memory of this is vague, but I have created an impression of being introduced to him by my grandmother, so it must be true.

Right: *Manuscript of a Kipling short story in the Haileybury Archive.*

Below: *Kipling Society membership card belonging to Mrs E. Lyon, Sir John Chapple's grandmother, signed by 'Stalky'.*

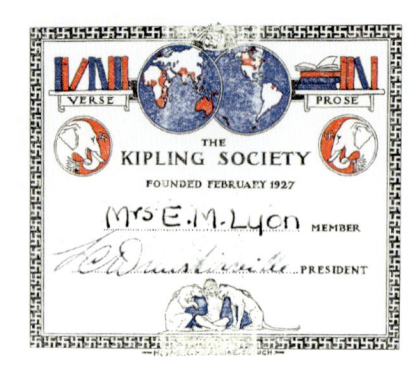

Later on I became a keen fan of the *Barrack Room Ballads* and the *Plain Tales from the Hills* and *Soldiers' Tales*. The *Barrack Room Ballads* have stayed with me all my life. I used to know almost all of them by heart. Many were well known in the Army and some, such as *Screw Guns*, were sung regularly in the Mess after dinner when there were special party evenings.

Whilst I was at Cambridge I got to know Charles Carrington (Staff 1921.2–24.2 and 1926.1–29.1), a noted Kipling scholar. I was at the time interested in the music hall tunes which, it was said, Kipling had used as settings for his

Below: *The Indian Railways editions of Kipling's stories.*

80

Chapter 4 — A CREATIVE SCHOOL

Right: *The cover of* The Skipper of the XI *(1915) by John Barnett.*

light verse. Carrington was also interested in this and he had done much research. He gave me a long list. Some of the music hall tunes remain well known, but most have faded from use. Unfortunately, I have mislaid the list of tunes.

About the same time, when I was in my late teens and early twenties, I started collecting Kipling books and other items. I don't really know why I did this. I already had a complete set of his published works, which have never been out of print. What I did was scour the secondhand bookshops in Charing Cross Road. There were lots of these shops. I searched through endless trays and shelves to find something of interest and picked up all of the Indian Railway editions of Kipling tales. These were paperback, each with two or three tales. They sold for one rupee. They were later printed in England and sold for one shilling and sixpence.

Much later, when serving in Malaya and Singapore, I shared a room with a fellow officer and we regularly quoted Kipling verse, one line alternately. We did this as our after-dinner act.

I joined the Kipling Society in 1954 and have been a member ever since. I was President of the Society for three years. I have never been a Kipling scholar, unlike many members of the Society, whose knowledge is truly remarkable.

When we moved house a few years ago I donated my collection of Kipling books, articles, etc. to the School's Archives. I hope this will be maintained and built up. I hope it will also have a reference library to record our most distinguished author.

John Chapple (K 1945.1)

THE SKIPPER

John Reginald Stagg (B 1891.3) was one of the 589 Haileyburians who gave their lives in the First World War, but when the 37-year-old died, 'the writer' John Barnett died along with him. As a pupil in Batten, Stagg made his reputation as a more than proficient batsman, but it was under the name John Barnett that he came to people's attention. The author of 12 novels, Stagg used his mother's maiden name as his *nom de plume*. He wrote for *Chatterbox* and *Cheer Boys Cheer*, two very popular boys' magazines, as well as working on his own novels.

One of the earliest novels, *Geoffrey Cheriton*, begins with a Cock House final at Haileybury, thinly disguised as Dunbury College. Two of Stagg's novels were about life at Haileybury/Dunbury, exploring the popular themes of hero worship, good sportsmanship and *noblesse oblige*. *The New Guv'nor* was published in 1913, having been serialized under the title *Wilding's First Term*. The reviewer for *The Field*, who liked the book, wrote: *It describes life at Haileybury so well as not to offend the susceptibilities of an Old Haileyburian, and those who know the school may be able to identify some of the characters or at least will be able to amuse themselves by thinking they can.*

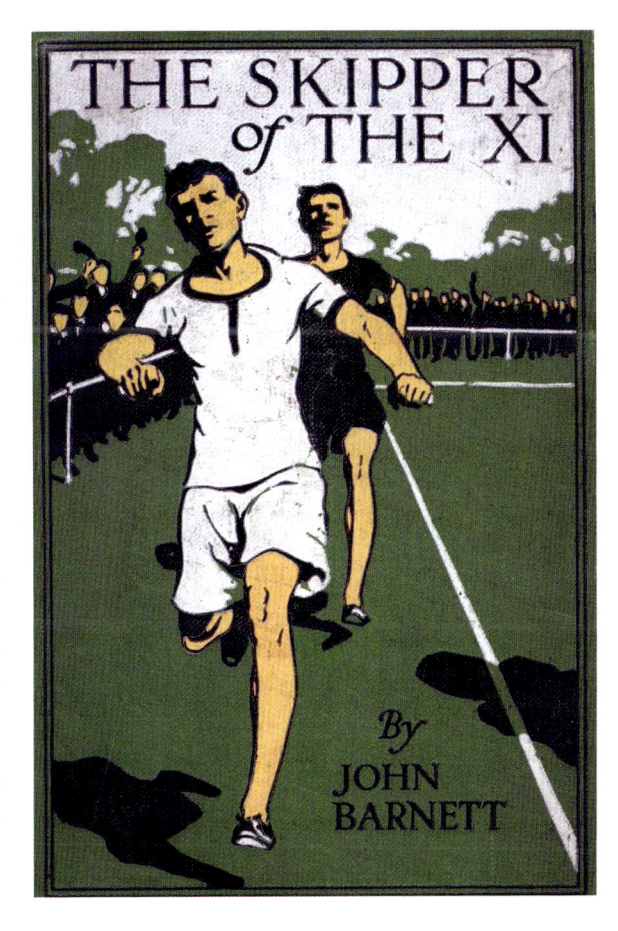

While serving on the Western Front in the Middlesex Regiment, Stagg wrote a companion volume, *The Skipper of the XI*. Published in 1915, *The Skipper* was his last novel – after being awarded the Distinguished Conduct Medal on 20 June 1916 for leading a patrol through heavy enemy fire and carrying one of the men to safety, he was killed in action on 17 September.

ATMP

HAILEYBURY DRAMA TOURS: 1990–98

For me now, trying to remember that period of Haileybury dramatic life, 21 years after our first European tour in 1990, is like revisiting another world. Recently Willy Lochtmans, manager of Concordia Theatre in Tongeren, Belgium, wrote to me: *Since the visits of Haileybury there have not been any performances of the kind at Concordia. It would be nice if there were, but, as you say, there probably is nobody who is crazy enough to take the risk*. As well-wishers used to say, 'Break a leg – as long as you have your E111!' (Now, of course, it would be your EHIC.)

On each of our six tours, we visited Tongeren and were treated by Willy and his wife, Miriam, like a teenage version of the National Theatre. We would send information about the plays in advance to the centres where we would perform, and this was distributed to local schools so that they would find it easier to understand the English text. The cast went into local schools to talk and answer questions. Hamish Loncaster's (Ha 1985.3) brilliant music for *Hamlet*, which underpinned the whole production, was aired on local radio. On the *Man for All Seasons* (1993) tour, the company was given a civic reception in Tongeren Town Hall, and the singers and organist James Fraser-Andrews (LS and K 1987.3) gave a concert in Tongeren Cathedral. This was enlivened by James leaving his music behind in Brussels and having it faxed through just in time for the recital.

Performance venues ranged from the open-air theatre in Valkenburg, the Netherlands, to the splendid civic theatre in Kerkrade. In Vondels Park in Amsterdam, Joe Dempsey (C 1985.3) as Hamlet was interrupted in mid-speech by a gang of bikers who asked what he was doing, stayed to watch, applauded loudly and then roared off into the night!

After the second tour we learned that our travel company had gone bankrupt, which explained some surprising changes of venue, including a pub in Maastricht, rather than the expected school, where the cast of *As You Like It* (1991) produced a near perfect performance to a small group of stunned beer drinkers. Kenton Bywater's (K 1987.3) athletic Touchstone and Jason Turney (Th 1987.3) and Kate Morley (Aby and E 1990.3) as Orlando and Rosalind rose to the occasion splendidly.

One interesting follow-up was that pupils from the International School in Bergen-am-Zee brought a production of *Antigone* in French to the Ayckbourn Theatre at Haileybury.

From the third tour, *The Alchemist* (1992), onwards, we relied on local contacts to find us accommodation, using host families, youth hostels, even a convent. Arriving very late in Nuremburg after a long, wet drive from Haileybury, and several circuits of the stadium where Hitler addressed mass rallies, we were delighted to be greeted at the youth hostel by a smiling Martin Dodd (Financial Controller 1989–2000). Other

The Hamlet *Tour, 1990.*

Chapter 4 — A CREATIVE SCHOOL

supporting adults on the tours included Roland Miles (Staff 1987.3–95.2) (occasionally on roller skates) and his wife Beverly, Ken Bartlett in his shorts looking for bombs under our vehicles each morning, my wife Jane (Staff 1988.3–2002.2) and Paula Thomson (Wardrobe), and the gap students, Stuart Marinus (Staff 1994.3–95.2) (who deconstructed anything, even his own power drill), Andrew Proctor (also a saxophonist in the jazz band for *Richard III* (1998)) and Andrew Moores-Grimshaw (Staff 1996.3–99.2). Colin, our Golden Boy bus driver, and his colleague Ray, enjoyed the tours so much that they helped us assemble and strike the sets.

Those on the tours will have their own special memories; maybe the sweatshirt with the poster design printed on it is at the back of a drawer or wardrobe. I recall Joe Dempsey (Hamlet) sweeping every stage before a performance as he created his own inner Denmark, and the menacing street fighting between the Montagues and the Capulets, orchestrated by the sinister Nigel Simpson (K 1989.3) as Tybalt. Few of the tech crew will ever forget the aromatic red deer skin used in *As You Like It*, which had been 'cured' by the boys behind the Ayckbourn. The overriding image of these tours for me is the teamwork of such disparate individuals pulling together – actors, musicians, tech crew and staff – solving problems on site to produce a *coup de théâtre*.

David Ross (Staff 1988.3–2002.2)

Above: Julius Caesar programme, 1932.

Right: Simon MacCorkindale.

THE GREEN ROOM

Since the first Pastimes performances which took the shape of plays put on by the Masters and their families to entertain the boys at Christmas time, through times of war and austerity and up until the present time, Haileybury has had a rich and varied history of drama. Such was the ambition of some that there was a tour of *Julius Caesar* to Poland in 1932, initiated by Edgar Matthews, as well a tour to New York in 1964. The production featured F.M. Haywood (M 1921.1, Staff 1931.3–35.2) as Julius Caesar, a previous Head Boy who had returned as a member of staff, and George Speaight (Le B 1928.3) as Cassius. George became a 'professor' (professional puppeteer), theatre historian and manager of Pollock's Toy Theatre, while his older brother, Robert (Le B 1918.1), became a celebrated Shakespearean actor and the first performer of the role of Beckett in *Murder in the Cathedral*. David Lloyd-James (Ha 1929.1), who played Brutus, later went on to become a BBC announcer.

For the most part productions were staged in Big School, which could easily accommodate the entire school but presented a real test to any performer given the lack of any amplification in the early years. One might assume that actors would have once been trained to project effectively and in recent years have lost that skill somewhat. During my first few months as the theatre technician in 2004 I found a document in my filing cabinet which had been written by a member of staff in 1979 which stated, *There were fundamentally only two things wrong with Big School as a performance space: 95 per cent of the audience could neither see nor hear anything that was going on on stage.* The findings may have helped the decision to convert the Gymnasium into what is now the Ayckbourn Theatre and in the years since 2004 it has taken on a completely new look under the direction of Rachel Beggs (Staff 2004.3–) as Head of Drama.

It goes without saying that one of Haileybury's most honoured pupils is Sir Alan Ayckbourn, one of the most influential British playwrights of the last two centuries. It would be remiss of us if we did not acknowledge the body of work he has produced, over half of which have been produced in the West End, and at 72 years of age he shows no signs of letting up. This is a larger oeuvre than that of the 'Bard' himself and at least we know Ayckbourn has actually written all of his plays.

Sadly, in October 2010 Simon MacCorkindale (B 1965.3) died from cancer at the age of 58. After his West End debut in 1974 he went on to act in, direct and produce successfully more than 60 productions for television and film, until his untimely death. He finished his career playing Dr Harry Harper as the star of the BBC drama *Casualty*. Simon once described his father's attitude to his acting career when he introduced him to Sir John Mills: 'Dad said, "I'm actually sitting here with someone who has a perfectly normal life. I guess it's possible for my son to not end up on skid row."'

In 1956 a production of *Macbeth* toured Canada and the US featuring a young Alan Ayckbourn as Macduff and Christopher Greatorex (B 1952.1) as Macbeth. A young Philip Franks (A 1969.3) who played Stanthorp in *Journey's End* (1973) would go on to study at Oxford and become a member of the Royal Shakespeare Company, proof that one can in fact have the best of both worlds. Franks continued to work on his career and has become a well-recognized artist, possibly best known for his work as Cedric 'Charley' Charlton in the television adaptation of *The Darling Buds of May*. He has also made appearances more recently in *Foyle's War*, *Casualty* and *My Dad's The Prime Minister*, to name a few. An earlier tour of Macbeth to Denmark in 1947 starred a young Gerald Harper (B 1942.3) as Macbeth. Harper went onto a career in television and on the stage, most famously as Adam Adamant in the 1960s. The uniqueness of having twin brothers as performers at one school, however, is only proven to be more unique by the Meyer brothers (B 1960.3), who both went on to have solid acting careers. They were able to use this to their benefit in the James Bond film *Octopussy* (1983), in which they played henchmen Mischka and Grischka.

Success has come to other Haileyburians in other areas of the theatrical world. Michael Aitkens (E 1961.3) has built a successful writing career, producing over 150 works with such well-known titles as *Waiting For God*, *Midsomer Murders* and *Fear Stress and Anger*. Stephen Mangan (A and Ha 1981.3) appeared in many School productions but did not think he would go on to have a career in acting and went on to study Law at Cambridge. Oddly enough, he did not think he would become a lawyer either so he returned to the stage. He apparently made the right choice and has carved out an excellent career in acting, recently playing Tony Blair in the comedy *The Hunt for Tony Blair* and taking a lead in *Episodes* (2011 and 2012).

I believe we owe a debt of gratitude to those who trod the boards before us and who were brave enough to follow their dream and pursue a life in theatre. But equally we must acknowledge those in recent years who have followed in the steps of their predecessors in various parts of the theatrical world. The list could easily fill a book with inspiring stories of those who make us laugh and cry, think and question.

Lee Wilkinson (Staff 2004–11)

Left: *Stephen Mangan and Miranda Greig (Hi, Aby and Th 1983.3) in a production of* Outside Edge *(1985), produced by Dan Hearn.*

Chapter 4 — A CREATIVE SCHOOL

Hoyt Richards in the unbeaten Haileybury XXX, 1980, seated second from right.

Bottom right: Fire Maidens from Outer Space *(1956), which provided a first screen outing for David Jones (Rodney Diak).*

Richard Leech (McClelland) as Henry VIII in A Man for all Seasons, *1960.*

Robert Speaight in Hamlet *at The Old Vic, 1930.*

AT THE MOVIES

With such a strong theatrical tradition it is perhaps to be expected that Haileyburians should have also played their part from its earliest days in the cinema. George Davy Burnaby (L 1894.2) was something of a celebrity in his lifetime and is now almost forgotten. The flamboyant and rotund Davy was a star of early British comedies. After studying at Haileybury and dropping out of Cambridge, he forged a career as a music hall singer and song writer, appearing in revues in both London and New York. In the early 1920s he formed a Pierrot troupe called the Co-optimists, which appeared to great acclaim at the Royalty Theatre in Soho, close to the studios where Marconi was experimenting with recording and radio broadcasts. The Co-optimists were one of the earliest acts to be recorded there and a recording still exists from 1922. In 1929, Davy appeared in his first film, *The Devil's Maze*, thereafter playing a succession of colonels and lords in over 30 comedies throughout the 1930s. His last appearance was in the Stewart Grainger film *Woman Hater*, in 1948.

The first known Haileyburian to star in films, however, was Howard Gaye (Le B 1892.3), who left his job as a reporter to follow his dreams in the US. Gaye acted from the earliest days of cinema in more than 40 titles and starred in two of the most famous films of the period, *Intolerance* (1916) and *Birth of a Nation* (1915). Since then other Haileyburians have appeared in major films: Stephen Mangan is best known for his television work but in fact appeared in the Oscar-nominated film *Billy Elliott* in 2000, while Hoyt Richards' (A 1980.3) chief claim to fame is as one of the first male supermodels, but he has appeared in Hollywood and independent films, albeit frequently playing male models.

Frank Vosper (Le B 1914.1) made his name as a writer as well as an actor. A popular figure in the movie business, he was often cast for his good looks and versatile voice. In 1934 he starred in Alfred Hitchcock's *The Man Who Knew Too Much* but drowned three years later, after falling from a transatlantic liner. Vosper was not the only OH to work with Hitchcock: the stage actor Stephen Haggard (Ha 1924.3) had a part in *Jamaica Inn* (1939) before playing Nelson in *Young Mister Pitt* (1942). Robert Speaight's career in film and theatre was a long and distinguished one which overlapped with those of Frank Vosper and William Fox (Th 1924.3) – in 1932 they all appeared in a production of *The Rose Without a Thorn* at the Duchess Theatre. Benjamin 'Robert' Flemyng

85

HAILEYBURY ~ *A 150th Anniversary Portrait*

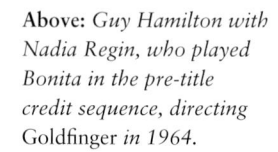

Above: *Guy Hamilton with Nadia Regin, who played Bonita in the pre-title credit sequence, directing* Goldfinger *in 1964.*

Left: *Shane Briant as Paul Durward in the 1974 Hammer Horror film,* Captain Kronos, Vampire Hunter.

(Le B 1925.3) had a part in the first performance of Frank Vosper's play *People Like Us*, which was banned by the Lord Chamberlain in his life time. Robert Flemyng's film career included *The Guinea Pig* (1948) (some of the filming was shot at the School), *Oh! What a Lovely War* (1969), *Battle of Britain* (1969) and *Funny Face* (1957). After leaving a career as a doctor in Ireland for the theatre, Richard McClelland (L 1936.3) became the first straight male actor on 'Binkie' Beaumont's books. Parts in films such as *Ice Cold in Alex* (1958), *The Shooting Party* (1985) and *Gandhi* (1982) came regularly from 1949 onwards, while he balanced a successful career on the stage. A serious contender for the title of the worst film ever made is *Fire Maidens from Outer Space* (1956), which was David Jones' (E 1938.2) (stage name Rodney Diak) first time on the silver screen. Luckily it did not kill his career, and two years later he was working with John Mills in *Dunkirk* (1958). Shane Briant (Ha 1960.3) continues to have an active career as a film actor and writer in Australia, but his best known works in the UK are four Hammer Horror films and a part in *The Naked Civil Servant* (1975) alongside John Hurt. The dubious honour of being the first murderer in the *Inspector Morse* series goes to Richard Durden-Smith (M 1957.3), who also starred in Tim Burton's *Batman* (1989).

In true Haileybury style, successful careers have also been carved out behind the scenes. Michael Stringer (Le B and C 1938.3), whose cartoons have been preserved in the School Archive, became a production designer and was nominated for an Academy Award for *Fiddler on the Roof* in 1971. He worked on many other films before moving into television. His resemblance to Harold Wilson led to on-camera cameos in both the 1968 film *Inspector*

Left: *Cartoon by Michael Stringer, Oscar-nominated production designer, of Raymond 'Twitch' Slater (Staff 1923.1–47.3), chief ARP officer.*

86

Chapter 4 — A CREATIVE SCHOOL

A HAILEYBURIAN IN HOLLYWOOD

In recent years Christopher Nolan has proved to be one of the most exciting, creative and successful filmmakers in the world. His first major film, *Memento* (2000), has become something of a cult classic amongst film fans. Based on a short story written by Nolan's brother, *Memento* is a thriller told in short bursts of time, starting at the end point of the narrative and with the plot unravelling in reverse. The protagonist has a form of amnesia which means he cannot make new memories and so tattoos himself with the clues to the murder (his wife's) that he is attempting to solve.

Nolan included a nod to his alma mater in the film; one of the tattoos (the murderer's car number plate) is SG13 7IU, which must be a real-life instance of the unreliability of memory as it is slightly wrong – the 'I' should be 'N' – but the director's commentary confirms that it is 'the zip code of the school I attended'.

Angus Head (Staff 2002.3–)

Above: *The licence plate, seen in* Memento.

Right: *Christopher Nolan directing* The Dark Knight Rises *in New York, November 2011.*

official James Bond director in 1964 and then again between 1971 and 1974. He directed a number of war films, such as *The Colditz Story* (1955), *Battle of Britain* and *Force 10 from Navarone* (1978), having actually worked for the French Resistance in Paris during the Nazi occupation. In the 1980s he was approached to direct a new film of *Batman*. It was, however, another Haileyburian whose name would be linked to Batman. Christopher Nolan (M 1984.3) is without doubt the most famous Haileyburian film director, credited with breathing new life into the genre of intelligent action films with his *Batman* trilogy. The second of his *Batman* films was nominated for eight Academy Awards and won two. He arrived at Haileybury in 1984 with an Art Exhibition and went on to study English literature at University College London, where he began making 16mm films in the College Film Society. His first major film was *Memento* (2000), which, together with *The Prestige* (2006), received multiple Academy Award nominations. More recently, in 2010, his film *Inception* was nominated for eight Academy Awards and won four. According to boxofficemojo.com, by the end of 2011 Nolan's films had taken $1.2bn at the box office worldwide.

ATMP

Clouseau and the television series *Paradise Postponed*. Peter Sharland (Ha 1931.1) was an actor and also produced TV series such as *Sexton Blake* and the BBC's *Ready Steady Go*. John Howard Davies' (BF 1953.1) film career started aged nine as the lead in David Lean's *Oliver Twist* (1948) and in *Tom Brown's Schooldays* (1951). Returning to the business as an adult, Davies directed and produced some of the first *Monty Python's Flying Circus* episodes, *The Goodies* and one series of *Steptoe and Son*. Other iconic series he produced were *Fawlty Towers* and *The Good Life*.

Remaining firmly behind the camera, Guy Hamilton (E 36.3) began his long directing career as an assistant to Carol Reed, going on to become the

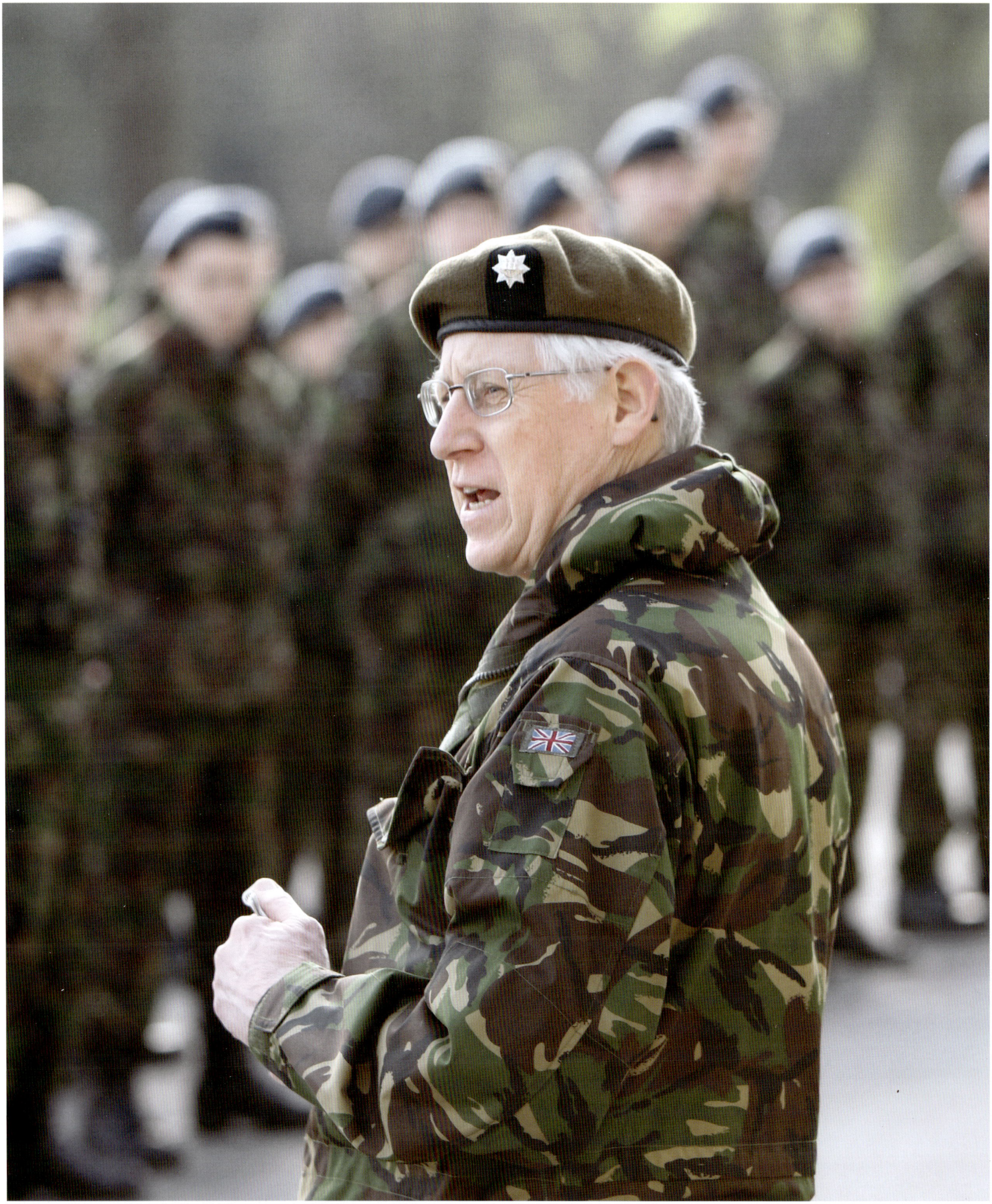

Chapter 5

THE COMMON ROOM

COMMON ROOM CLERIHEWS

Behind a scholarly and placid exterior, members of Common Room have always enjoyed sniping at each other from time to time. One such exponent of refined bitchiness was Geoff Wright (Staff 1938.2–72.2), as he was known to his colleagues. The boys referred to him as Daddy Wright (though he was childless) and the *Red Book* gave him his opulent four initials G.B.W.P. Wright. He introduced to Haileybury his version of the clerihew. This form was invented by and is named after Edmund Clerihew Bentley. When he was a 16-year-old pupil at St Paul's School in 1906, these lines came into Bentley's head during a science class:

Sir Humphry Davy
Was not fond of gravy.
He lived in the odium
Of having discovered sodium.

This was not exactly a witty poem, but Bentley's invention prospered. His next effort was more praiseworthy:

George the Third
Ought never to have occurred.
One can only wonder
At so grotesque a blunder.

So the rules of the clerihew are simple. Line one must introduce the name of the subject. Lines two, three and four should be as rude and uncomplimentary (and even untrue) as possible.

The clerihew flourished, inspiring many imitators, not least Geoff Wright, who wrote the following scurrilous and entirely libellous clerihews on his fellow beaks:

First come I – my name is Bonhote,
Anti-sex is what I connote.
Here I brood like any vulture,
Black against your art and culture.

Next come I – my name is Lloyd,
Of all enthusiasm void.
For thirty years I've struggled daily
Against unnatural vice in Hailey.

Next come I – my name is Cook,
With my suburban butcher's look.
I hope to save from the Old Bailey
The great majority of Hailey.

Jack Thomas

Opposite: *Robin Bishop (Staff 1984.3–), HM of Batten for 11 years, Head of Economics for 10 years and currently CCF Commanding Officer.*

Below: *Joe Davies and Steve Dixon (Staff 2001.1–) in the Common Room, 2012.*

HAILEYBURY NONDESCRIPTS

Originally a Common Room team formed well before the war, Nonders still offers the joy of playing cricket entirely for fun. Of very mixed ability, it often included, among the rabbits, players of real quality – Tony Mallett (Staff 1950.3–56.3) (Kent), Jim Seabrook (Captain of Gloucestershire), David Richards (Staff 1957.3–68.2) (Captain of Wiltshire), Peter Ellis (Middlesex) and Geoff Howarth (Captain of New Zealand). On warm summer evenings, at village grounds where occasionally cows grazed and care was needed when fielding, the settings were a poet's dream. Sadly, few records have survived (the games were not important enough to preserve details) but some incidents remain fixed in memory – lightning-fast bowler Mallett struck colossally over the churchyard wall at Essendon; not quite so fast Reverend Philip Morgan (Staff 1958.3–73.3) hit for six over the slips at Little Berkhamsted to lose an epic match; a defeat at West Mill by an innings, and a century by Richard Skelly (Staff 1977.3–88.1) at Little Berkhamsted, both very rare in a 20-over match.

In the 1960s, tours of Kent and Sussex introduced Nonders to Hambledon, the home of cricket, and, even better, to The Bat & Ball pub. During term time a Nonders side which included 'non-cricketing' boys played the same local villages on Lower Pavilion, our third pitch, but, even so, a great deal better than the village grounds. It seems strange that 20-over cricket should have become the most popular form of the modern game. I wonder if Nonders pioneered it?

Andrew Hambling

ARRIVING AT POST-WAR HAILEYBURY

I arrived at Haileybury in the last year of Canon Bonhote's Mastership. In his quiet, patient way he had managed the difficult task of bringing two schools together, Haileybury and the Imperial Service College at Windsor.

With the war over there was a shuffling of the staff. Young men appeared to give fresh blood and to replace those who had for the duration held the fort and to give what their National Service had trained them to do, a close care of those in their charge. It was a task that used up all our energies and brought a deep satisfaction. There were 522 in the School and a staff of 57. There was no Half-term holiday, just a few lessons off on Friday and Saturday one weekend. The contact between boys and parents was little, except by letter. For those new to boarding this was quite a challenging life. We ran round the playing fields and once a week we became soldiers again.

Haileybury was quite a gaunt place, even by the standards of those days, seeking to heat itself and make the rations go round and with memories of a terrible winter. I remember sitting in my overcoat, huddled over a coal fire with an electric fire also in my bachelor rooms on the ground floor in Clock House. It was largely a

---

'THE MOST DEVOTED HAILEYBURIAN THAT EVER LIVED'

Thus wrote the Master, Edward Lyttelton, in *The Times* about Lionel Sumner Milford. Milford was the first to write a history of Haileybury. Published in 1909, *Haileybury College* is not so much a history as a personal recollection, drawing on a remarkable memory, a voluminous correspondence with former pupils over the years and a deep love of the school which had been his life from the age of 11 apart from a five-year break during which he studied at Pembroke College, Oxford.

In his tribute to Milford, his successor as chronicler of Haileybury, R.L. Ashcroft (Staff 1919.3–57.2) quoted Seeley's *Ecce Homo*: 'There is no moral influence comparable to that of a good schoolmaster', and went on to say that 'if anyone justifies that remark, L.S.M. does'. He was Housemaster of Bartle Frere from 1887 to 1903 and stayed on past his scheduled retirement in 1915 through the trauma of the war casualties until 1919. Thereafter he was a member of Council for 15 years and edited four editions of the *Haileybury Register*. *Haileybury College* is a delightful book, unusual in its structure, always finding the best in people, yet never afraid to register comments about the directions the School took in those early years. It gives an insight into a bygone era but remains essential reading for anyone wishing to appreciate the foundations upon which the School was built.

PRW

bachelor establishment and many of the Housemasters were bachelors. Common Room provided quite a luxurious living style and there was a prevailing sense of camaraderie, humour and a British sense of making fun of whatever came to hand. After a day of serious endeavour it was good to laugh. There was little petrol and few cars. A journey to Hertford was quite an expedition. We were in our own little world.

As with the rest of the country, there was a challenge to make the best of hard times. Peace brought challenges but also a determination to succeed.

Richard Rhodes-James (Staff 1947.3–81.2)

Below: *A Lempriere board outside the Dining Hall. The nature of the various epidemics is of interest.*

THE LEMPRIERE BOARDS

The Lempriere Boards adorn the Common Room side of the Dining Hall and act as a memorial to the days when pupils spent days in the Sick House and the Sanatorium recovering from various ailments. Although the carved wooden boards were named after the Resident Medical Officer, Dr Lancelot Lempriere (C 1886.3, Staff 1903.2–38.2), the tradition of pupils carving their names into panels while recuperating from illness began at an earlier date. There are 23 boards on display in Memorial Quad and one other, slightly damaged, panel in the Archives. Many of them not only have the carver's name but are augmented by the inclusion of their House badge, one individual proudly asserting his home as the Irish Free State.

In one of his 'Haileybury Letters', 'Praeteritus' (the *nom de plume* of L.S. Milford) wrote that the boards were first provided to the convalescents around 1880 but the custom died out shortly after and was restarted in a systematized way in 1885. The carved boards were originally arranged around the downstairs sitting room in the Sanatorium at the level of the dado.

Lempriere was fully committed to the life of the School outside of the Sanatorium and Sick House, helping out on the athletics track, at the Bath and in the Gymnasium. In a controversial letter to the *Daily Telegraph* on 21 February 1992, Maurice Willoughby (B 1927.3) remembered once telling Lempriere that he had mumps and was rewarded for this observation with six of the best for 'giving a medical opinion', after which he was dosed with castor oil and admitted to the Sanatorium.

ATMP

Chapter 5 — THE Common Room

First Impressions, Last Impressions

Haileybury seemed large certainly in 1956, but very spartan, with not many carpets or curtains, big iron pipes and radiators conveying modest heat, benches and iron beds, desks of splintery wood, and a walk outside to bathroom and toilet. The geography was bewildering – where were the White City, the Grubber, Talbot's Mound or Caesar's Grave, the Dardanelles, the Mississippi, XX Acre, Terrace and Pavilion? What were Hoips, the Hour, Little Tea, Groise? And noises – the chatter and clatter of the Dining Hall, running footsteps towards Chapel, *Jerusalem* at *fortissimo*, the occasional shout of 'Fag!' and, above all, the bell, from rising to day's end – the bell.

The Master, C.P.C. Smith (1948.3–63.2), perhaps a little shy, played squarely by the book and seemed all-knowing. A bachelor, he lived in the Lodge and a summons there, for beak or boy, was fraught with anxiety. His memory for names and faces was phenomenal, with little *aides-memoires* tucked into boys' files – 'mother wears silly hats', 'father limps – war wounds?'. The senior beaks seemed super-intellectual, critical of the boys, mostly war veterans; the middle group determined to trick the new beak into embarrassing situations with misdirections and confusing advice – the hierarchy exact, particularly

Above: *Opening of the Stephen Austin Room by Philip Cohen (right), Managing Director of Stephen Austin and Sons, 2003, with Andrew Hambling (left) then Hon. Archivist.*

at breakfast – everything was very masculine and seemingly very controlled.

'Boy power', invested in the prefects, seemed all-embracing and the rules bewildering, the Head of School awesome, and Elysium just what it means. 'Dates' were prolific and corporal punishment the norm, even prestigious, yet there were lots of smiles and Quad never 'echoed to the swish of the cane', as suggested in one newspaper article recently. Lessons were an unwelcome interruption to sports and everything was compulsory. Most boys were destined to National Service (until 1960) so the CCF gave a taste of what was to come; the great Inspection Parade and 'Army Bugle' were highlights of military achievement. Food rationing had ended, but you might never have guessed; all meals were formal, starch and stodge essential to the growing boy. Long dormitories were part of life, creating a special camaraderie, and it didn't take long to 'belong' to a vibrant if traditional school.

Thirty-six years and three Masters later, when I left in 1991, some things remained familiar – the Lodge with its huge wooden doors, the Quad and its grey surrounds, the bells. Sixth Form girls had, for nearly 20 years, impacted on social, academic and cultural life. Gone was the use of formal surnames; no one 'ticked' any longer (ie acknowledged teachers by raising the finger); prefects lead by persuasion; caning and fagging had long gone. Compulsion had given way to choice, in the classroom and on the games fields, and meals were less formal and a great deal more palatable, the gong seldom heard.

The internet and league tables were on the horizon, but the number of administrators was increasing and 'rule by committee' emerging. Significant developments were quickening and were in discussion: the ending of long dormitories and the re-alignment of Houses, the replacement of the Swimming Pool and all-weather playing facilities, IT and IB, even co-education from 11+. Yet it was a time of economic anxiety, boarding was in decline so there were many more day boys, even a day-boy House, and numbers were decreasing. However, a bequest worth several million pounds had created optimism and somehow the Dome, brooding over Quad and reminding people from afar that Haileybury was there, suggested a permanence and purpose as it entered the last decade of the 20th century.

Andrew Hambling

A New Beak

At the start of 1960.3 I arrived by Greenline bus, which miraculously went all the way from Trinity Road tube station, quite near my family home in Wandsworth Common, to the front gates of Haileybury – two heavy bags were no problem. By the start of 1961 the Greenline was no longer needed as I was the owner of a small, clapped-out car, which cost £35 and died after one year. Beaks at that time got paid by cheque at the end of term, but new beaks could request an advance from the Bursar to keep them viable – I did.

For my first year I was in bottom-rung bachelor accommodation on the ground floor of Clock House, but it was definitely a step up from my Cambridge bedsit. My sitting room was to the left of the Quad door of Clock House (at present the Archives office), and my small bedroom was adjacent, behind the sitting room. Bathroom and lavatory (happily separate) were upstairs and were shared with the other three bachelor residents of Clock House, so to get to them Ken Rimmer (Staff 1958.3–92.2) and I, ground floor, had to venture out into the open 'tunnel' connecting Quad and Memorial Quad; thus we each needed to time our morning ablutions carefully to avoid the Dining Hall breakfast traffic, as well as the other three residents.

Below: *Christopher Smith, Master 1948.3–63.2.*

Bottom: *R.L. Ashcroft, MC, TD, Housemaster of Lawrence and Allenby, Second Master, Life Governor and member of Council 1957–63, chronicler of Haileybury.*

Chapter 5 — THE COMMON ROOM

Above: *'Jaggers' Johnston (Staff 1901.3–32.3 and 1941.2–42.2) some time Housemaster of Colvin, caricatured as the bulldog of Clock House.*

Below right: *Clock House, which now houses the School Archives, was previously used as staff accommodation. During the days of the EIC, it was home to Thomas Malthus and, more recently, to the Colvin Housemaster and junior members of staff.*

But while our personal accommodation was pretty basic, in other respects bachelors' domestic arrangements were, if not luxurious, quite pampered. In those days the domestic staff included some usually quite elderly stalwarts known as 'House Tobies', who performed various cleaning and sewing duties in the Houses and at House tables in the Dining Hall, but who each also looked after one or more bachelor beaks, a bit like military batmen for officers. They made our beds and cleaned our shoes, if we wanted them to, and they delivered 'rations' – butter, tea, milk and a daily bun – for tea: there was a ring in the sitting room on which to boil a kettle, but no other cooking facilities. My 'Toby', Bill Brown, performed these duties with no obvious enthusiasm, but quite efficiently.

In addition, very importantly, bachelors enjoyed the facilities of the Common Room, with its elegant and spacious ante and dining rooms. At breakfast we each had our own set place, with our newspaper laid out, and silence was the custom – even a 'Good morning' was frowned upon, especially a cheerful one. The lunchtime atmosphere was more relaxed: the food was the same as the boys had in Hall, except that there was a cheeseboard. Beaks normally lunched in the Dining Hall only if they were on 'carving' duty at one of their two House tables – every beak was allocated to a House as a 'carver' (in my first year mine was Hailey), which involved dishing out the food from the head of the table, but happily no actual carving! At supper time there was a drinks trolley in the ante room (gin and sherry, to be signed for, with an end-of-term Common Room bill, but very cheap), and a three-course meal, with free beer on the table.

Married staff ate meals in the Common Room dining room only by invitation of bachelors, whose dining room it was (they had no other). No woman entered Common Room – the sole exception was for tea on Speech Day, when certain special College guests were invited, such as the daughter of the Reverend A.G. Butler, the first Master of Haileybury (surprising, but true!).

I ran the Chess Club, where at first the best players comfortably beat me (later I improved), and the Astronomical Society, where I made my first task to arrange for the Clerk of Works Department and the metal work teacher to build the College Observatory. Also it

Left: The Observatory today, and a pupil using the refracting telescope in the 1960s.

was wonderful to introduce the top Fifth Form set to calculus, and the Sixth Form double mathematicians to that most beautiful and elegant branch of mathematics, projective geometry (sadly long since dropped from the syllabus). These sets contained some very able students, including two of the best three I ever taught.

John Chick (Staff 1960.3–96.2)

Interview Questions and What Followed

Bill Stewart, the new Master of Haileybury, had written to the OURFC Captain in November 1964 to ask whether any member of his team wished to teach. Apparently, 'any subject would do'. Without much thought my application was duly despatched.

My 'interview' was bizarre for I was offered the job before the interview officially began. The Master opened with a perplexing question: 'I wish to appoint a Christian and a gentleman. What are you?' This was followed later by Richard Rhodes-James's (Head of Economics) penetrative one-liner: 'I am pre-Keynesian. What are you?'

I took up my appointment two weeks into the Christmas term of 1965. I had been granted leave of absence (salary duly docked) in order to complete an Oxbridge rugby tour of South America. This did not go down well with Common Room where neither beak nor boy was expected to step out of line. Service and duty were the watchwords.

On day one I was appointed a House tutor. The HM informed me that this was on condition I produced a winning House rugby team. As an aside, he told me I was to teach economics to a Sixth Former who was far too clever for me.

Haileybury was run on a hierarchical structure, power flowing from top to bottom. Everyone knew their place. So when a boy passed a beak in Quad he 'ticked' you (a mini salute) as a mark of respect.

The Master was a somewhat isolated figure, but he certainly had presence. The bachelor-dominated Common Room was the centre of power. They set the tone for practically everything. For example, if you wished to direct a school play you pinned up the cast list for Common Room approval. The Common Room was run like an officers' mess. The 27 bachelors sat at breakfast in order of seniority. Silence was observed. Each member read *The Times* and only *The Times*.

THINGS THAT GO BUMP …

I recall 'Dad' Wright trying to teach his Form-room directly above the Reverend Val Roger's (Staff 1936.3–54.1) English Upper Fifth and becoming exasperated with Val Roger's deafening declamation of *King Lear* below. He raised his chair above his head and dropped it to the floor directly above Roger's head in the Form-room below, bringing him to a sudden halt.

David Bolton (Th 1948.2)

Chapter 5 — THE COMMON ROOM

Above: Harold Pamphlion, who served in the Book Room from 1918–79.

Below right: Cartoon of 'Daddy' Whyte by Nevill Coghill (Tr 1913.1), nephew of the V.C. laureate at Isandlwana. John Whyte (Staff 1878.3–1918.3) died on 27 November 1918 after falling from Terrace. Coghill went on to become a leading authority on Chaucer and Merton Professor of English Literature at Oxford University in 1957.

The head steward, Mr Bell, surveyed his empire with quiet dignity.

The Heads of Department had considerably less influence than later in my career. They met perhaps once a term, sometimes not even that. Staff in charge of games held the real power, determining all things sporting, including picking the Captains of Rugby and Cricket. A pupil would be strongly advised not to allow his Oxbridge interview to clash with a rugby Cock House match. Soccer in any shape or form was banned. House boxing matches were an Easter term event overseen by an RSM.

Staff were expected to take games and/or to help run the Corps. I was one of the first staff intake not to have seen active service or National Service. Annual Corps camps, Field Days, Army Bugle competition and General Inspection were major events in the School calendar. Haileybury, like Cheltenham or Wellington, was considered a major source of army officer intake.

The Resident Medical Officer was a former Naval Surgeon Captain. Almost daily he would cross Quad in his white coat, stethoscope and clip board in evidence. He could carry 'grave news' of impending flu epidemics and 'off games' lists. The doctor's decisions were sacrosanct. The doctor was once outranked by Rear Admiral Sir Charles Darlington (Staff 1965.3–75.2) (a member of the Maths Department) when asked for a sixpenny cornet!

Dan Hearn

Trevelyan Days

My abiding memory as Housemaster is of the (now legendary) dormitory, where 48 beds stretched away from the Housemaster's study like a Crimean hospital ward – allowing for a cheerful social life and the scene, too, of House suppers and House entertainments and 'hags' bags' and bedtime stories for the Removes and Middles before lights out. Except for swimming, Trevelyan did not generally excel at sport – but we did have a House orchestra and we produced House plays over the years. In a memorable production of *Sweeney Todd* (1978) the Housemaster was obliged to demonstrate the effectiveness of the barber's chair, which flung him into outer darkness under the stage, to everyone's delight, and we held 'Trevelyan Days' when we put on exhibitions and concerts.

My first year coincided with the second Sixth Form girls' entry – which made us notionally 'co-educational' – and those first arrivals seemed to me to be hand-picked and startlingly bright and beautiful. For my older colleagues it was quite a lot to swallow. Facilities improved by leaps and bounds (thanks to some generous bequests) – the Sports Centre, for example, and later the indoor Swimming Pool, the emergence of Quitchells and the transmogrification of the Reading Room into the Council Room then into the Attlee Room.

Haileybury was never a dull place: it owes a huge debt to successions of talented and totally committed individuals, domestic and teaching staff alike, who gave it everything they had. The most legendary character of all was, perhaps, Harold Pamphlion, who ran the Book Room for generations: he had an encyclopaedic memory for Haileyburians, remembering Attlee (for example) by his House, subjects and school number, but without fully appreciating that he became Prime Minister! In Trevelyan my wife, typically, was involved in many aspects of the boys' lives, as well as working in the 'San' and entertaining parents and visitors on a relentless scale.

HAILEYBURY ~ *A 150th Anniversary Portrait*

Chapter 5 — THE COMMON ROOM

SPY CATCHER

E.F. Williams, who was tasked with teaching me German, was in the Intelligence Corps during the war and always spent the last ten minutes of his excellent lessons giving practical examples of the application of the language.

Maybe it was an early thirst for tales of espionage and derring-do that caught my young imagination but, to this day, I remember very clearly his fail-safe method for catching a German spy:

Give the suspect a sum to work out using long division and watch the method of doing this. Germans never know the English system and it is an immediate give-away.

Frederick E. Pearson (B 1948.3)

The role of our wives in this peculiarly male society cannot be overstated. How willingly they cheered their Houses on the touchline and wiped the eyes of homesick boys and ministered to distracted husbands and checked the breath of illicit drinkers.

David Hunt (Staff 1974.3–94.3)

Simple Joys

White House is now a gracious private residence off the main road running past the College. When I first arrived at Haileybury in 1976 it was divided into three flats for members of staff. It was there at a rather lively late-night staff party that I first got to know Ken Bartlett, one of the great members of Common Room, later to be Housemaster of Kipling. As the noise level increased, Ken suddenly appeared in our midst, perched on a bicycle which he was riding down the stairs, hotly pursued by the future Master of Wellington, while the future Headmaster of Cheltenham was banging on the walls in frustration at the unacceptable amount of noise keeping him awake. I quickly realised that I was going to enjoy my time at Haileybury.

In its glory days the Pool offered some of the most magical moments of the school year. In the summer term when the bell rang at the end of second prep (or in some Houses some time beforehand) swarms of pupils erupted from their boarding Houses and headed in an excited rush to what was the splendid open-air swimming pool on Pavilion. Having been cooped up in stifling prep rooms during the sweltering evening, individuals grabbed the chance to cool off and release their pent-up energies before bedtime. What a nightmare it would give today's health and safety experts! In the gathering gloom one or two staff with a semblance of supervision chatted amiably amongst themselves as the water churned and swallows swooped in graceful arcs through the shadows. Reluctantly, as the lights from distant boarding Houses grew brighter against the darkening sky, the last individual was summoned from the water, a rough head count was taken, and pupils disappeared into the dusk back to their Houses. What a marvellous way to end a summer's day.

In the rugby season it was one of the Yearlings A great fixtures – an away game against Harrow. After the pressures of coaching the School 1st XV I seized the chance to join forces with Mark Seymour, now Headmaster of Winchester House, in trying to expand the skills of our first-year intake. We'd had a good journey over to Harrow, the Masters' Common Room had indulged us with their customary hospitality, and Mark and I reunited with our young sportsmen in the in-goal area for a pre-match team talk. With the time for kick-off drawing nearer, our exhortations increased in urgency as we rehearsed all the drills; every situation was covered, every player reminded of his responsibilities. An All Black changing room could not have been more electric. Every single thought was concentrated on those critical first 30 seconds: commitment, aggression, focus. Mark's rousing oratory had me sweating; both of us were more than ready to run onto the field ourselves.

Right: *The Victorian Bath, 1890s.*

Opposite: Haileybury – Past, Present and to come *(Anon.)* a painting presented to Colin Cobb. This painting contains many intriguing details and a so-far not fully deciphered narrative.

ROGER WESTLEY: A LIFE CUT SHORT

When I went to Haileybury in 1972, I was taught maths by Roger Westley (Staff 1969.3–74.2 and 1976.1–82.2). He would have been around 25 years old at the time, but seemed a fair bit older as he had receded in a manner reminiscent of Coco the Clown.

It must have been during the summer term of that first academic year that Roger burst into the classroom late to announce that his wife had just given birth to a daughter. 'I think you'll be able to work on your own for 40 minutes, gentlemen,' he said, a huge smile spreading across his face and beaming back to us from his bronzed crown. No one complained.

On another occasion, Roger called one of the class up to his desk for providing an answer that very closely resembled the one given in the back of the book but without any corroborative 'working'. 'Stephens [I'll give the boy a false name to save his blushes – he's probably a judge or an IB curriculum director now], let me have your book.'

Stephens handed over his maths book. 'Let this be a lesson to you, lad,' said Roger, as he tore the answer pages out of the book, before handing it back.

'Sir,' cried Stephens rather feebly.

'What is it, lad?'

'This is your book, sir.'

And Roger, like the true gent he was, gave Stephens back his copy, keeping for himself the book he'd just butchered.

I got to know Roger best when I was in his cricket XI in 1976 and 1977. He and the coach, Peter Ellis, besides being a fine coaching team, were also no mean double act. The fact that one was never sure if Peter was aware he was playing the straight man somehow only made it funnier. One of the stories that went the rounds about Roger was that he had dropped a goal with his left foot from the halfway line to win the match for Bedford against their arch rivals in his one and only appearance for the Club, having been drafted in because they were one short. I don't know about that, but it wouldn't surprise me. Roger was a great man and a wonderful friend, who died all too young.

Hugh Tyrwhitt-Drake (BF 1972.3)

Left: *Roger Westley (left) during one of the many ski trips which he led.*

The whistle blew, the ball spiralled skywards and the Harrow forwards thundered menacingly down on our receiver. As we held our breaths, a Yearlings player positioned close to the touchline suddenly turned to Mark and without a shred of emotion very politely enquired: 'Excuse me, Sir, what time did you say we could change into casuals after the game?' Oh, the innocence of youth, and the harsh realities of school teaching.

R.G. Bass (Staff 1976.3–78.2 and 1981.3–99.2)

SPEECH DAYS

Speech Day at Haileybury, as at many schools, is a high day full of event, show and ritual. And, because of the drama, mishaps, which inevitably occur, tend to be writ large. Many will recall the recent visit of Gerhard Schröder, the former Chancellor of Germany, as Guest of Honour. He processed through the Sports Hall to the stage – along with the Master, the Chairman of the Governors and other members of Council – to the loud accompaniment of the *Ode to Joy* from Beethoven's *Ninth Symphony*, the anthem, of course, of the European Union. Haileybury was saying to the great man, 'We are all Europeans together'. But

Chapter 5 — THE COMMON ROOM

Above: *The Commemoration Service, Speech Day, 2012: (left) Chris Darnell (M 1965.3), President, Haileybury Society 2011–12 and (right) the Right Reverend Christopher Herbert, former Bishop of St Albans and President of Council 1995–2009.*

Below right: *David Summerscale, Master 1976.1–86.1.*

unfortunately there was no coincidence between the time it took the processing party to reach the stage and to form up there facing the audience (short) and the time it took to complete Beethoven's magnificent passage (very long). As a result the group on the stage stood to attention with increasingly rigid smiles facing an audience also standing but not on display in the same way, for what seemed an interminable period as the Great Hymn pounded on and on and on.

Another mishap of timing occurred in David Summerscale's period as Master. Summerscale, having taught at St Stephen's College, Delhi, knew India well and had invited the Indian High Commissioner to be Guest of Honour. Like many Headmasters, Summerscale was an extremely good speaker and waxed eloquently to the assembled pupils, staff and parents. But he also waxed long. In the result the High Commissioner's speech began as follows: *The Master has been crystal clear in his instructions to me that we must all be out of this Hall (Big School) by 12.30pm. As you can all see (he pointed to the big clock in the balcony) it is now 12.29pm. This puts me in a difficulty.* He continued deft, humorous but very brief.

Two mishaps at Speech Days which involved me personally were these. In my last year the Guest of Honour was Lord Attlee, Haileybury's only Prime Minister. He was known as a man of very few words – terse economy, straight to the point. I was fortunate enough to have been awarded some prizes, which meant that I clambered up on to the stage to receive a book from him more than once. On the last occasion Attlee decided to say something to me and he leaned forward and whispered briefly in my ear. As he was also known to be calm and wholly undemonstrative, he must have looked with favour on my complete lack of reaction or response. For my part I had clearly received a succinct chunk of wisdom that would be totally transformative of my life. This was the message that would make all the difference. Unfortunately, just before I went to Haileybury I had had a major operation on my right ear and was, as a result, stone deaf in the ear into which he dropped the pearl. It was lost irretrievably, my life was untransformed and I have wondered ever since what he said.

Much later, in my time as a member of Council, the Guest of Honour was Lord Goodman, a solicitor and, as Arnold Goodman, the founder of the firm Goodman Derrick. He was prominent in public life and often used by the Government to mediate and settle disputes at home and abroad. He was very fat and known as 'Two Dinners Goodman'. I had had no part in the invitation to him but, as I knew him, I was asked to look after him during the day. He climbed up the steps on to the stage in Big School, with the rest of us, and when his moment came made a characteristically witty speech. The Bishop of St Albans brought proceedings to a close and the moment arrived for the stage party, headed by the

99

Bishop, Lord Goodman and the Master, to go back down the steps and process out of the hall. Lord Goodman looked round for me and beckoned me over. 'The audience is now going to witness a bizarre spectacle. I am suffering from vertigo. I must go down these steps on my bottom. You will help me to sit down on the top step and pull me to my feet from the bottom.' And so he did (and I did) to a respectful and awed silence. He was indeed a very fat man.

Edward Walker-Arnott

SCHOOL SONGS

School songs seemed to be going out of fashion until a couple of years ago, but the foundation of new, academically ambitious academies means they are now making a comeback.

Haileybury's first School song at the 1865 Speech Day was *Hurrah for the Holidays*, a stirring round-up of everything that should be celebrated at school. However, the name of the writer and its music has been lost to history.

Hurrah for the Holidays

Hurrah! for the holidays – time full of leisure
May we drink our full of their joys and their pleasure.
First of all we will cheer our Head Master dear,
Whom we are all so glad to see again here.
Three cheers for the Council – long may they live –
For the week more they've granted three cheers let us give.
Hurrah! for the Masters whose rule we enjoy.
Who their time in our good and our pleasure enjoy.
Next, three hearty cheers for the Head of School,
And three for the prefects, and well they rule.
For the Prizemen we'll give too a hearty three,
Let us hope that next year greater honours they'll see.
Three cheers for the Eleven, we all hope they score
Next year may be equal to this year's and more;
Their victories next season shall not be so few,
When the new ground is old, and the old ground new.
Three cheers for three fellows now going to leave,
For their life at this College ne'er may they grieve.
For old and the new Members let's give a loud three,
Though hostile their colours true friends may they be.
Three times three for the Ladies both yellow and blue,
Whatever their colour, it must match their fair hue.
Three cheers for our Sovereign, long may she reign;
And Britain's great glory ne'er under her wane.

Apart from *Hurrah for the Holidays*, Haileybury adopted Winchester College's rousing end-of-term song, *The Dulce Domum*, and this was sung at the end of the year and at Speech Day. *The Dulce* remained in the book *Songs Sung at Haileybury* until 1913 even though Haileybury had a number of its own songs by then. The second school song was written by the poet Francis Bourdillion (E 1865.3) and set to the tune *So Hurrah for the pipe so rich and ripe*, first published in March 1872 in *The Haileyburian*. *The Phoenix* was a song which linked the East India College with Haileybury and celebrated this link, in the chorus: 'So here's to all whose deeds have won/For Haileybury glory!/Ours to be the aim to uphold their fame, And prove the Phoenix story.' Bourdillion emphasised Haileybury's past and present associations. Also in that year W.E. Smith (Tr 1868.2) wrote *A new 'Haileybury' version to an old song* based on *Auld Lang Syne*, with 13 verses. *Horae Subsecivae* by

Inset: Sursum corda, Haileybury's motto until 1942. Lift up your hearts, by Henry Montagu Butler is now adopted as the School hymn. H.M. Butler served as a member of Council and was father of Montagu Butler (Tr 1886.3), Governor of Central Province, India, and Master of Pembroke College, Cambridge. Montagu Butler's son, 'Rab' was a cabinet minister when Clement Attlee was deputy Prime Minister.

JOHN ARTHUR HENRY BEHREND

John Arthur Henry Behrend (E 1869.2) was a composer and theatre manager whose score for the hit song *Daddy* sold more than a million copies. Behrend, the scion of a Danzig banking house, had music in his blood as the maternal grandson of composer Michael Balfe. When Behrend left Haileybury he spent a year at the Royal Academy of Music and then went to Leipzig to study under Ernest Richter and Carl Reinecke. Throughout the Victorian and Edwardian periods, Behrend worked with Frederic Weatherly and other librettists to produce popular songs which were performed in the music and concert halls across the country and then were sold in their tens of thousands to eager audiences. Four of Behrend's ballads were performed at the Proms in 1896 and 1899 and over the whole of his career he composed at least 200 songs, four cantatas and six operas.

ATMP

Chapter 5 — THE COMMON ROOM

Right: *A wine list from the Common Room, late 19th century.*

Below: *Cartoon depicting a match between Bartle Frere and Highfield with players wearing the Whites and Stripes jerseys, by Richard Gubbins (C 1882.2).*

the Reverend James Robertson, the third Master of Haileybury (1884.1–90.1), was a rather turgid effort combining Latin with English, and with rhymes such as: *Our game was done, and our race was won,/And the hour was come and gone;/We crept into School feeing rather a fool,/And thus we said our con.* Unsurprisingly, *Horae Subsecivae* survived for only one edition in the Haileybury song book. James Robertson's legacy was certainly not musical.

Three football songs were written for Haileybury in its first 20 years. The first was by James Rhoades, a poet and the first Housemaster of Highfield, to a tune written by J.A.H. Behrend (Ha 1867.2), who became a composer and theatre manager. The Choir Master, George H. Sunderland Lewis (Staff 1886.1–1915.3), reset the words of Rhoades's *Football Song* some time in the early 1900s. The message of Rhoades's song was one of good sportsmanship, reinforced with patriotic dogma. The second football song was written by another beak, Henry Cottrell (Staff 1873.3–75.1), whose song is based on the Below Big Side matches between Whites and Stripes that took place on Haileybury's rugby fields. Rhoades asked for his players to 'collar' the opposition, but Cottrell asks for more from his musical team, encouraging the players to 'scrag' and 'maul' but reminding them at the same time that:

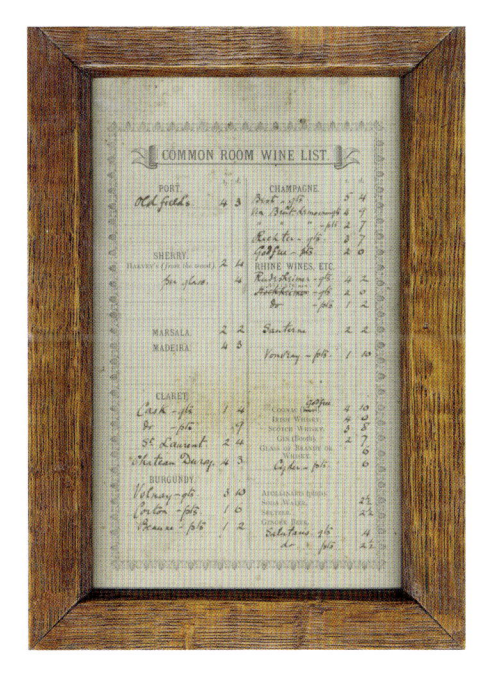

When schooldays are o'er,
The Football is no more;
Keep ever well in sight
The Noble and the right.

Cottrell's and Rhoades's messages of muscular Christianity were not alone and the concept appears in most of the School songs. The final football song was written and arranged by Alfred Koe (BF 1880.2), Captain of XV, in 1884.

Why a school should need so many songs is perhaps a reasonable question to ask but one that can be answered simply: pride. In *The Haileyburian* for 25 November 1882, a plea was published for School songs, the correspondent claiming that there were only four School songs for Haileybury. W.H. Savile (Tr 1873.2) responded with *School Song* a couple of months later, a piece which was not a great success, and the poet, Frederic Trench (M 1880.2), replied in 1883, with *Sur Sum Corda*. The organist M. Haywood wrote the score and the song was performed at OH and Haileybury concerts:

Upward, triumphant, strong
Lift we our heart and song
Echo it Loud and Long – Sur Sum Corda

Trench's song was for a while sung at the end of School and OH concerts in the same way as the official song, Bradby's *Carmen*, such was its popularity. Sadly, Haywood's score has not survived the vagaries of time and like many of the older songs, Trench's stirring piece has faded.

HAILEYBURY — *A 150th Anniversary Portrait*

Haileybury is perhaps unusual in that it now has two official School songs, but they are rarely sung. After 1865 no 'School song' was performed at Speech Day until 4 July 1874 when Bradby's *Carmen Haileyburiense* was sung. The second song, *Vivat Haileyburia*, written by Arthur Butler, was not sung at a Speech Day until 1912, when it was performed in the evening at the end of a torch-lit display to celebrate the School's jubilee. It appears that the *Vivat* was the 'second string' school song, designed to be sung at OH reunions, School concerts and Entertainments. Originally the words of the *Vivat* were sung to the tune of *O Tannenbaum*, but this setting was altered because some thought that a British song deserved a British tune, a change that did not fully convince L.S. Milford. In the book *Songs Sung at Haileybury*, only five verses were printed, but Butler had composed one verse to be inserted after verse two on special occasions:

So may each conquering match be won
Vivat Haileyburia!
'Gainst Uppingham and Wellington:
Vivat Haileyburia!
And yet more glorious may we be
In nobler fights by land and sea,
And either University.
Vivat Haileyburia

By the publication of the fourth edition of *Songs Sung at Haileybury* in 1925, the *Vivat* had dwindled to two verses and Butler's creative intentions were no longer conveyed. The second verse carries the hopes of the 30-year-old school and one which perhaps should still be our mantra:

Then shout five hundred voices all,
Vivat Haileyburia!
Our days of old we first recall,
Vivat Haileyburia!
But whatso'er their fame of yore,
We've yet a mind to make more,
Our age of gold still lies before.
Vivat Haileyburia!

The Boys' Own Paper on 29 December 1906 wrote that the *English song of Haileybury has a swing and a go which are very alluring ... Next to Harrow's* Forty Years *there is no doubt that* Vivat Haileyburia *is the finest school song written in English. Haileybury may rest secure in her belief that it will take some beating.* In the Second World War, J.W.C. More (Th 1924.2), was taken prisoner by the Japanese and while imprisoned wrote a variation on the *Vivat* called *Vivat Rangoon Jail Birds All*, on Japanese Army loo paper. The prison anthem was:

The Britons are a stupid race
They built a jail right at this place
Vivat Rangoon Jail Birds All.

The Britons came and passed away,
Japs soon followed – they're here today,
Vivat Rangoon Jail Birds All.

Then we came here one bloody day
And here we are and here we stay.
Vivat Rangoon Jail Birds All.

And all through life, where ere we be,
Oh bloody jail we'll think of thee.
Vivat Rangoon Jail Birds All.

So lift your tin and in cold tea
We'll drink the toast with three times three –
Vivat Rangoon Jail Birds All.

ATMP

MANY THANKS

I was very lucky to have gone to Haileybury in the third term of 1948. It was the term that Christopher Smith arrived as the Master. He made a special point of learning every student's first name, and as he passed through the Quadrangle he would stop and look at a student and you could see his mind turning over. He would then break into a big smile and call you by your first name.

Also I was lucky enough to go into Allenby House, where the Second Master, Mr R.L. Ashcroft, was Housemaster. He was a very proud man and very proud of his House. We had to be the best, we had to win Cock House, we had to win everything – and we did. We seemed to dominate all the games and sports events for two or three years.

Thanks to the Master and Housemaster who recommended me for a scholarship through the English Speaking Union, I was able to go to Harvard School in California on a year's scholarship. This continued to help with my development and it was a fantastic experience which has stayed with me all my life.

Martin Skan (A 1948.3)

Opposite: *The Master, Joe Davies, meets with staff in the Common Room at the weekly Wednesday briefing, 2012.*

Chapter 5 — THE COMMON ROOM

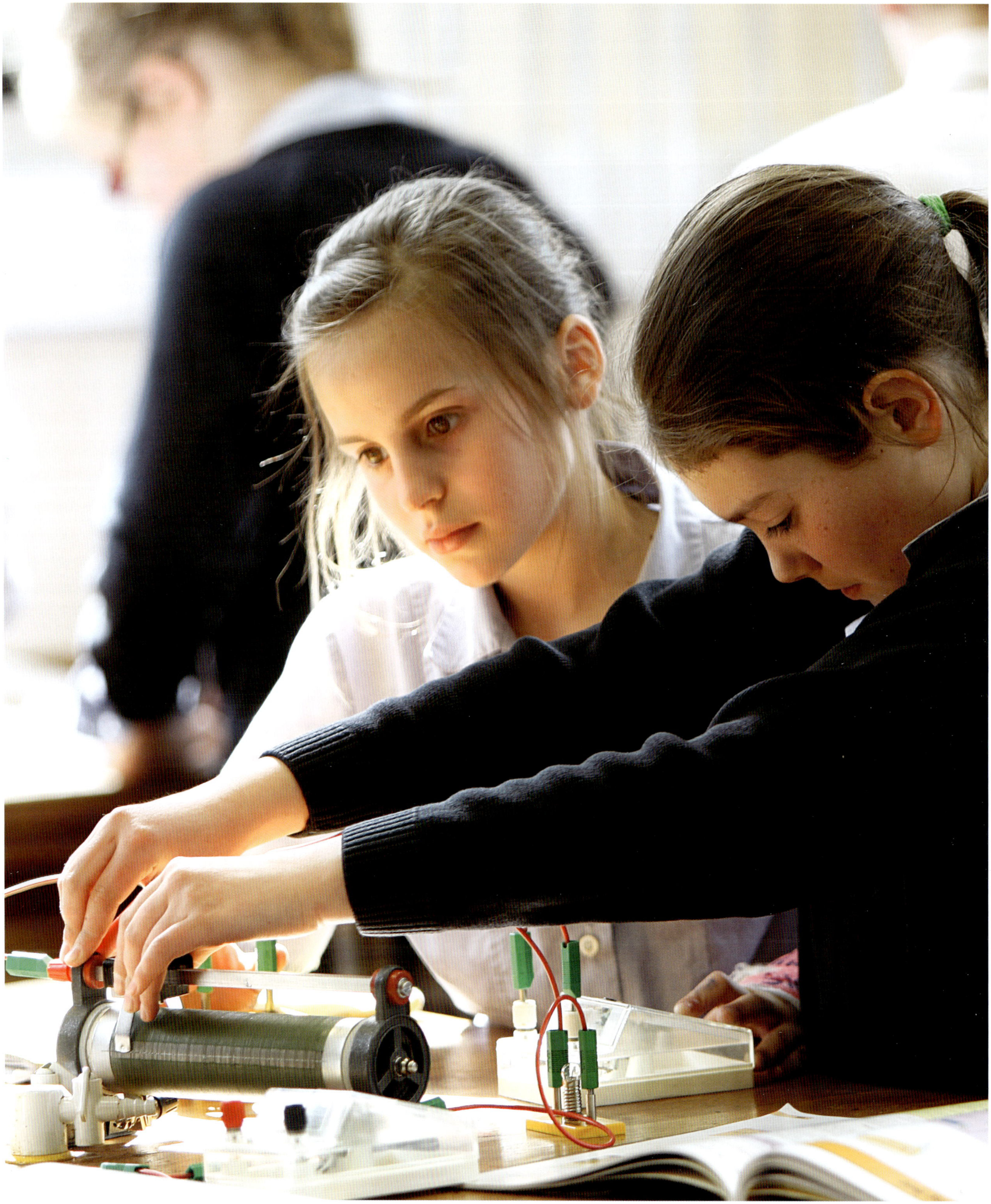

Chapter 6

SCHOOL LIFE

Silk Stocking Stories and Evensong

When I went to the School in September 1935 there were five other new boys or New Governors in my House, Batten. They were John Campling, Bryan Gavin, Val Ohlenschlager, Alec Sheldon and Charles Vane-Tempest, and our Housemaster was Edgar Matthews.

Every morning at 6.30, winter and summer, we would wash in cold water. There were many windows in the 'dorm' into which the prevailing icy wind always blew. After dressing one attended at 7.15am a short service in the Chapel, followed by breakfast in the memorial Dining Hall. Each House was allocated two long tables. At breakfast we had a choice of porridge or cornflakes. The sugar and milk were placed on the table and replenished by the House Toby (servant), who also served tea from huge metal teapots. Porridge and the cooked breakfast were obtained from the serving hatches situated along the wall dividing the hall from the kitchens. There was a choice of type of egg and also bacon, sausage and fried bread. Butter, toast and marmalade were also collected from there. This was without doubt the best meal of the day.

On weekdays we wore a pair of grey flannel trousers and a dark jacket. As a New Governor you had to keep the coat fully buttoned up. You were allowed to undo a button for each year you were at the School so that in your fourth year your jacket was fully undone. If you went outside the College grounds you wore a House cap. As a New Governor it had to be worn with the peak well over your eyes and as you became more senior the peak position was raised so that in your last year the cap was balanced on the back of your head. On Sundays a navy blue suit with a black tie was the required dress, with the same button rules. A straw boater with House ribbon replaced the dormitory cap.

The six New Governors shared a large room called the Dormitory Class Room (DCR), close to the House itself, together with six other boys who had been at the School for up to a year. These boys were each allocated a New Governor and their task was to teach them how to behave as a member of Batten. This did

SIDE

Old House photographs record the changing nature of uniform and the caps pictured in them appear to be worn in rather individualistic ways. Wearing a cap to denote one's place in the School, known as 'side', was a distinctly Haileybury tradition and was as complex in its message as the wearing of braid was by Rugbeians. To 'sport side' was lost to Haileybury when Canon Bonhote abolished the wearing of caps and introduced a new but prosaic mark of clannishness, the House tie.

What, then, was side? Side was a series of ways in which to wear the cap in order to express one's place in the School's pecking order. Side separated the New Governor from the Prefect and the Second Termer from a Blood.

Caps had been worn at Haileybury from the beginning but it was not until the 1880s that a series of conventions arose in the way that caps should be worn to denote one's position or aspirations within the School. A New Governor was required to hide their fringe with the cap. To achieve the required 'no side', the Governor had to pull their cap down as firmly as possible. The resulting effect of 'no side' was that a line appeared at the back of the head, caused by the parting of the hair, and this was known as a 'bug run', presumably because it created an improved highway for head lice to travel along. 'Side' could be worn only by men who were in their second year at School when a small amount of fringe revealed was considered seemly; any attempt to sport side before the second year was dealt with severely as an affront to the natural order. As a pupil progressed through the School, they were able to wear side in more flamboyant manner. 'Bloods' and those who aspired to be 'Bloods' would push the cap to the very back of the head so that it resembled a kippah. The practical nature of a cap was pushed to breaking point by the 1890s and it became a serious topic of discussion in the letters section of the *Haileyburian*. Correspondents in the *Haileyburian* noted that the design of the caps needed to be altered so that extreme 'side' was no longer 'sported'. A 'side' cap was one which was shallow and worn several sizes too small so that it could not perform any other role than sitting back on the crown of the head. The caps worn by Governors were deeper in their manufacture and had to be the right head size or indeed slightly larger, so that side was not inadvertently sported; these caps were known as 'Gov'nors' Lids'. The flamboyant wearing of side, which continued for around 50 years, eventually caused the authorities to kill off the House or dormitory cap, but other, unofficial, 'sides' continued to survive and evolve. The lowliest members of the School, the New Governors, Second Termers and Third Termers, developed their own customs, such as handkerchief and button 'side', as spurious methods of separating themselves. After all, one term was a very long time at Haileybury in the 1900s.

ATMP

Right: *New Guv'nor with large, firmly planted 'Guv'nor's Lid', no side worn.*

Far right: *Miniscule side cap worn by a 'Blood' (member of the XV) at the back of the head.*

Chapter 6 — SCHOOL LIFE

Right: *'The Boot', Canon Edward Bonhote, Master 1934.2–48.2, watching planes overhead during the war, by Michael Stringer.*

not take very long as it amounted to only one thing, which was to do what one was told by everybody who was more senior, i.e. the whole School.

Saturday was a favourite day for visits by the family and one could be taken out until lock-up time, which was 6pm in the winter and spring terms and 7pm in the summer. On Sunday one was free after lunch until one attended Chapel for Evensong. During the five years I was at the School I was visited only once and that was by my brother, Joe. He had just been commissioned as a Sub-lieutenant. Edgar Matthews insisted on seeing him before I was allowed out and he told Joe that I must not be taken into licensed premises or to a cinema. We went and had lunch at the Old East India College Arms and then went to Hertford to see a film. As far as I know, Edgar never found out and I believe that this breaking of the rules was common.

One thing I remember only too well from my time in DCR was being shown how to spit accurately. The chief exponent of this art was George Banes (B 1934.2), who was senior to me by one year and one term. He was able to lie back in a comfortable armchair and spit at the metal lampshade hanging from the ceiling. George was so skilled in his ability to control his spitting that every time he did it his spittle landed on the top surface of the lamp shade and remained there until he could be persuaded to wipe it off. A disgusting habit, but one which showed great determination, which may have helped him win his Military Cross some ten years later in 1944.

The Batten DCR was situated on the other side of the Quad from the House and was close by the House of the Master, Canon E.F. Bonhote, known by all as 'The Boot'. He was a single man who was devoted to the Christian life, but very low church. One of the results of this was that the Chapel, which had been decorated in typical Victorian style – colourful paintings all over the walls of saints and scenes from the life of Jesus – was repainted with a light cream paint and thus became almost bare except for four large circles of gold on the ceiling of a new inner pierced dome beneath the big dome. The existing apse was demolished and a new one built extending some 15ft further into the Quad.

'The Boot' was famous also for his methods in teaching elementary physics. He used to climb up a rope, which was hanging from the ceiling in one of the classrooms in the Science lab, and drop weights from the top to illustrate the force of gravity. On one occasion he fell off the rope, much to the very controlled amusement of the class.

After approximately two years in the DCR, one qualified for a shared study. There were five of us in my first study, all roughly 15 or 16 years old. During our second term in the study we decided to investigate under the floorboards. In order to do this we had to cut a square hole. We found that the study was supported on either side by small brick walls which divided each study from its neighbour but that there was a void below the underside of the flooring of some 3ft in which we could sit. We considered it too dangerous to use the space below our own study, so we removed some of the top bricks from one of the small walls, repeating this under the neighbouring study until we reached the space under the study two away from our own. We considered that this would be far enough away and so we covered the floor of this space with old rugs and cushions. We used a flex to carry lighting down to this refuge and as a general rule we kept our conversation to as little as possible and conducted it in whispers. Some of us used the space so that we could have a cigarette and all looked at the most sensational sex magazine of the time, *Silk Stocking Stories*. This featured lots of pictures of girls showing their stocking tops with suspenders or garters. The stories were equally thrilling, describing how the girls' skirts were raised by strong winds, falling off bicycles or by becoming caught on unseen nails, etc.

We occupied this study for some four or five terms and our secret remained undiscovered. Later we moved to a different study on the opposite side of the corridor. A few terms later I was offered a double study for two terms and then a single study on my own. It was during my time in a single study that our excavations were discovered and the floor repaired. Questions were asked of all the previous and present occupants of our old study but no one admitted any knowledge and the matter was never discussed again.

Thomas David Chitty (B 1935.3)

A Life-Changing Decision

When I got off the Green Line coach at the main entrance to Haileybury and ISC and walked down the Chestnut Avenue past the obelisk and the bicycle shed at the start of my first term, I was terrified. I was a 13-year-old orphan and I was afraid that I was not good public school material. My worst fears were soon realised when, minutes later, I found myself in the Allenby DCR amid five other New Governors and a dozen giant and highly superior-looking Second Termers, all of whom I soon discovered were licensed to bully. It was they who were actually authorised by the authorities to inflict 'six of the best' on those New Governors who in their eyes were committing any misdemeanours. I was the first to experience this privilege a week later by failing to pass the traditional 'New Governors' test' when the Second Termers gave you a written exam

Above: *Prep in Big School, 1961.*

Chapter 6 — SCHOOL LIFE

Above: Edmonstone DCR, 1932 in Big School.

Right: White City, the notorious lavatory block, which was demolished in 1961.

on the geography and nomenclature of the numerous Haileybury buildings and traditions.

In the cold, bare dormitory I was reunited with my tuck box and my trunk, both of which instilled a touch of warmth. My battered tuck box represented the only pleasant memory of three dismal years in a boarding school evacuated to the safety of North Devon. The trunk reminded me of my ATS sister, five years my senior, who had taken some leave to do my necessary school clothes shopping; with clothes rationing in full force, there was plenty of space in the trunk.

I found myself lacking adequate learning and was always bottom of my class. More sadly, with inadequate sporting ability, when team captains selected their teams at the start of a game from those waiting in an expectant group, I was invariably the last choice, the oip of the Hoips. The food hastily gobbled down in the new Dining Hall between more important events like homework, Chapel and exercise was inadequate, to say the least. In fairness, I later realised this was more the fault of U-boats in the Atlantic than of inefficiency and economy in the kitchens. Water temperature in the sinks of the ablution block was never more than tepid. In order to get to the ablution block in the morning we juniors had to run from our beds naked through an archway of seniors painfully whipping our bottoms with their towels. The School lavatory block was unbelievably revolting through lack of staff to clean it, I presume. I have since become somewhat of an authority on water closets and public conveniences the world over, having had good reason to experience those in such famous slums as the relatively nearby East End of London and the Gorbals of Glasgow; my experience later extended to Karachi, Cairo, Mexico City and the world-class slums of Nairobi, and never have I come across any more repulsive toilets than 'The White City' of Haileybury.

As well as being a poor sportsman and hopeless at learning, I was a coward. It was compulsory that New Governors competed in the boxing championships that were held every term. I gave my opponent a whole week of pocket money in return for his looking as if he was fighting hard but in such a way that he did not hurt me.

I had a lisp, which originally earned me the nickname of 'Cecil', but which I managed to convert to the more dignified 'Sid'. I could not even learn the four lines of script that the smallest part in the House play demanded. Beatings and how to lessen their hurt became one of the few areas in which I excelled. If one sheet of newspaper was inserted between the skin and underpants it was less likely to be detected than were it inserted between the underpants and trouser. By the end of the first term I had experienced two Second-Termer floggings, three Dormitory Prefect floggings and four Assistant Housemaster floggings. I narrowly missed a School Prefect's beating from an organisation called Elysium, the top of the top College prefects, a consortium of six, the purpose of which seemed to be only for the enforcement of corporal punishment.

109

HAILEYBURY — *A 150th Anniversary Portrait*

Above: *Elysium tie, still worn by the Head and Deputy Head of the School.*
Left: *Elysium, 1878.*

Even socially I was a misfit. When other children were enthusiastically recounting tales of their pre-war visits to Paris, Vienna, Naples, the Alps and the South of France, I would meekly try to make my trip to Worthing in one of my father's Bedford lorries carrying equipment for our unfurnished seaside bungalow sound exciting.

Halfway through my stint at Haileybury I had to make the greatest choice of my life to date; volunteers were called to restart Melvill House. Discussions in the drying rooms about the topic of abandoning Allenby to go into a School House were endless. Ten years later my decision to emigrate and renounce the Queen was, by comparison, a matter of tiny importance to that of changing Houses.

From then on contentedness, if not blissful happiness, replaced my first impressions of bullying, beatings and boxing. I must thank my peer Nigel Harley (A and M 1943.2) – who, unlike me, positively shone over the School for six years and headed it twice – for encouraging me to make my small contribution by instituting a House magazine, gaining my House rugger colours and winning the Army Bugle for Melvill. It has, however, taken a long lifetime for me to fully appreciate those distant days in that dear old home beneath the dome and even longer to realise that, where other institutions have let me down, the traditional ethics of Haileybury I have never found wanting. Now I can appreciate fully one of her several mottoes, this one emblazoned in Latin in golden letters around the dome and its full meaning of 'You have received much, give much'. I am proud to have been a part of this tradition.

Richard Hedges (A and M 1943.2)

Above: *Elysium, 1941. Standing: Souter and Milner; seated: Purkiss, Crowder, and Fairbairn.*

110

'LICKING BABIES FOR LOAFING': SCHOOL SLANG

Every school has its own traditions, customs and words, and Haileybury is no different. While many readers will know what 'to rag' means, a general public school term, how many would know what 'paupers', 'favours' and 'below the line' mean?

To act as a pauper or 'to pauperise' is a Haileybury term which appeared in the pupil lexicon in the 1860s. 'Pauperise' meant to behave in an undignified manner in a public place such as Quad, but it could also mean that an older pupil was behaving in a manner beneath themselves. A New Guv'nor could never be a pauper because they did not know any better. If a senior pupil allowed or encouraged poor behaviour amongst the junior forms he was accused of 'babylove' and was, undoubtedly, 'a pauper'. 'Babies' were members of the Lower School and when the Red House Run, the shortest of all School runs, was started it was known as the 'baby arena'. Pauperish behaviour in the studies would ultimately lead to one being 'prepped', meaning sent into Big School to join the juniors in a supervised prep. 'Mashers' and 'chappies' were terms for dandies awarded by other pupils while, in the 1890s, a clique of peacocks took to calling themselves 'Johnnies'. The cry *cave* was used to warn of a beak's imminent arrival and halt 'pigeon shooting', a primitive initiation in the Form-room involving the new pupil running the length of the room while others pitched dictionaries at them. The Ghost of the New Gov'nor formed part of the lore of the dormitory classroom; it was said that the spirit of a new pupil haunted the School after he had a heart attack when he realised he was late for Chapel. 'Lates', whose names were marked by the prefects on 'blacklists', were deemed to have failed to enter the Cloisters before the last peal of the Chapel Bell, which is why it became known as 'The Sanctuary'. The only Chapel a First Termer was ever allowed to miss was the New Guv'nors' service at the beginning of the new academic year, which was in fact an annual hoax.

For the Cock House final, 'changs' or men (there were no boys at Haileybury) would decide which House they should support and purchase the appropriate ribbon of House colours (usually worn around the 'basher') from the Cap Room. For two to three days before the match the men would look like distinguished soldiers, with ribbons or 'favours' pinned to their chests. The winning team was granted the right to 'carry the ball', once around the Great Quad with the whole House in procession, followed by a 'cup supper'. Originally, the Captain of Cock House (the XV Captain) carried the match ball, but this was replaced by the silver rugby ball, the competition's trophy, and later still it was replaced by the match ball again. The most detested position to come in the 'ranking of the Ball' was second and it was for this reason that choosing of favours was vital to men whose House was not in the final but might have a score to settle.

One of the most invidious positions for a man to find himself in at Haileybury was 'below the line'. To act 'below the line' was to behave like a 'cad' (a non-School man), the term coming from the placing of a pupil's name, found to have cheated in an examination, below the printed line that marked the end of his form on the examination list. If a 'chang' made regular serious transgressions from the customs or rules of the School, they were 'sent up' by the members of 'Olympus' (Common Room) to the Master for a flogging and might be asked to 'walk the School' (expelled).

ATMP

Getting Away with It

I recall Rick Came's (Th 1946.3) exploit as Head of Thomason: the surreptitious extraction of the fire emergency key from its glass-encased box, making a duplicate from a soap impression to open the padlocked grille, going down to the coal cellar to stoke the furnace for late-night baths until he accidentally shovelled in the key and had to climb back into College over White City undetected. Sotheby's later entrusted themselves to his wily acumen.

I also witnessed Mick Murrell's (Ha 1946.3) silver cigarette case leap from his jacket pocket, fly open and cascade its contents down the stairway of the crowded Form Room Block on our way to classes. He survived and became Haileybury Society representative in Vancouver.

David Bolton (Th 1948.2)

A Family Connection

Reminiscing about Haileybury is a bit of a family tradition. The centenary of the School took place the year before I arrived as a 'New Guv'. The Queen visited and my grandfather, Sir Clement Jones (Tr 1893.3), a Governor of the School at the time, contributed to a special edition of the *Haileyburian*. He described events during the 1890s and in particular the review in Windsor Great Park of public school cadets by Queen Victoria in her Diamond Jubilee Year of 1897. All the boys wore spiked helmets and scarlet tunics and 'the Queen passed so close you could have touched her'.

My own experiences in the spring term of 1963 involved a great deal less formality; in fact, the best possible breakdown of the established order as a result of unprecedented winter weather. As the Trevelyan House magazine, the *Maltese Cross*, recorded: 'All rugger was cancelled this year on account of the worst snow of the century'. Thick snow remained on the ground for weeks. Instead of the rigid routine of daily games, for weeks on end in the spring term we were able to head off to the woods next to XX Acre.

We brought with us a collection of improvised toboggans – mainly tin trays – and older and younger boys alike sped down the snowy slopes through the trees. It was exhilarating and a wonderful – and probably completely misleading – introduction to school life. The hierarchy of House year groups changed, too, a glimpse of what the modern School is like. How could the House Prefects be seen in the same light once we had seen them horsing around in the snow?

Tim Clement-Jones (Tr 1963.1)

Left: *Members of the Haileybury College Rifle Volunteer Corps, c.1894. Sir Clement Jones' recollection is incorrect as the Corps uniform was grey until after 1897 when they adopted scarlet.*

Top: *The Centenary edition of The Haileyburian.*

Above: *Skating on the Bath c.1895. Note the hole in the ice in the foreground.*

Right: *Allenby Little Quad cricket, 1941.*

The Perils of Little Quad Cricket

It was towards the end of the summer term, in July 1962. This was the Haileybury centenary year. I was in Allenby House and within the House was a Little Quad, in which we played 'Little Quad' cricket. There was a set of rules, one of which was that if you hit a six, which took the ball outside the Quad onto 'Triangle' (a triangular area of grass and trees, bordered by two roads and a path), you were out and, of course, you had to go out to retrieve it. On this occasion I hit a six, was duly out and had to go and collect the ball. On picking it up, I threw it back towards Little Quad, but unfortunately my aim was a little off and to my horror, the ball was heading fast towards the senior dormitory window. My heart was in my mouth; there was nothing I could do but await the sound of tinkling glass and then later, no doubt, a suitable punishment. My poor father would have to pay the bill, unless my pocket money was docked. As I watched, helplessly, from the vantage point of 'Triangle', I noticed that the dormitory windows were slightly open, from the bottom up, and miracle of miracles, the tennis ball went straight through the opening of one of them. Silence! Phew, what a relief. I headed up to the dormitory to ask for 'my ball back, please', but then, on the way down the stairs, I twisted my ankle, which meant that I could not go to the CCF Army Camp.

Humphrey Gillott (A 1958.3)

Winter Term

I remember the particularly spartan conditions inside my House, Allenby, during my first term in 1965, especially in the dormitory. The sheets were damp; the windows would not shut properly; there was no heating; and you would wake up to snow on top of you. To keep warm we slept in tracksuits and rugger socks. No wonder so many Allenby boys ended up in the San that term. I sent my parents a letter: *The dormitory is perishing cold and we have to walk to our classrooms in blizzards. The food is fair, but am always hungry and I have to ration my food … could you please send my black jersey, some boys wear three jerseys, and I have only a short-sleeved one.*

Peter Rye

Straightening Me Out

My Haileybury career was not typical in the sense that it did not span the five years from age 13 to 18. It started in the Fifths as I'd been overseas in Malaysia with my family living the life of a colonial boy.

I arrived at Haileybury aged 15, spotty, poorly prepared academically and thoroughly unprepared for a boarding education. Fortunately, I was quite sporty and had an approach that allowed me to adapt and get on with things – once I'd had my protest.

I was in the bottom set of all subjects and hated the associated stigma. Some of my peers sneered at my lack of Haileybury experience and background. So I tried my hand at smoking and breaking bounds and ended up in the Master's study where Bill Stewart gave me six of the best and straightened me out.

I had a tolerant and compassionate Housemaster in Melvill, Richard Rhodes-James. Later, when I learned of his background in the war, in Burma during the 2nd Chindit campaign, I realised he was a man of experience and wisdom who deserved at the very least a young man's respect. I hope, when I was his Head of House and he had married the lovely Rachel, that I paid back his tolerance, care and support in some small way.

There were a number of teachers (beaks) in the Fifths who tried valiantly to straighten out my erratic education in order to fit me for the 'O' Level examinations. Andrew Hambling, Dan Hearn and Ken Rimmer I remember with particular fondness, and in the event I achieved most of the required exam targets.

Sport was central to my Haileybury life. I was lucky and proud to be a member of the Melvill teams that won both Cock House rugby and cricket. I was Captain of Swimming, played fly-half in the XXX and left wing in the Hockey XI. I met John Barber (K 1963.3) through rugby and we became lifelong friends. His family – one of the great Haileybury families – became very precious to me as I spent long summers with them during Haileybury days and afterwards in Casablanca.

You didn't always end up in a study with the friends you wanted to, but I was very lucky. I shared an Old Study with Anthony Watson (M 1964.1) who was reading Classics and would spout Xenophon at me to no avail. He made it to Oxford. Our foursome in the Centenary Studies comprised Hugh Becker (M 1963.3), Charles Burnett (M 1962.3) and one of the US 'students', J. 'Jim' B. Harvie IV (M 1966.3), who was killing time before going to Harvard. What a time we had! Charles Burnett became a lifelong friend.

Extra-murally Ken Rimmer's adventurous training expedition stands out. It was during the Easter holidays and we walked the 180 miles from Pforzhheim to Basel in ten days, through the snow of the *Westweg*. I wore shorts because my father had worn shorts when he was in the RAF Mountain Rescue Team. The trip kept reminding us all of Horst Jankowski's *A Walk in the Black Forest*, which had been a big hit when it was released in 1965.

Then there was the Haileybury skiing trip to Zermatt; the 'ski train' from London, with the beautiful, unattainable girls from whichever school, who made up the noisy, colourful group on board. Prannoy Roy (Tr 1967.1), the founder of New Delhi TV, had come to Haileybury for the Sixth Form and was on the trip. We were friends and, as friends do, he lent me his new fashionable moccasin shoes for the evenings out after skiing. The shoes really suffered in the snow. After the Public School's Relay Competition at the Swiss Cottage Baths, I would spend an exeat weekend at Prannoy's mother's, somewhere in Hampstead if I remember correctly, and we would venture out to the Purple Pussycat disco on the Finchley Road. They've made films about this type of scenario and the reader knows they all end in broken hearts and pain.

I must have been adequately reconstructed because Bill Stewart made me a College Prefect and it was the proudest moment in my life. Then R.-J. made me his Head of House. The Head of School in my final term was Peter Thomas (Ha 1964.3), and Andrew Bulmer (BF 1963.3) was Deputy Head of School. The three of us comprised Elysium, which was a special privilege, with its own tie, crested writing paper and unique dining arrangements. I sometimes reflect on our three contrasting characters: Peter was scholarly and with a phenomenal and surprising knowledge of emerging rock bands – he introduced me to The Doors. Andrew was a stunning sportsman and athlete with a strong Christian faith. And I was an average scholar, an average sportsman, but I held Christian beliefs and loved rock music. I loved Haileybury, too.

Chris Darnell

SCHOOL FOOD

Memories of food are often strong when associated with school, especially for boarders. Dining Hall and the Grubber are two of the centres of the School, servicing the needs of several hundred people every day and, as such, they have elicited strong responses from pupils and staff over 150 years. Geoffrey Allchin (Le B 1908.3) wrote to his mother during his first week at Haileybury saying simply, 'We have excellent food here' and reiterated the view of Robert Stafford (Le B 1904.1), who considered it a great improvement on his prep school's catering. In 1904 dinner might consist of one of the following: hot roast beef, mutton chops, Vienna beef steak, boiled fish (known as College shark) or potato pie, perhaps ending with boiled macaroni and rhubarb or bread and butter pudding. The Steward designed the menus before the First World War on a three-weekly cycle, but when the war came the memories became much more negative. Root pie, a meatless dish served two or three times a week, was despised by all and even those seeking solace in the Grubber's selection were to be disappointed; a 'brown lunch' biscuit seemed to have been made out of straw. Edmund Allenby's favourite Grub Shop delicacy was a 'three corner', a pastry, while in the 1920s a 'Mrs Wright', a jam sponge sandwich with pink and white icing, was a particular favourite, named after a music teacher.

The rationing in the Second World War did not seem to have damaged the quality of the catering as much as the shortages felt in 1914–18. There is a

Chapter 6 ~ SCHOOL LIFE

Below: *The old Dining Hall (now the Attlee Room), c.1900, with Hall waiters in attendance.*

Bottom: *The Memorial Dining Hall in use, 2004, when the new layout was introduced.*

story about Canon Bonhote being unhappy about the limited rations that Haileybury pupils had. Bonhote wrote to the Ministry of Food, informing them of the injustice of the state school pupils receiving a meal at school and their ordinary rations while his charges did not. There was no reply to Bonhote's letter, so when he wrote again explaining the situation, he also informed the officials that he would start sending 200 pupils a day to have lunch at a local hotel. Needless to say, the response was rapid and the rations enlarged.

115

HAILEYBURY — *A 150th Anniversary Portrait*

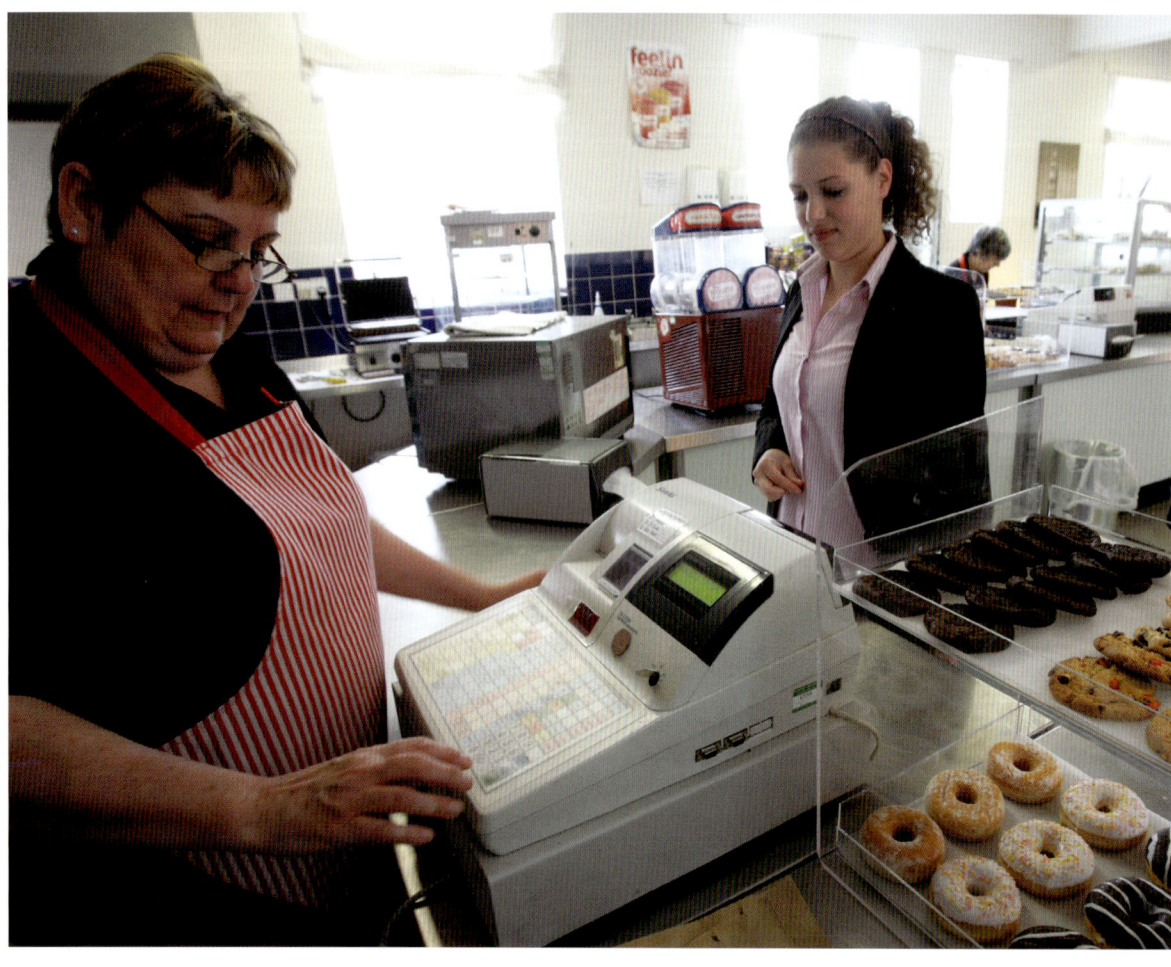

Left: *The Grubber, 2012.*

Below: *Food petition, 1945.*

In the first days of the School's existence the Steward, who had only organised catering for the worldly students of the East India College, served up pickles with all the meals and found that a month's supply vanished in a matter of days. Benjamin Jones's error was not repeated again and even in 1973 the Caterer was claiming that vinegar was too expensive to be served with chips in Hall.

In 1988 it was decided by Council that the Dining Hall should adopt a cafeteria style and in 2004 the present system of multiple stations was adopted, offering a choice of food to suit all tastes.

ATMP

War-time food was adequate if uninspiring. Reputedly it provided a balanced diet, devised and presided over by the Lady Dietician, Miss Howard Mercer, who no doubt did a good job in difficult circumstances. She often appeared at mealtimes and was wont to stress the benefits of extra meat ration if a foreign body was found in the cabbage. Some monotony in the menus was demonstrated by a petition signed by nearly half the school and received by me when Head of School in 1945; the original heading, crossed out but still legible, was, 'The following suggest that less stew be served for lunch'. It must have been realised that this was open to misinterpretation, for the wording was changed to 'The following suggest that fewer stews be served for lunch'. I hope some improvement resulted.

John Brock (A 1941.1)

116

Chapter 6 — SCHOOL LIFE

LUNCH MENUS: PLUS ÇA CHANGE
2011
Beef and Ale Pie
Mashed Potatoes / Carrots / Cabbage
Sponge Pudding
1988
Beef Stew and Dumplings
Parsley Potatoes / Roast Parsnips
Pears and Chocolate Sauce
1945
Toad in the Hole
Cabbage / Mashed Potatoes
Spotted Dick
1904
Steak Pie
Potatoes / Greens
Treacle Pudding

Below: *The interior of Dining Hall in the year of its opening, 1932.*

Below right: *The Dining Hall exterior, designed by Sir Herbert Baker, 1932.*

Fire Drills and Field Days

I remember the horror I felt at my first Kipling dormitory fire drill, which involved having to climb down a rope (not a rope ladder) suspended from the ceiling which went down through a hole in our floor and then down into the Batten dormitory below and onto its floor. The thought of 50 of us making that escape with a fire raging doesn't bear thinking about. I don't think anyone worried about health and safety in those days.

I also remember one Field Day where I was responsible for defending an area of a wood with my platoon. I put everyone in their positions and told them to make themselves invisible and not to move. I think the day went well and eventually we all went back to Hall for tea. After a couple of hours I realised that one of my platoon wasn't having tea and we all wondered where he was. I suddenly had an awful feeling, rushed back to where I had placed him in the wood many hours earlier, and found him. I apologised profusely for having forgotten him but he was very good about it. Naturally, I congratulated him on following his orders to the letter.

Anthony Harper (K 1960.1)

A Sense of the Sixth Form

From the sight of hundreds of upturned pairs of male eyes appraising us with curiosity as we, the new girls, trooped onto the balcony for lunch on induction day, to the sound of over 500 male voices belting out *Hark the Herald* as I sobbed my heart out up in the choir stalls on my last day after seven terms in the Sixth Form, my memories of Haileybury can be conjured up in a series of intensely vivid sensory perceptions.

There is the glorious sound of Jack Hindmarsh or Derek Longman on the Chapel organ resonating across Quad on Sunday mornings. There is the inglorious but no less thrilling Saturday night sound of rock music blasting out of every window in the Old Studies. There is the beautiful purity of the madrigals echoing across Amwell Pool at the annual 'mini-choir' performance and the raucous laughter as the Masters made fools of themselves (or displayed admirable comic talent, depending on your point of view) during Pastimes.

There is the sonorous sound of the gong bidding silence before lunch in the Dining Hall and the occasional self-imposed (and unnatural) silence during the meal as we demonstrated solidarity with one of our number expelled for (in our view) a feat of great daring. And there is the mellifluous dignity of David Summerscale's rendition of *Journey of the Magi* at the Carol Service and, in the Chemistry Labs, Harry 'Hotplate' Hargreaves' (Staff 1948.3–81.2) urgent admonition and sharp intake of breath as he inverted test tubes of acid on his thumbs: 'Ooh, never do this! Never do this!'

I remember the sickly sweet smell of the cherry brandy which we naively thought the Masters would never recognise on our breath and, much worse, the choking clouds of cigarette smoke in the girls' toilet in the Music School (a place the boys thought the Masters would never check). I remember the exhilaration of walking in the dark all the way across School from Alban's (then the girls' House) to the Biology Labs for evening lessons and the even more exciting night-time adventure meeting one's beloved by the Whatton Block shrubbery for the all-too-short 15-minute stroll together between evening preps.

From the feeling of the first hesitant incision with a scalpel blade into the skin of a warm, newly dead rat during our first dissection (Mr Woodburn strolling around the room half smiling, half despairing at our incompetence) to the final clicking back on of the pen lid with relief and exhaustion at the end of the last Oxbridge entrance exam, these are just a very few of the Haileybury experiences imprinted on my senses which, like Proust's madeleine, invoke a stream of memories, brimful of everything and everyone.

Jo Burch (Alb and K 1980.3)

Above: Study, May 1965.

Above: Marno Nagtegaal (Tr 1994.3), Matthew Williams (LS, RD and M 1992.3) and Andrew Coward (L 1996.3) in the Technology Centre, 1999.

Chapter 6 — SCHOOL LIFE

HAILEYBURIANARAMA

*Gazing out a factory window in Kathmandu
I recall a fairytale I once travelled through …*

*Of pristine quadrangles with language fandangled,
running with books and excuses entangled*

*Twenty acres of drama, five X for cheek
coco 'n' bun fights in the Half once a week*

*A drunk band of brothers, imaginary lovers,
fags in the woods and lying for others*

*Jokes after lights-out that got you in trouble
and answering back that meant it was double*

*Styling your uniform and fighting for fashion
and House matches fought with implausible passion*

*Quoting King Lear, Broxbourne beer, Housemaster fear,
Hedgehogs cheer …
Loyalty and love and adventure were near …*

*A Victorian hangover … architecturally grand
a Big School … a legend of our Green and Pleasant land.*

Joe Sixth Form Centre says … I miss you guys!

Mark Alex Bloom (E 1978.3)

Top right: *Dance, 2012, a popular Wednesday afternoon activity.*

Far right: *Rob Turnbull, on his way to Chapel. He retired at the end of the Summer Term, 2012, after 33 years service which included eleven years as Second Master.*

Below: *Boat-building in Shops.*

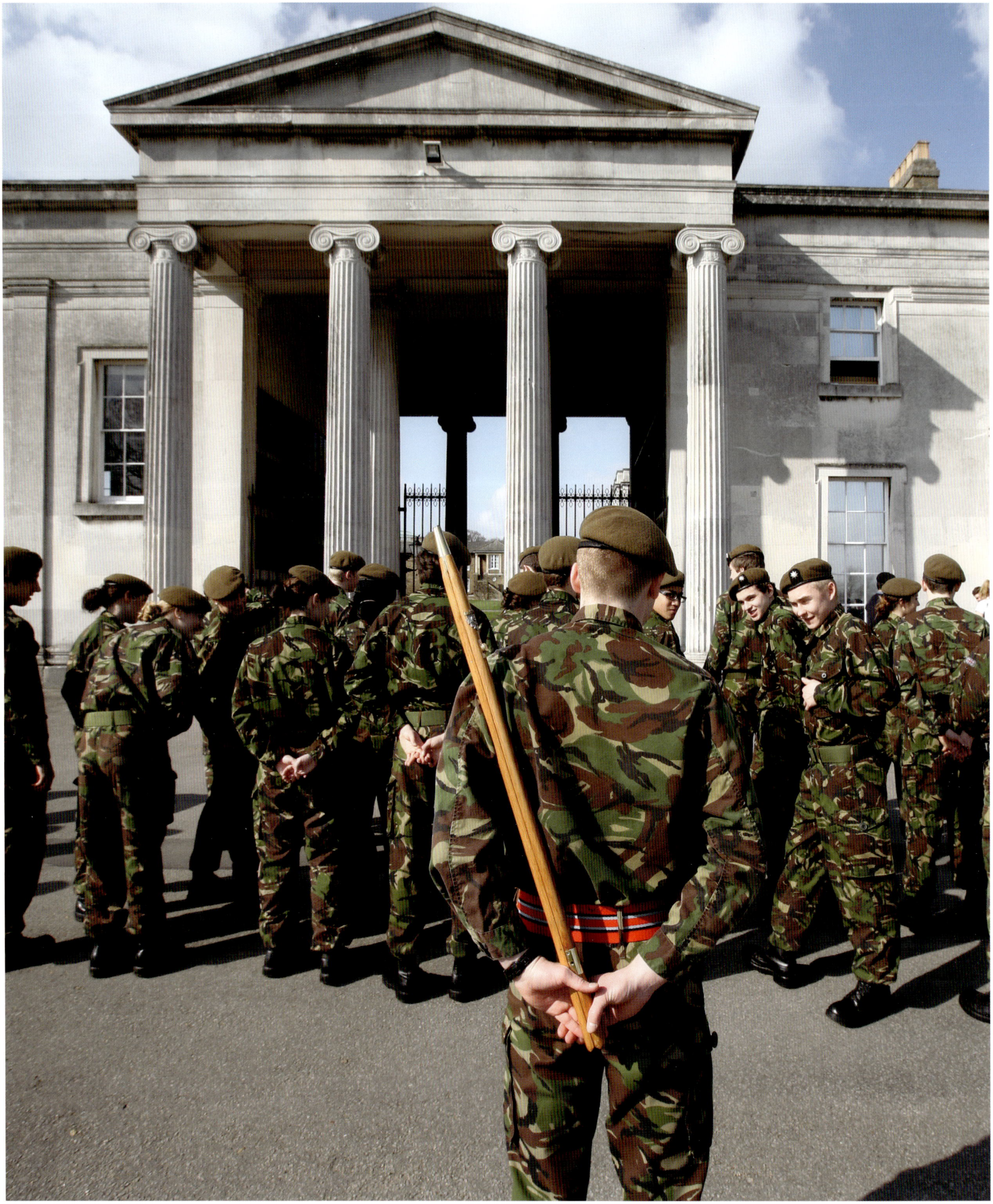

Chapter 7

SERVICE BEFORE SELF

Opposite: *Mustering for the weekly CCF parade, 2012.*

HAILEYBURY REACHES OUT TO THE COMMUNITY

When I started Community Service, I didn't really know what it was. At about this time last year, I undertook some service hours for my International Baccalaureate (IB) and the Duke of Edinburgh's Award and agreed to take the place of one of last year's Upper Sixth students at Wheatcroft Primary School in Hoddesdon.

Looking back on what I have done, I feel a certain degree of pride, not only as it is important for pupils privileged enough to be at a school like this to give something back to the community, but also, I felt, for the first time in my life, I could do something beneficial for others.

The children we worked with certainly enjoyed our presence. Working with them involved helping the Year One and Year Two pupils with computer or ICT work, reading and writing exercises, as well as messy artwork and even cooking. In addition to those 'school activities' we helped them by building a ramp for their toy cars that they play with in break time. We usually worked with a class of about 25 pupils and one teacher, who really valued our help. After a couple of weeks the teacher will work out what you enjoy doing and then employ you purposefully. At the beginning it felt a bit strange, with lots of little people asking questions ('where are you from?', 'what is your favourite football team?', 'do you have a girlfriend?' – it can get quite personal!). After a while you learn how to get the best out of them, with races or rewards in the form of sweets. I really enjoyed taking the option of community service at a primary school and can certainly recommend it.

Simon Haug (BF 2000.3)

There are many misconceptions, myths and fears between people brought up in inner-city areas and those who come from more prosperous areas of the UK.

In 1989 a project was set up by a group of people who were deeply concerned about such issues and this became the Inner Cities Young People's Project (ICYPP). The aim of the project was to bring together young people from these different backgrounds and let them experience and learn about each other's communities in the hope of eradicating some of these prejudices.

I was fortunate enough to take part in the ICYPP residential course with Alexia Kaila (Aby 2000.3). There were three parts to the course, the first of which was a three-day weekend in Elephant and Castle called the 'Familiarisation' weekend, where we met the others who were to be in our group, some from public schools like ourselves, and some from inner-city schools. During the weekend we spent much of our time in the confined space of a small church and had the opportunity to share our experiences and opinions with the group. We also visited a community centre in King's Cross where we organised activities for the children.

The second part of the course was the inner-city school experience in London, which was a chance for the independent school pupils to experience inner-city school life. We spent a day shadowing the inner-city school students, going to their lessons and meeting their friends. For me this was the most eye-opening part of the course. Before I went I imagined the school to be quite disjointed and perhaps violent, but it was not long before I was proven wrong. Despite the occasional strange look from some of the pupils, everyone was very friendly and the atmosphere of the school was informal and relaxed. But what struck me the most was the attitude of the pupils, who seem to be there more because they wanted to be there, not just because they were forced to. There was a real will to learn.

During the rest of the inner-city break we had the opportunity to discuss among ourselves a variety of issues, ranging from teenage pregnancies and abortion to recreational drug use. This was a good opportunity to hear the views of people from very different backgrounds, and it certainly made me reconsider some of the beliefs that I held before the experience.

The third and final part of the course was a four-day stay at Charterhouse, giving us a chance to see the reaction of the state school students in this environment. For them it was a chance to experience the formality and regimented structure of independent school life.

When people ask me what I have got from the Inner Cities Young People's Project I find it hard to give a straight answer. It has given me a wider perspective on life, but what I have really gained is the experience, which is what ICYPP is all about. What we have learned is not something that you can read about and teach yourself but something that you have to experience personally. I was lucky enough to have this experience and at the same time I really enjoyed myself and met some great people.

Richard Dimock (B 1994.3)

During the summer I spent a week in Liverpool helping at a special needs play scheme. The play scheme took place in an area called Fazakerley and was for children aged between five and 16, with a variety of disabilities such as Down's syndrome, deafness and ADD. The play scheme was run so that the special needs children in the area had something to do during their holidays and so that their parents had time off from looking after them. There were different activities every day, including swimming, pottery, football and visits to playgrounds, parks, a farm and Chester Zoo, all of which I got a chance to help with.

At times I found it extremely challenging as some of the children had multiple disabilities and so it was difficult to communicate with them. I did get to learn some sign language, which was really useful, and when I could communicate with them it was very rewarding.

Apart from the play scheme, I also got to see around Liverpool, which was very different to how I expected as everyone was so friendly. This was very helpful for making friends, some of whom I am still in contact with.

While I was there, many people asked me why I was taking part in the project and I didn't know. But now that I have done it, I realise I have learned so much: I have gained confidence as I went up to Liverpool where I knew no one, on my own. I am more accepting of other people and other communities. I have got satisfaction from helping others. I have handled responsibility for children in my care. And above all I had a fantastic time which was enjoyable, rewarding and fun, and met lots of new and interesting people.

Everyone gets something different out of their Inner Cities Young People's Project experience.

Elizabeth Williams (Alb 2000.3)

Above: *Lily Köhler (C 2008.3) with Mrs Mathilde Krajewski, long-time resident of Hertford Heath and former matron of Kipling.*

HAILEYBURY AND ISC MISSIONS

The Stepney Club and the Haileybury Guild are well-known aspects of Haileybury's history, but there are other two missions that form a part of the School's heritage, one in India and another in the East End of London.

The mission at St John's College, Agra was started by the second Master, Edward Bradby, in 1873. The pupils, members of Common Room and OHs, contributed money every year for the maintenance of a lecturer called the Haileybury Master or Missioner. The College had been founded in 1850 by the Reverend Thomas Valpy French with the support of three East Indiamen who had been educated at Haileybury: James Thomason (EIC 1820), John Colvin (EIC 1823) and Sir William Muir (EIC 1836). St John's provided an education for Muslims, Hindus and Christians, but there was a huge problem in persuading the three groups to mix. The Agra fund was chosen by Bradby to support 'Indian idealism and Christian ideals' because of the School's Indian connections. Surviving members of the East India College, such as Lord Lawrence (EIC 1827), Edward Thornton (EIC 1828) and John Hallet Batten (EIC 1827), publicly lent their support for the rest of their lives alongside the modern Haileyburians. In 1885 Bradby wrote from his mission at St Katherine's Dock to the readers of the *Haileyburian* to explain the importance of a school-supported mission outside of England: *They were fain to hope that something of what was best in the genius of the old college had descended to its young successor, and that they might be able to claim a real moral as well as a local continuity. But if this were to be done, then India, and the duties which Englishmen owe to India, must always have a prominent place in thoughts and interests ... Home Missions are excellent things. Living where I am now living I see daily evidence of the good they may work; and we may well rejoice that, since the foundation of our fund, many of our public schools have been move to undertake them. But they do not exhaust the whole duty of a citizen of this great Empire, much less a Christian. In both capacities we have wider relations, and owe a debt to our fellow subjects in India no less than England.*

At a meeting of Old Haileyburians on Monday 7 July 1890 Edward Lyttelton made a speech, in which he suggested that OHs should support the clergy in British cities. The Reverend Edwyn Hoskyns (Tr 1865.1) then suggested the formation of a Haileybury Guild, which would not affect the Agra Mission but rather *show clearly to the world that Haileybury had a heart that could beat in full accord with the most distant of our possessions and at the same time had sufficient warmth to listen to the cries of those who were so near their homes.*

At the end of the meeting a resolution was agreed upon and a council for the Haileybury Guild was formed. The first meeting of the Council was held at Haileybury on 21 July 1890 and it was decided that the Guild would have a dual nature. First, the Guild would allow relationships between the OHs and

Below: St John's College, Agra, recipient of monies raised by the Haileybury Agra fund.

HAILEYBURY — *A 150th Anniversary Portrait*

BOYS' CLUB CADETS

In 1945 the School was given a half holiday to mark the appointment of Clement Attlee as Prime Minister. Attlee's socialist leanings stemmed from his time at the Haileybury Boys' Club in Stepney. In my day the Club remained an active and successful organisation. Although its buildings were destroyed in the London blitz, it continued to function at Territorial Army headquarters in Mile End Road. After five years in the army and at Cambridge, I attended a year's course from 1950 to 1951 at London University in preparation for appointment in the then Colonial Service. Michael Copinger (L 1935.2), a brewer with Charringtons in Stockwell, was in overall charge of the Club, but I, priding myself (overmuch, I fear) on my military competence and experience, was happy to take over from him the running of the cadet company, the parent regiment being the Rifle Brigade, whose depot was at Winchester.

I loved my time at the Club, all of whose members were true 'East Enders'. We had parade and club nights each week and highly enjoyable and rewarding weekends at both Winchester and Haileybury. Alas! My time there was all too short, for in 1951 I sailed to seek adventure in Africa, and any hopes I might have entertained of becoming a socialist Prime Minister were irrevocably dashed.

John Brock

My recollection of the Boys' Club in Stepney is our annual rugger game which was played indoors, so you can imagine how bruised we were when we left, having, inevitably, been beaten. I also remember one of the Club boys asking me where I learned to speak my strange language!

Peter B. Maynard (L 1936.2)

Above: *Clement Attlee, a manager of the Haileybury Club from 1907 to 1914, with boys from the Club.*

the local populations, and second, to encourage 'all influences, social, physical, mental and spiritual'. The development at Stepney (Hoskyns' own parish) was not originally intended to be the sole focus of the Guild but merely one manifestation of the Guild's work. At Stepney the mission grew dramatically, adding a set of rooms for classes and meetings, designed by Reginald Blomfield, which was opened in 1896 by HRH Princess Christian of Schleswig-Holstein, and six years later Haileybury House was built to provide accommodation for a resident manager and five others. While Clement Attlee's time at the Stepney Club has been written about before, what is less well known is that John Slessor (L 1911.2) spent several weeks in 1915 assisting Oswald Watson (L 1899.3) before he joined the Royal Flying Corps.

The Imperial Service College mission was at St Mary's, Cable Street, St George-in-the-East, an inheritance from the Army School. Edward Beckwith, before he was Headmaster of the ISC (1912.1–35.1),

124

Chapter 7 — SERVICE BEFORE SELF

ran the Army School at Hollyport and asked the Bishop of London to allot a poor area in the diocese to be his school mission. St Mary's parish was chosen for the Army School and the Mission of the Good Shepherd at Dean Street was founded. In 1912, when the Army School merged with the ISC, the Mission of the Good Shepherd became the ISC Mission, although it was not known as such until 1916. Sadly, the Dean Street Mission was closed because of the expense of maintaining it and the ISC support went to St Mary's Institute in the same parish. The ISC Mission buildings, owned by the Mercers' Company, were used as Sunday schools, social clubs, meeting rooms and for London County Council instruction classes. The money raised paid for the upkeep of the Institute. Every Whit Monday the ISC would play host to about 70 parishioners from St Mary's, a cricket match would be held and an evening service in the School Chapel would be attended by the visitors.

In 1942 St Mary's was devastated when Haileybury and ISC amalgamated, the contributions to the mission dropped and the financial burden on the parish grew immensely. The ISC Mission did not end in 1942 but only small donations were made from the School Offertory Fund and by 1945 it appears to have largely passed into history.

ATMP

Right: *Haileybury Youth Trust beneficiaries in Kizigo, Uganda. The money for the water tank was raised by the pupils in Trevelyan in 2011.*

HAILEYBURY YOUTH TRUST

A century after Clement Attlee's life was transformed by his work among the poor of London, his old school continues to improve lives, albeit in East Africa rather than the East End. It was at the Haileybury Boys' Club that the young Attlee first visited in 1905, having just come down from Oxford. It was his first real encounter with social deprivation and was, he wrote later, 'a day that was destined to alter the whole course of my life'. Attlee became a Manager of the Haileybury Club and lived at Haileybury House until the outbreak of war. It was his experiences in Stepney that led him to a career in socialist politics.

After a century of working in the East End, however, Haileybury's support was no longer needed. The people of Tower Hamlets were adept at finding other sources of funds and the old Boys' Club was sold back to the borough. Yet the spirit of service continued and the trustees of Haileybury Youth Trust (HYT), as it had become, looked for new opportunities for the privileged of Haileybury to serve and learn alongside the impoverished youth of another community. I had introduced Jim Cogan, late of Westminster School and founder of the gap year charity SPW, to Uganda and he had introduced me to a remarkable appropriate technology that could transform lives in sub-Saharan Africa. There seemed to be an opportunity for the wider

School community to engage in useful development a world away from Haileybury – and to be enriched by it.

HYT has embarked on a programme of sustainable development in rural Uganda that is different from other, more conventional, school partnerships. Although many British independent schools enjoy fruitful links with schools in Africa and support building projects such as classrooms, science labs and libraries, there is perhaps not always an awareness of the environmental consequences of such aid.

Traditional construction in much of Africa uses hand-moulded clay bricks. The widespread use of these bricks is, however, devastating the landscape as vast quantities of firewood are required for the kilns that produce them. Not only that, huge amounts of carbon dioxide are emitted in the firing of the brick kilns and fragile biodiversity is further depleted. It is estimated that 140,000 new homes are required every year in Uganda and that it takes land clearance of an area the size of two tennis courts to produce the bricks for each of these homes. That's 280,000 tennis courts' worth of trees lost every year. Free and universal primary education means that many new schools are also needed for this fast growing and youthful population. Eager charities and indeed British schools unwittingly contribute to this emerging environmental catastrophe as they continue to build with traditional fired bricks.

HYT, however, promotes an appropriate construction technology that could have a far-reaching impact across sub-Saharan Africa. The Trust encourages the adoption of an Interlocking Stabilised Soil Block (ISSB) which compresses a moistened mixture of subsoil and a small amount of cement in a mould that produces oblong blocks which are cured, not fired. No firewood is used and no trees chopped down. Ancient forests and biodiversity are preserved and CO_2 emissions drastically reduced. The interlocking features of the block means it is stronger, cheaper and quicker for construction purposes.

Not only does the use of the ISSB technology meet basic humanitarian needs while preserving the environment and reducing carbon emissions, it also offers employment and income-generating opportunities. HYT has recently completed the first phase of a five-year project, *One Village at a Time*, where ten rural villages will be transformed in a programme of sustainable development which will include training, education and construction. Schools are an effective focus for its promotion, as they often have large roof areas (good for rainwater harvesting and storage in ISSB-built water tanks), a diverse community of children, parents and teachers, and can offer training opportunities for future employment. Pupils can also make blocks in their spare time, earning pocket money and acquiring skills, while recognizing the need to safeguard their beautiful but fragile environment.

Working alongside its permanent staff, Ugandan engineers and local trainees, pre- and post-university gap year students from Haileybury spend time volunteering for the Trust deep in the African bush, pioneering the use of this simple block. The United Nations Department for Human Settlement, UN Habitat, has visited projects, endorsing HYT's work, as has the Department for International Development. The project is a life-enhancing experience for the privileged young people of Haileybury, just as it was for the Haileyburians who spent time at the Stepney Club, while also contributing in a small but important way to development in some of Africa's poorest communities.

With Haileyburians and Ugandans working shoulder to shoulder, this technology provides a solution to an African crisis, without costing the earth. We like to think Attlee would be pleased.

Russell Matcham (Staff 1999.3–)

Above: *James Clarke (K 2005.3) with children at Kizigo – one of the* One Village at a Time *sites in Uganda.*

Chapter 7 — SERVICE BEFORE SELF

Amongst the Afghans

Sunday in Afghanistan is the first day of the week. I have been working for Tearfund's Disaster Management Team for the last six years. Tearfund's programmes in Afghanistan reach tens of thousands of people a year, providing water treatment for safe drinking water, water-management reservoirs, food security improvement through animal and seed distribution in drought-prone areas leading to improved nutrition, hygiene and sanitation education, flood protection walls, and disaster risk-reduction education. As the Country Director for these programmes I got to see the direct beneficiaries only every few months when I visited the field sites in Jawzjan, Faryab, Kapisa and Kandahar. Sometimes this meant wearing the full *burqa* and other times simply the *salwar kameez* and headscarf. With some conversational Dari I was able to converse with them directly, which was a great asset. But it is my staff in the field sites who have a direct impact on these people's lives. If I leave behind a handful of better managers for Afghanistan then I feel I have done my job. If I have led by example and ushered my colleagues through difficult situations, times of panic and pressure, to choosing compassionate and considered ways to deal with things, then I have done my job.

Below: *Kate Bowen, Tearfund Disaster Management Team.*

It is sometimes hard to remain positive about the areas of the world I work in that have such endemic problems, so I reduce my expectations for the impact I can have on a few individuals. It is a more realistic and achievable endeavour. My faith in God gives me hope in situations that seem so hopeless. The inscription from Revelation on the Chapel dome that I saw every morning sticks in my mind: '*Esto fidelis usque ad mortem et dabo tibi coronam vitae*' – 'Be faithful unto death and I will give you the crown of life' – *Revelation 2:10*.

It reminds me to be faithful to what I believe in and the passions I have in me.

Kate Bowen (Alb and K 1994.3)

Mine-Clearing in Angola and elsewhere

Having been looking for something interesting to do, HALO's six-month intensive training package for 'enthusiastic, fit, well-educated men' came just at the right time. Haileybury can take credit for the third characteristic.

Established in 1988, HALO Trust is the world's leading humanitarian mine-clearance charity, working in nine countries – Abkhazia, Afghanistan, Angola, Cambodia, Kosovo, Mozambique, Nagorno Karabakh, Somaliland and Sri Lanka. My HALO career began with training in Angola. During this time I was trained in all the aspects of a mine-clearance programme, including de-mining, explosives, survey, mechanics, medical training, finance and location management. While I never thought mine clearance was a particularly glamorous job, five hours a day on my knees in sweltering heat clearing mines was certainly a reality check. De-mining is essentially a very simple, although pretty laborious, process. It basically involves one de-miner in a 1m-wide lane with a metal detector and a bunch of excavation tools. Key to clearing an area quickly is scale – deploying as many de-miners as possible.

After Angola I was given my first posting as a location manager in Cambodia. I would often see the entire process of a minefield being cleared and then witness it quickly transform into a paddy field or expanded part of a village. After Cambodia I returned to Angola and started my current job of operations officer west for the provinces of Benguela and Huambo. It is not the easiest country to work in – just its sheer size and poor roads make logistics difficult. What makes the frustrations easier to bear is that I have the opportunity really to effect change and make things happen. HALO has a lean management structure so if I have an idea to change something and my boss agrees then I can crack on with it. Over 12,000 mines and two million square metres were cleared in 2007. Just as I thought when I began this odd career, it is fun doing something a bit different.

Roly Clark (L 1997.3)

ARMED SERVICE

At Speech Day in 1910, Lord Salisbury suggested that every pupil at Haileybury must have felt that they had a Field Marshal's baton rattling in their pockets after listening to the distinctions won by Old Haileyburians and the rousing speech given by Lord Roberts. In 2012 Haileybury pupils can no longer carry a Field Marshal's baton in their pockets because five-star (Admiral of the Fleet, Field Marshal and Marshal of the RAF) appointments have been placed in abeyance since the military reforms of the mid-1990s but they can still aspire to becoming leaders in their chosen field of work. Haileybury has produced two Field Marshals and two Marshals of the RAF, all of whom were appointed in the 20th century: Edmund Allenby, John Chapple, John Slessor and William Dickson (H 1912.3).

ATMP

Corps

Since its foundation, Haileybury has had a proud military tradition, though today's pupils may not be aware of it, or of the thousands of Haileyburians who have served in the armed forces during the 150 years of the College's history, many making the ultimate sacrifice in foreign fields. Not surprisingly, such awareness was much stronger when I started my four years at Haileybury in the summer of 1945. The war in Europe ended in May that year, and many of the beaks were returning to College, taking classes still dressed in their service uniform.

National Service for all young men was to follow, and I can remember Speech Days when scores of OHs attended proudly dressed as officers, providing a very military atmosphere to the proceedings. Many OHs embarked on careers in the armed forces, and there was a services Sixth Form preparing boys for the entrance examinations for the three services. On arrival at Sandhurst in 1949 I found that I was one of 20 OHs in the Academy.

Left: *Roly Clark removing buried munitions in Afghanistan in 2008.*

Below: *The brass relief on the top of the Victoria Cross Memorial on Terrace.*

Chapter 7 — SERVICE BEFORE SELF

Right: *L–r: John Chapple, Bryan Webster, Oliver Kingdon (L 1944.2) and George Richey (L 1944.3), 1948. Interestingly, John Chapple went on to be Chief of the General Staff (1992), Bryan Webster became a Major General and Director of Army Quartering (1982) and George Richey was a Lieutenant-Colonel in the Royal Artillery.*

Right: *General Sir Alexander Godley (Th 1880.1 and USC 1882.1) inspecting the Corps before unveiling the Memorial Cross on 7 July 1923. The Cross of Sacrifice was designed by Reginald Blomfield, one of the three major architects of the War Graves Commission.*

During my time at Haileybury, all boys were expected to join the JTC, and each term the Corps would set off, headed by our drums and fifes, for Field Days in the Hertfordshire countryside. I still treasure the memory of heading the khaki-clad column, as Drum Major, through the small village of Hoddesdon with the (possibly) appreciative villagers lining the route. Then, having reached the battlefield, we would spend the rest of the day crouched in damp fields clutching a heavy Lee Enfield rifle and throwing thunder flashes at the advancing enemy.

In his book *Random Recollections of Haileybury* (1956), R.L. Ashcroft lists the School's contribution to the Army – one Field Marshal (Allenby), seven Generals, four Lieutenant Generals, 32 Major Generals, and 106 Brigadiers. More have been added since then, including our second Field Marshal, Sir John Chapple.

I write, of course, of a different era. With unbroken world peace for an unprecedented period (except for conflicts in which our part is being undertaken by smaller, all regular armed forces), and a change in national attitudes towards conflict, it is natural that the School's military flavour has diminished, but it is reassuring to see that the tradition of service at Haileybury is still, in a wider context, as strong as ever.

Bryan Webster (M 1945.2)

HAILEYBURY ~ A 150th Anniversary Portrait

PER ARDUA AD ASTRA: THE ROYAL AIR FORCE AND HAILEYBURY

On 29 May 1985 at 11.45am a magnificent silver RAF Gazelle helicopter landed out of a clear blue sky on Terrace in front of the Lightning Oak. An old Haileyburian, the senior Marshal of the Royal Air Force, Sir William Dickson, resplendent in full uniform, stepped out of the plane. He had come to unveil the 'Haileybury and ISC RAF Honours Board', which recognises the enormous contribution that he and other officers have made to the service. All, like Sir William Dickson, had once been pupils at the School. After lunch with many distinguished RAF Haileyburians and their wives, his motorcade swept him down past the Armoury, then the Grubber and Swimming Pool to the RAF headquarters, where he inspected an RAF cadet Guard of Honour. He then gave the following address:

Before I unveil this honours board and declare this new headquarters open, I think one or two things need to be said. The first is what gave rise to this occasion.

Everyone knows of the proud record Haileybury and the ISC have of service to their country over many years, especially in the Empire and the Commonwealth. What is not known so well is the outstanding part Haileyburians have played in the Royal Air Force from its beginning and in what is sometimes called 'The conquest of the air'. That is why the Master and the Housemaster of Colvin decided that there should be a commemoration to give recognition to all those who, after being at school at Haileybury and the ISC, went on to serve in the Royal Air Force.

It is also to bring to the notice of present pupils in the School and those in the future the fine, proud link that Haileybury and the ISC have with the Royal Air Force. It is a record which is second to no other school in the United Kingdom. It is a tradition which, I think, every boy and girl at Haileybury should know of and be proud of. The Royal Air Force also recognises the part that Haileyburians have played in the service and that is why they have flown me here to represent the Royal Air Force at this ceremony.

This board, which it is my honour to unveil, records the names of the most senior and most distinguished Air Force Haileyburians. It does not, and could not, record the names of the very many other Haileyburians who served in the RAF during its short but famous history. The board is therefore a tribute to them also, especially to those who gave their lives in the Air Force service.

The School may wonder what it was that attracted Haileyburians into the Air Force. There is no doubt what it was to start with. It was the novelty, the challenge and the adventure of flying. In 1914, when I was at Haileybury, it was only ten years since man made his first flight in a powered aircraft – that was after thousands of years watching and envying the birds. Before the war started, people stopped in the streets to stare and marvel at an aeroplane in the sky. So, you may imagine what effects the exploits of airmen fighting the war in the air had on young men coming from a school with traditions like Haileybury.

The attraction of the Air Force to Haileyburians after the war was something different. The war in the air in 1914–18 not only established a new dimension in warfare, it started a new chapter in man's life on earth – his use of the air. The RAF had a pioneering role to play. It was reorganised into a small, regular air force with foundations and a front line to meet our requirements at home and our many commitments across the world.

Below: *The Marshal of the RAF Sir William Dickson, unveiling the RAF Honours Board in 1985. On the right is David Blakeway Smith, Officer Commander, RAF Section, Haileybury. On the left is David Summerscale, the then Master.*

130

Chapter 7 — SERVICE BEFORE SELF

Above: *Portrait of Sir John Slessor (L 1911.2) by A.R. Thomson, RA.*

The first list of permanent commissions came out and Haileybury was well represented.

It is hard to describe what it was like to be in that band of dedicated enthusiasts. There was, of course, the thrill of flying and the possibility of doing something new every time you went up. But uppermost there was the feeling of responsibility and the challenge to everyone to develop this new air power in every way possible and to show what the Air Force could do. This was especially important where the Air Force could greatly assist in our control and defence of large areas in India, the Middle and Far East. This challenge has a special appeal to Haileyburians because of the School's links with India and the East. Everyone was inspired to aim high and to strive. Per Ardua Ad Astra was the chosen motto.

It was the enthusiasm and the example of these first Air Force Haileyburians which led more Haileyburians to join the Air Force and others to follow them. If they could not get permanent commissions they took short service commissions, an idea that the Air Force pioneered. This idea suited both parties. It suited the individual because he could enjoy the adventure of Air Force service and Air Force life, and the training he received and the man it made him increased his chances and value in civil life. It suited the Air Force because it gave them a valuable reserve air crew. The idea continues today. That was how the Haileybury/Air Force link started and grew and it explains the distinguished part OHs played in the last war and why many of them reached high places, some the highest.

Haileyburians were also prominent in the Air Force after the war. At one time there were three of them together on the Air Council. Thanks to those who showed the way, the spirit in the Air Force today is the same. Morale and pride of service continue to be very high. They feel the same challenge of the air and their responsibilities and they strive to carry them out in a typically, excellent Air Force way.

Before I pull this cord I say to members of the RAF Section that whatever you choose to do in life, and it may not be in the Air Force, I suggest that you aim high like your predecessors. You may not feel you have it in you now, but you acquire character and standards here which give you great advantage, especially to meet the challenge when it comes. So, *Sursum Corda* and good luck.

In the afternoon, sitting on one of the benches overlooking Pavilion, Sir William Dickson was shown by a young cadet, Lance Corporal James Tschaikowsky (M 1974.3), how to fly his radio-controlled Sopwith Pup aircraft over Pavilion. As he had the controls Sir William was heard quietly to comment, 'I learned to fly in one of these on Lake Windermere in 1916.'

Marshal of the Royal Air Force Sir William Dickson, as one would expect of a great-great-grandson of Lord Nelson, joined the Royal Navy and then transferred to the Royal Naval Air Service. He learned to fly on Lake Windermere and, soon afterwards, was involved in the first experiments to take off and land an aircraft on to a ship. On 19 July 1918, flying one of a formation of seven Sopwith Camels from *HMS Furious*, he took part in a highly successful bombing raid on the Zeppelin

131

HAILEYBURY — *A 150th Anniversary Portrait*

base at Tondern – the only seaborne raid from a carrier during the First World War.

Through rapid promotion in the Second World War he became, first, Director of Plans, then Fighter Command followed by Air Officer Commanding the Middle East Air Force in Italy, Marshal of the RAF and, finally, the first Chief of the Defence Staff, a post he relinquished to Lord Mountbatten – altogether a fine record of service.

When told of Dickson's engagement in 1932, a gruff Lord Trenchard, founder of the RAF, told his intended, 'Good choice. He's brave as a lion and clever as a monkey.'

Marshal of the Royal Air Force Sir John Slessor was rejected for the Army because he had had polio, walked with a limp and was 'unfit for all military service', but he managed to join the Royal Flying Corps. He directed plans and served on the Air Staff and his high point came as Air Officer Commanding Coastal Command in 1943 at the height of the Battle of the Atlantic. With his leadership, great determination and the close cooperation between all the services and Washington, victory against the U boats and their threat to our ships was eventually achieved. After his death his family found in his desk, recorded in his diary, a prayer he had written on the day he took over as Chief of the Air Staff. It tells of the fears and dangers he faced and the quality of the man:

O God, my Father, grant me Strength and Courage to face bravely the High demands that will be made upon me in the coming time.
Let me always remember the high responsibilities that I bear to my country and to the Royal Air Force.
Strengthen my soul and help it to triumph over my nerves.
Grant me a sound judgement and a valiant heart and help me to bring our country and the world to a safer haven, Amen.

After the war, through his deep thinking, writing and consciousness of the Soviet threat, he influenced the strategic nuclear defence policy right through to the end of the Cold War.

Left: *Sir Brian Baker (L 1910.3) during Haileybury Cricket Week, 1959.*

Air Chief Marshal Sir Trafford Leigh-Mallory (M 1906.2) flew in the Royal Flying Corps in the First World War. In 1940 he was Air Officer Commanding 12 Fighter Group during the crucial Battle of Britain and formulated the famous 'Big Wing' policy. Then, in 1941, he became AOC Fighter Command. On D-Day in 1944, under General Eisenhower, Leigh-Mallory was Commander-in-Chief of all the British and US air forces in the greatest air armada in history for the invasion of Europe. After this success, Lord Louis Mountbatten appointed him to be Commander-in-Chief of the combined British and US Air Forces in India against the Japanese. Sadly, he was killed in an accident while flying out to the Far East in November 1944, the most senior Air Force officer to lose his life in the war.

Air Marshal Sir Brian Baker (L 1910.3) had a brilliant career as a junior officer in the First World War. In 1917 he commanded No. 48 Squadron and, flying a Bristol BE2, he became a Royal Flying Corps 'ace' and was credited with more than 12 victories. He rose to high command and was responsible in 1944 for 'corking' the English Channel on D-Day and so prevented any enemy aircraft or ships from interfering with the Normandy landings. He was so successful that, of the vast fleet which crossed the Channel, only one ship was torpedoed in the crucial first four weeks. He was appointed to be Commander-in-Chief of RAF Transport Command, a key and crucial responsibility, and planned the difficult but successful breaking of the 'Berlin Blockade' with the remarkable Berlin Airlift.

Air Chief Marshal Sir Thomas Prickett (E 1927.1) flew Wellingtons and Lancasters in the Second World

Chapter 7 — SERVICE BEFORE SELF

War and took part in the successful bombing raid on the Peenemunde Army Research Centre, where V1 and V2 rockets were being built. Later, he led one of the Pathfinder squadrons in the heavy bombing raids on the Ruhr and reported on the effectiveness of 'window' radar counter measures which had just been employed for the first time. After the war he became Commander-in-Chief RAF Middle East, and in 1964 Commander British Forces Cyprus. He was heavily involved in the planning for the Allied Air Task Force for the politically disastrous, though operationally successful, Suez Crisis in 1956.

Air Marshal Sir John Whitley (Th 1919.3) was a senior commander of the RAF in the Second World War who took escape and evasion seriously. This proved to be extremely worthwhile for, when he was shot down in 1943, he made a classic escape back through France to Gibraltar and then back to England. He commanded No. 4 Bomber Command Group, using the Pathfinder Squadrons, to lead the main bombing campaign over Germany. After the war he became Air Officer Commanding No. 1 Group, Air Member for Personnel, a member of the Air Council and, finally, Inspector General of the RAF in 1959.

Air Vice-Marshal G.A.H. Pidcock (E 1911.3) was a Royal Flying Corps 'ace' pilot with six victories in the First World War and became one of Churchill's closest RAF advisors and Director General of Armaments in the Second World War.

David Blakeway Smith (Staff 1970.3–93.2)

HAILEYBURY'S EARLY AVIATORS

While Haileybury's connection with the RAF is well known and the names John Slessor, 'Wings' Day (C 1912.3) and Brian Baker are celebrated, what is less well known is our role in the formation of the Royal Flying Corps and the developments in aviation as a whole. Edward Maitland Maitland (E 1894.1) was a dashing young lieutenant when he experimented with ballooning, starting in 1908 with ascents made from Crystal Palace, one of which was a record-breaking journey of 1,117 miles to Russia in 36 hours. By 1909 Maitland had turned his attentions towards aeroplanes, exhibiting a Voisin biplane at Doncaster, which was the first aviation meeting in England. In spite of an accident at Larkhill in August 1910 that left Maitland with two broken ankles, he attempted to claim the £4,000 prize offered by Baron Forest for an Englishman to fly over the Channel using his Howard Wright biplane and a co-pilot, but it crashed yet again before the journey had begun. The Howard Wright No. 2 biplane that Maitland had built and then damaged on a number of occasions was sold for just over £600 to the British army and became the model for the B.E. 6, serial number 206, built at the Royal Aircraft Factory. Maitland was seconded to the Royal Engineers Air Battalion in 1911 and was appointed its commanding officer in 1912.

In 1912 Henry Brooke-Popham (L 1891.3) returned to Haileybury to lecture on military aviation in front of a rapt audience of 500 boys. Brooke-Popham, having gained his pilot's licence in 1911, like Maitland, transferred to the Royal Engineers Air

Right: Edward Maitland Maitland (hands on hips), at RNAS Pulham, Norfolk, where he was the Commanding Officer, c.1916.

Below: Henry Brooke-Popham (fourth from right in front of propeller), commanding the newly formed 3rd Squadron, R.F.C., 1912.

133

Left: *Cadets waiting to board the York aircraft that was taking them to Spring Camp at RAF Chivenor from RAF Bassingbourn, 1950.*

Battalion and commanded the Aeroplane Company. When the Royal Flying Corps was formed on 13 May 1912, Haileyburians commanded the first two squadrons and when the third was formed a number of days later, Brooke-Popham transferred there.

Towards the end of 1913 Maitland successfully experimented with a parachute, managing to jump 2,000ft and later 10,000ft without any injury from balloons and airships. By 1914 Maitland had become a colourful figure in the public's imagination, and he refused to experiment in the air using other people if he was able to undertake the role himself. In 1914 he was transferred to command the Balloon Detachment of the Royal Naval Air Service, which was urgently required to provide support for the Navy. Maitland's understanding of the military possibilities of the airship allowed him to pioneer anti-submarine techniques. In 1917 he jumped from an airship over the sea from a height of 1,000ft and was awarded the Distinguished Service Order 'in recognition of valuable and gallant work in connection with airships' and parachute experiments, some of which were under enemy fire, and at huge personal risk. On 24 August 1921 Maitland was killed when the R38, at the time the world's largest airship, plunged into the Humber estuary, cutting short the life of one of the most fascinating figures in military aviation.

While Brooke-Popham and Maitland were some of the earliest pioneers in military aviation, Alan Reginald Boyle (L 1902.2) was the first Haileyburian to hold a pilot's licence, number 13. Like Edward Maitland, Boyle built his own plane, but in 1910 he suffered a serious injury after he was thrown from it and was unconscious for over an hour. Boyle was the founder of the Scottish Aeroplane Syndicate and he was responsible for the construction of the first British monoplane.

During the First World War large numbers of Haileyburians joined the Royal Flying Corps or Royal Navy Air Service – of the boys who entered the school in 1912.3, 12 took to the sky. Of those 12 boys, four became highly decorated pilots, two became Air Marshals and one became a fighter ace who later died while attempting to break his own non-stop flight record. One of this distinguished group of pilots wrote for the *Daily Mail* on aviation matters under the name 'Wings' and came to national attention when he was attacked by seven German aircraft and managed to beat them off even though his right arm was smashed to pieces by an enemy tracer bullet. In spite of the injury 'Wings' was able to make a perfect landing and then walk to the casualty clearing station where his right arm was amputated above the elbow. 'Wings', or rather Sir Arthur Sanders' (E 1912.3) actions were considered to be without a superior in the records of the RFC in 1917.

ATMP

Chapter 7 — SERVICE BEFORE SELF

Above: *Sir Arthur Sanders entering Westminster Abbey, c.1950.*

Right: *Jack Benham who took up parachuting out of boredom with civilian life.*

TIGERS AND CHIPMUNKS

The flight to Spring camp was a very rough one and I think a number of us were lighter when we arrived than when we left. I had to learn to overcome airsickness when I was subsequently training as a pilot in the RAF. The camp was fun, not least because we all got a trip in the then new RAF light training aircraft, the Chipmunk. It was a delightful aircraft, one that I got to know very well when I was giving air experience myself to air cadets as a reserve pilot in the 1960s.

I owe a lot to the RAF section because it helped to develop my keenness for flying, aided and abetted by flights in RAF aircraft at Panshanger, a nearby airfield. Particularly enjoyable were flights in the Tiger Moth with Flying Officer David Darbishire (Staff 1949.3–55.2), a beak at school. He introduced me to aerobatics and I can still remember spinning over the School Swimming Pool. The next time I spun in a Tiger was over Lincoln Cathedral during my RAF flying training and that, too, was memorable! The Tiger's spin was near vertical. After I got my 'wings', I found myself back at Chivenor for fighter training in 1954/5. So the wheel had turned full circle.

John Allinson (Tr 1947.3)

JACK BENHAM

Wing Commander Jack Benham (Th 1914.3) ran away from school in November 1915, aged 15, to join the Army. His Housemaster, 'Gussy' Lea (Staff 1883.3–1919.3), managed to telegraph Benham's mother in time and his uncle brought him back to Haileybury. In 1918 Benham was still desperate to serve in the First World War and he attended the Royal Naval Air Service (RNAS) selection board on 14 March. RNAS amalgamated with the Royal Flying Corps on 1 April 1918 and Benham was posted to Egypt, where he spent a year as a pilot.

After the First World War Benham worked in the cigar trade and it is believed that he designed the iconic 'trim' or label for the Monte Cristo brand. Civilian life was rather dull for Benham, according to *Flight* magazine, and so he started to learn how to parachute jump. In 1940 Winston Churchill demanded that the British forces be skilled in using parachutes and the Central Landing School was founded. Jack Benham was appointed the Chief Ground Instructor and he set about training the newly formed Commando units, the Parachute Regiment and SOE agents. Benham became a respected figure in security circles and was moved to act as Despatch Officer for the SOE squadrons. The training that he provided was unique and it is surprising to read the official papers of the time which state that he was one of only three RAF officers with any experience in parachuting.

On 28 January 1942, Jack Benham was reported missing on the return journey from a triple SOE mission. Why Benham was travelling in the Whitley V Bomber is not known, but his loss seriously damaged the support and training of the Special Operations Executive for a while.

ATMP

FOUR-FIFTY MILES TO FREEDOM

After the failure of the British defence of Kut-el-Amara, six Haileyburians were taken prisoner by the Turkish army. One of them was James Harris (BF 1911.1), a territorial officer in the Hampshire Regiment, who was captured on 29 April 1916. The conditions at Yozgad were terrible and many prisoners were left to starve to death. Harris and seven other officers formed an escape group and they managed, through sheer determination and good luck, to make a success of their plans. The escape from Yozgad was a true adventure, which involved a 37-day trek covering 330 miles by land and 120 miles by sea.

Harris, known as 'Loony', and his companions existed on minimal food throughout their time at large and in one of his diary entries he recorded that he existed on two biscuits, 4oz of sultanas and 1oz of chocolate a day. He was also forced to give up his only spare clothing to buy the silence of a goatherd as they crossed the Taurus Mountains. Surviving attacks from brigands, frequently walking through the day and night with only one hour's rest and hiding from the Turkish army, Harris's feat was perhaps one of the most physically demanding escapes in either of the two world wars. By the 30th day of their escape Harris and his group were forced to take three or four days to rest, plan, pick wheat, grind it and collect supplies before they were able to steal a boat and head for Cyprus. Harris spent the entire journey working the engine's clutch to prevent it from cutting out. On the 37th day after their escape, Harris and the other officers arrived at Cyprus where they were given a bath, shave and warm welcome.

ATMP

QUIET DIPLOMATIC BRAVERY

In the second half of the 1890s two cousins entered Hailey. They worked hard, served as College Prefects and later became two of the key figures in British diplomacy during the Second World War. Sir Ronald Campbell (Ha 1897.1), having been British Minister in Belgrade, was appointed Ambassador to Paris in 1939. The posting became a mammoth task after the German invasion, forcing Campbell to manage both diplomatic and strategic military matters. After the occupation of France, Campbell was moved to neutral Lisbon where, according to his obituary, 'he gave invaluable services to his country … though much of his work has had to remain secret'. What we do know about his achievements is that he persuaded the Portuguese to allow the Azores to be used as a vital base for the Allies in the Battle of the Atlantic.

Campbell's cousin, Sir D'Arcy Osborne (Ha 1898.3), who succeeded to the Dukedom of Leeds after he retired, arrived in Rome in February 1936 to take up the post of Minister to the Holy See. He had worked at the British embassy in Rome during 1909–13 under Sir Renell Rodd (C 1871.2) and developed a real love for the city. Osborne was not the first Haileyburian to be appointed Minister to the Holy See; three years earlier Sir Robert Clive (M 1891.3) had held the post for a year before he was sent to Tokyo. When Italy declared war on Great Britain, the Minister to the Holy See became a front-line diplomat and Osborne was forced to retreat into the Vatican, where he lived for four years in a position that put him at the centre of European politics and even involved him in a plot to assassinate Hitler.

Osborne was disgusted by the treatment of the Jews and urged the Pope to speak out. It was a difficult job for Osborne to support the British war effort and not compromise the neutrality of the Vatican, but against the odds he managed to do just that. Personally, Osborne was involved in rescuing and sheltering escaped prisoners of war and Roman Jews avoiding deportation to the concentration camps, even though

Below: Life in the Ravine, *an illustration by Hal King from* Four-Fifty Miles to Freedom *(1919) by M.A.B. Johnston and K.D. Yearsley, which recounts the story of their escape from a Turkish prisoner of war camp in 1916.*

Right: CCF Naval Section trip to Gibraltar, 1966.

ON THE ROCK

In my last year I was Coxswain in charge of the CCF Naval Section. At the end of my last summer term, we went on a naval trip to Gibraltar. There were about 20 of us, travelling on board a Sea Cat Destroyer, HMS *Agincourt*. Among our number was a certain Leading Seaman Jonathon Band (A 1964.1), later to become First Sea Lord. Just like all the rest of us he was to rough it with the ratings below decks as we slept on our journey from Portsmouth to Gibraltar, either in hammocks, on benches or in other ratings' bunks. It was very tight and there was no officer luxury. On the Saturday, Jonathon Band and I had the afternoon off. I suggested we go to the five-star Rock Hotel and, though we may not have been suitably dressed for a five-star hotel, I had been there with my parents in the past and was able to be brash and lead the way to the lounge where there was a television. There we duly watched the England vs Germany football World Cup Final of 1966!

Colin Barber (K 1961.3)

his actions could have caused the Germans to invade the Vatican. He needed someone to help him in this enterprise and this support came in the person of Monsignor Hugh O'Flaherty, a charming Irish priest. Osborne raised large sums of money through loans from the Vatican Bank, the UK government acting as guarantor, allowing him to support approximately 3,925 prisoners of war and Jews hiding in Rome and the surrounding area during 1944. This monumental humanitarian effort was undertaken while Rome was occupied by the Germans and inspired the 1983 TV film *The Scarlet and the Black*, with Peter Burton playing the role of Sir D'Arcy Osborne. Meanwhile, in Lisbon, Ronald Campbell was organising a rescue mission for rabbis in central Europe, providing them with entrance visas into Portugal. Over 1,000 rabbis and their families were saved by Campbell's scheme in June 1944, an act about which he never spoke again, even to his family.

The altruism that Campbell and Osborne displayed during the Second World War, despite the rigid diplomatic protocols imposed on them, should never be forgotten by Haileyburians.

ATMP

THE GREAT ESCAPER

Harry Melville Arbuthnot Day became a prisoner of war in October 1939 after being shot down on his first mission over Germany and he spent the Second World War dedicated to escaping from his captors. Day, a Wing Commander in the RAF and a recipient of the Albert Medal for gallantry in the First World War, escaped no less than seven times before he was finally able to link up with the US forces at Trento in 1945.

As senior British officer in many of the prison camps in which he was incarcerated, Day briefed all of the new prisoners on the importance of not accepting that the war was over for them. Day pointed out to his fellow captives that one escaped prisoner took tens of Germans out of the war effort, thus helping the allied war effort. Day first escaped from Dulag Luft by digging a tunnel; from Stalag Luft III he escaped twice; and at Oflag XXI B he successfully tunnelled out and evaded capture for a couple of days. Perhaps the most daring and now most famous escape that Day helped to organise was the Great Escape in Stalag Luft III in 1944. Almost 80 officers escaped, including Day, and 50 of the recaptured PoWs were executed on the orders of Himmler. Somehow Day avoided death and he managed to escape via a tunnel from Sachsenhausen. For the remainder of his imprisonment as a PoW, Day spent most of his time at Flossenberg and Dachau concentration camps. At the end of the war he was awarded the Distinguished Service Order for his leadership in the PoW camps and promoted to the rank of Group Captain.

ATMP

HAILEYBURY DURING THE WAR

In 1939, the memory of the last war was still fresh in most people's minds.

It seemed on arrival as if the School, like the country as a whole, had suddenly awoken to the war; for the first week or two working parties of boys were formed into squads after lunch to fill sand bags, which, once filled, were built across the ground floor windows of House dormitories or House rooms to form blast walls. Once this work had been accomplished, the ground-floor House rooms were converted into dormitories so that while Bartle Frere, Colvin and Edmonstone Houses were used normally during the day, at night the boys used to put on pullovers and trousers over their pyjamas, don overcoats, scarves and Wellington boots, and troop across Quad to their ground-floor bedrooms, each of which was provided with a bucket in case anyone needed to urinate during the night. We never discovered whether the related misuse of Wellington boots was deliberate or not.

'Proper' air raid shelters had been built in the orchard between Trevelyan and the Sanatorium, but as I recall, they were used only once and that appeared to be as a drill. It was all the more bewildering therefore to be woken up one night by the most terrifying explosions, which went on for some half an hour, without a summons to the shelters. I lay in my bed, blue with funk, expecting any minute to be my last. The next morning we learned that a mobile anti-aircraft battery had moved into Hailey Lane and been firing on German planes. I suspect, however, it was a demonstration firing for the Home Guard.

The lathes in Shops were required to produce a weekly quota of mushroom-shaped pegs for the Air Ministry, otherwise, we were told, the antiquated wood lathes would have been requisitioned. Those of us doing Extra Shops were therefore put on to

In 1951, Rear-Admiral Sir Michael Denny, Third Lord of the Admiralty, was the inspecting officer for the annual inspection of the CCF. After the ceremonial march-past he inspected cadets in training. The Naval Section had been instructed to rig a pair of shearlegs to enable a breeches buoy across the Swimming Pool. Admiral Denny asked if it would carry a man across the water, and when assured that it would, without taking off his cap, climbed on and was ferried across! With his back to the photographer is Curtis Delmar-Morgan (Staff 1938.2–54.3), Head of Art and winner of the DSC whilst serving with the Atlantic convoys, here Officer Commanding the Naval Section.

John Rice (A 1947.2)

'mushroom' production before we were allowed to turn out our fruit bowls, egg cups and napkin rings. The Science School, too, had to make its contribution to the war effort and one of the ground-floor lecture rooms was used as some sort of analytical laboratory. The presence of this lab was of benefit to both boys and School alike; the lab used to pay 6d. (2.5p) for frogs we collected from the Heath. The money was good, however, and I doubt that the knowledge that the frogs were being used for pregnancy tests would have made any difference.

Apart from providing working parties for the local farmers, the School also grew its own potatoes. The seed potatoes were stored, one year at least, in the Rackets Court; as there was no coach, rackets were

Chapter 7 — SERVICE BEFORE SELF

FIELD DAY
OCT. 31ST 1945
(Drawn from rough sketches and a little imagination)

The attack takes a short cut along a railway line —

— which leads them through a cutting —

— and back to the original track.

The grub and ammo arrives —

— and fighting begins.

[Under orders!]

Nigel Racine.

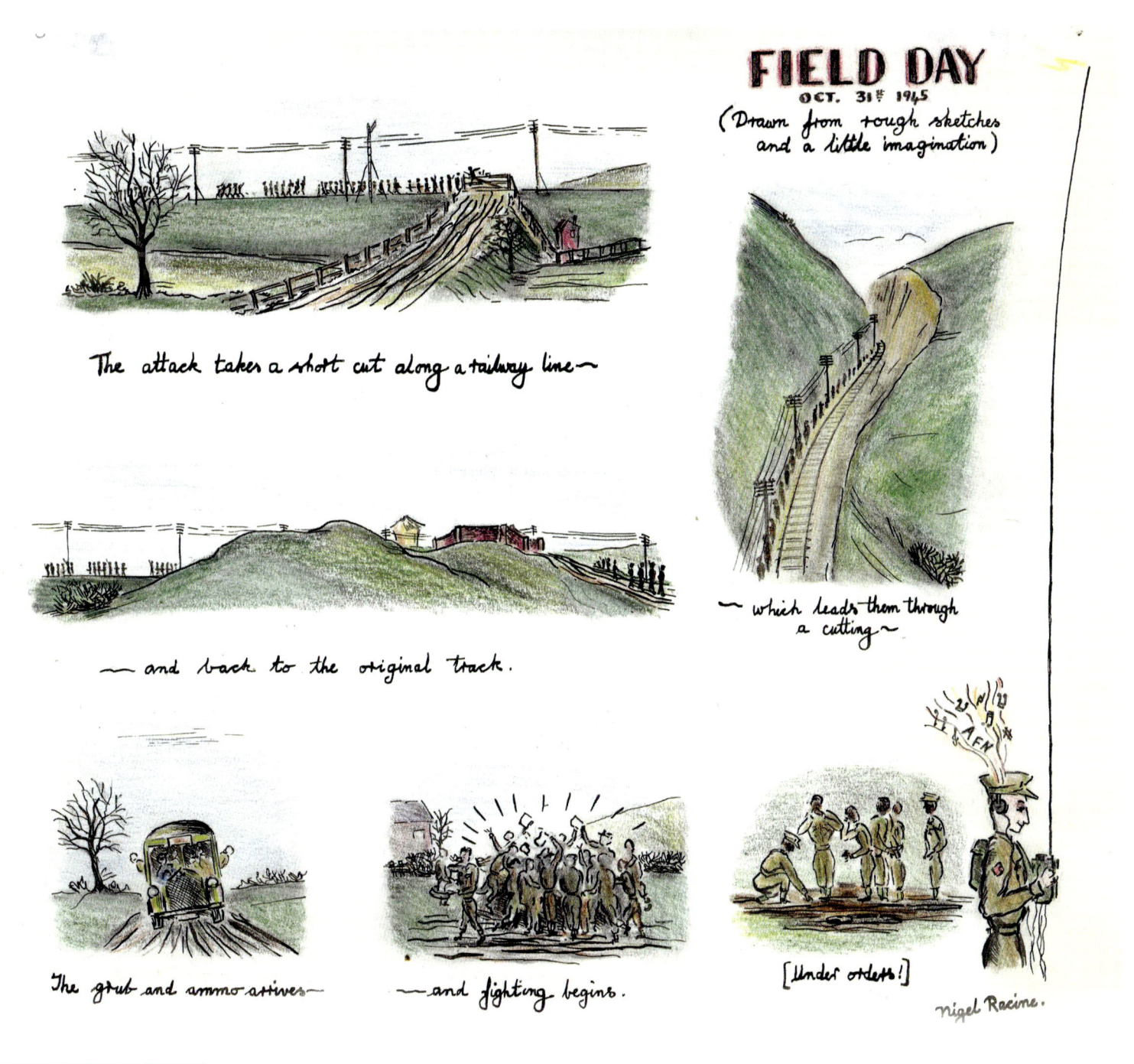

Above: *Field Day 31 October 1945 by Nigel Racine Jaques (Tr 1942.2).*

not played during the war. It also happened that the two galleries were used to store furniture belonging to someone on the staff. Even in the cold, dry conditions of the rackets court, quite a few of the seed potatoes had rotted down to a black, slimy mess. Which clown it was that decided to take an armful of these up to the gallery and pelt the working parties, one from each House, below with them, I do not know. I do remember getting one in the small of the back as I was loading potatoes into a wheelbarrow. It was not long before a wild battle was raging, with as many sound potatoes hurled as rotten ones. Unfortunately, the defenders in the galleries sought refuge behind the furniture and, our aim not being too good, a great deal of damage had been done to the furniture – looking glasses smashed, matchboard backs to wardrobes

139

Cartoon of the School by Michael Stringer, 1941.

Chapter 7 ~ SERVICE BEFORE SELF

HAILEYBURY COLLEGE IN 1941   A CARTOON by MICHAEL STRINGER (Le BAS & COLVIN (1939-1942)

THIS WATERCOLOUR PAINTING WAS EXHIBITED IN THE BRADBY HALL IN 1941 IN AN ART EXHIBITION ORGANISED BY MICHAEL STRINGER WHEN THERE WAS NO ART SCHOOL FACILITY IN THE COLLEGE. THE ART MASTER C. DELMAR MORGAN WAS AWAY ON ACTIVE SERVICE IN THE ROYAL NAVY AT THIS TIME. LE BAS HOUSE HAD BEEN CLOSED AND TRANSFORMED INTO AN EMERGENCY HOSPITAL, AND MOST OF THE HOUSE MOVED INTO COLVIN.

THE FOLLOWING INDEX MAY HELP TO IDENTIFY SOME OF THE PEOPLE IN THE PAINTING :-

1. "The BOOT" CANON E.F. BONHOTE M.A. The MASTER
2. "ERNIE" PARKER D.B.E. PARKER M.A. ENGLISH MASTER
3. Mr ADAMS MATHS MASTER
4. "The BULL" MAJOR FAIR HOUSEMASTER of TREVELYAN
5. Mr TREGENZA HOUSEMASTER of EDMONSTONE
6. Mr SLATER HOUSEMASTER of COLVIN
7. "GROISEY WHISKERS" and "GROISEY HAIRS" The TWO P.T. INSTRUCTORS. "GROISE" WAS THE NICKNAME FOR BUTTER AND MARGARINE IN THE 1940s AT HAILEYBURY.
8. Mr LLOYD HOUSEMASTER of HAILEY
9. Mr SARGYL
10. MICHAEL STRINGER IN J.T.C. UNIFORM
11. F.J. SEABROOK M.A. GEOGRAPHY MASTER AND 1ST XI CRICKET COACH
12. THE EMERGENCY HOSPITAL
13. Mr DEAKES The SCHOOL CARETAKER
14. J.T.C. PARADES

Michael Stringer

splintered – before a College Prefect arrived and brought hostilities to an end. The ringleaders were reported to the Boot and received six of the best.

There was no lock-up in those days, of course, because the air raid shelters were outside Quad. It was inevitable, therefore, that parties of boys would 'break out' after hours and I remember the exhilaration of these illegal 'space walks'. We had to keep a sharp lookout for beaks, no doubt going about their legitimate business but always suspected by us in a pejorative way of 'coming back from the pub'.

We followed the course of the war closely through news bulletins on the wireless and reports in the press. In the early days I used to feel a deep sense of loss at setbacks such as the sinking of HMS *Hood*, the fall of Singapore or Rommel's victories in North Africa. But even in those dark days the thought that we might lose the war was inconceivable.

Of our camping excursions it was the farming camp at Evesbatch in Herefordshire that I remember with most pleasure. I think I only went on two, the summers of 1943 and 1944. These were run by Edgar Matthews and his family. It was my contact with him that prevented my time at Haileybury from being a dreary penance. As my Form-master for School Certificate year he enthused not only me but my classmates. He told us what he expected of us and then by encouragement over the year, he got it.

The School closed early at the end of the summer term 1944. After a doodle-bomb landed in Hertford Heath, the Master, Canon Bonhote, must have concluded that the next flying bomb might cause loss of life and so closed the School after the School and Higher Certificates had been sat. I had one term after that and received my call-up papers for the Royal Navy on my 18th birthday in January 1945.

John Nichols

The summers of 1938 and 1939 were good for me, but by the time we returned to 'Coll' the following summer everything had become, somehow, greyer. Invasion was expected any minute. Those of us who were old enough transformed from OTC cadets to LDV and then to Home Guard, though how we would have defended Windsor Castle, I dread to think.

As a part of our normal House duties, Dougie introduced fire watching. Cambridge ('A') House stood by the 'Coll' main gate like a barrack guardroom. Opposite was Lawrence ('C') House. Both were rather stark brick and stone buildings, three storeys high plus an attic. The attics had skylights with the most splendid views across the Thames Valley. We had buckets of sand, buckets of water, a sort of rake and 'dustpan' in which incendiary bombs were supposedly to be collected, and a stirrup pump to use with the water buckets to put out any fires.

Diagonally across Big Side cricket field from us lay the tuck shop, a mere wooden hut of some considerable age. In those days, despite war-time shortages, it still had a substantial supply of chocolate, sweets, potato crisps, and the School chef still was able to produce freshly baked loaves of bread of which we could purchase half for tuppence. Then, one night, the bombers started to drop incendiaries over Windsor. Most of them fell on open ground and we watched several burn themselves out on Big Side. However, it only needed one stray incendiary to create tragedy. Yes, one fell straight through the roof of the tuck shop and we watched helplessly as our precious chocolate went up in flames.

Michael Balcon (ISC (A) 1938.1)

When I arrived at Hailey in September 1940 the School was coping with many boys being evacuated to North America, and combining Houses because of reduced numbers. It must have been tough for the Master and staff to handle all this, but we New Guv'nors hardly noticed as we were too busy adapting to a new and initially strange way of life.

Fortunately, I was introduced to chemistry and physics – under 'Twitch' Slater (Staff 1923.1–47.3) and 'Bloody R.' Roberts (Staff 1932.3–64.2). They and Mr Pickles (Staff 1913.1–45.2) for the Chemistry VIth ensured that I got a place at Oxford to read Chemistry (and nothing else).

Another delight of Haileybury was no compulsory cricket. Instead, some of us used half holiday afternoons to bike to local airfields – Hunsdon to see secret night fighters with searchlights in their noses, years before they were revealed in the press; Radlett to look at the latest bombers Handley Page were building; and Hatfield for other secret planes. It was easy to find tracks that led to the perimeter fences, to get a good view. At Radlett we were only 150 yards from the entrance to the final assembly hangar, whose doors were usually open. Some fast riding was needed to get back for the infuriating 4pm roll call.

In 1944, after D-Day, V1 flying bomb attacks started. On a summer evening, still light after lights out, I got up to look south out of my dormitory window (each Hailey cubicle had its own), heard a thudding V1 engine cut and then saw the bomb diving silently to explode on some unfortunates nearby. It must have been only half a mile away. I can still see that bomb diving so clearly in my mind's eye. But as an ordinary schoolboy at a rather military school I thought of it merely as part of the war we were then winning and went back to untroubled sleep.

Christopher Saunders (Ha 1940.3)

A major reason for my entering Allenby as a New Guv'nor in January 1941 was that the School had not been evacuated. My father, having served with distinction in the First World War, did not believe in evacuation; he advocated standing firm in face of the enemy. At home we had no protection against air raids; spurning an air raid shelter, which he dismissed as a 'funk hole', he never changed his views, even

Bottom: *Air-raid shelter on the east side of the Dining Hall, 1940.*

Below: *1938, ARP preparations.*

Below right: *A Fire Party in anti-gas clothing, part of the Munich preparations, 1938.*

after our house in Kent was bombed and destroyed in October 1940.

In 1942 two floors of the Military Hospital were de-requisitioned to permit the amalgamation of the School with the Imperial Service College. To us boys the amalgamation, though not generally welcome, passed off smoothly and uneventfully, surely much to the credit of the staff, not least the Master, Canon Bonhote ('the Boot').

At that time there were no day boys and no half-term holidays or exeats, the one and only day's holiday in term time throughout the year being on Ascension Day, when, with petrol rationed and in short supply, nearly everyone took to bicycles and sallied forth into the surrounding countryside. We all had bicycles, and cycling, walking and a limited but controlled diet contributed to our good health. I remember in 1941 the whole School walking down to and back from Hertford to see Charlie Chaplin in the film *The Great Dictator*.

John Brock

Like the tales of Harry Potter, the term began with a mass of boys catching a train from King's Cross station to Broxbourne and on to Haileybury College. There would be the renewal of old friendships and the challenge of a term ahead. For me these were happy days, with few unpleasant memories. Even being caned with other boys for using a farmer's haystack as an exciting slide, doing the stack no good, of course, left me at the time a little proud of the red-blue stripes on my behind rather than anything else.

Soon after arrival the New Guv'nors had two weeks to learn about Haileybury, its traditions and customs, its Masters and Houses. This was all taught by the older boys in the Junior Common Room, who were new boys only a term or two before. Threat of dire consequences if one failed the test hung over one's head in those first two weeks.

Arriving at Haileybury in 1944, World War Two was of course the background to many things. The Corps had some meaning and launched many a boy into life as an officer in the armed forces. Self-propelled flying bombs were being launched at night against London. Some over flew into Hertfordshire and over Haileybury. One could hear the drone of the engine as it approached, but at the point when the engine stopped, we would all dive under our beds as the silence meant that the missile would fall and explode on impact. Some did land in the grounds around Haileybury, although none caused serious harm or damage.

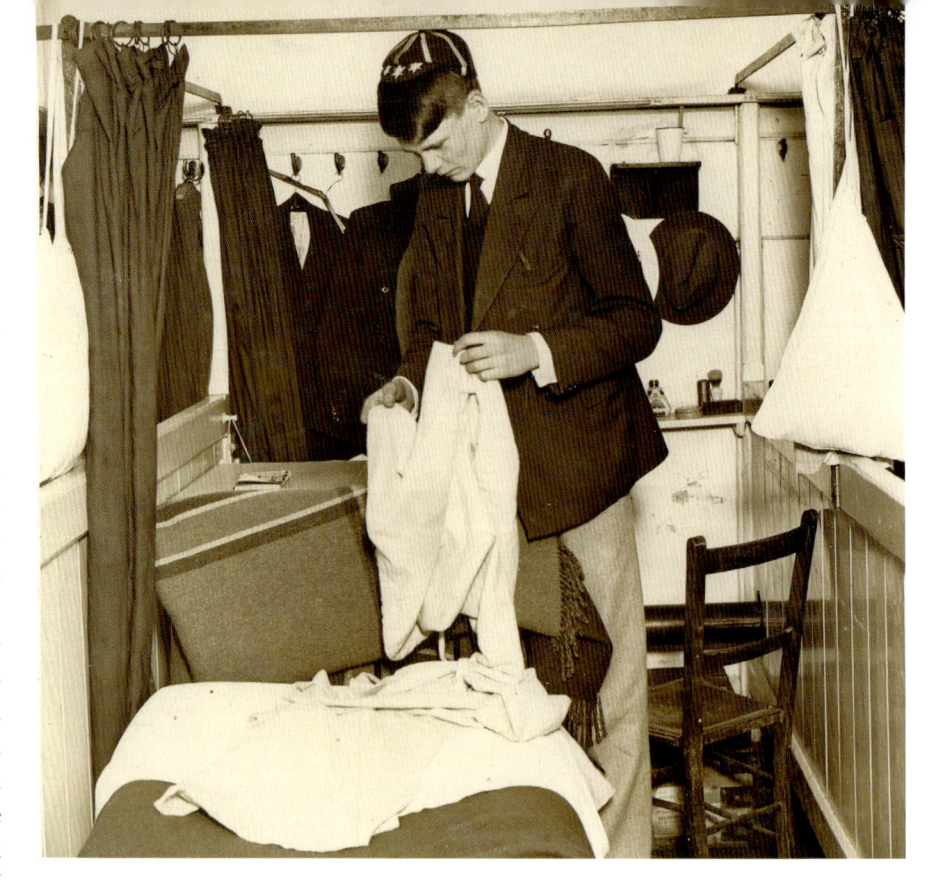

I remember well the day in May 1945 that the war in Europe ended. News spread through the School like wild fire. All the boys on the Common Rooms around the Quad began cheering. Dustbins were beaten with anything that would make a noise.

Sports and the classroom were equal partners in the life at Haileybury. The value of friendships, the responsibilities and discipline when House and School Prefect were learned without knowing. I have no doubt that all these played a significant part in my entrance into medical school and my life as a physician, which took me to Canada and the expanded opportunities that I and my family have had here.

Robin Andrews (Tr 1944.3)

The New Guv'nor with a private life bounded by a dormitory 'compart', the traditional compulsory song, meeting new people in new surroundings and lessons in a form probably too high: it all seemed tough in the first term, relieved by the opportunity to face the great Alan Fairbairn, Captain of the 1st XI, in a House match. There were lessons before breakfast, Chapel each morning, meals at House tables in Hall, war-time cold meals once a week, Latin grace by College Prefects, evening prayers in House, the blackout, Quad closed at night, Hailey and Allenby the only 'out' Houses.

Above: Alexander Abraham (E 1929.2) in his Compart, 1932.

Opposite: The South African War Memorial, which stands at the main gate on London Road, was designed by Reginald Blomfield and is a memorial to the Haileyburians who died in the Boer War, 1899–1902. Each plaque commemorates a specific engagement.

SVRSVM

HAILEYBURY — *A 150th Anniversary Portrait*

Chapter 7 — SERVICE BEFORE SELF

Right: *The '40 Year Board' in the Social Club (celebrating its 75th birthday in 2012) is a testament to the service and commitment of the employees of the School. In many cases, working at the School has been a family affair for as long as the School has existed; Sylvie Race (1945–2002) was the daughter of Rose Hornett (1912–62) and her daughter Lynda and nieces, Nina and Carol, work at the School. Another daughter, Anne, and granddaughter, Kim, have also worked at Haileybury, giving in total 180 years of service to the School. Another family who have given long service after arriving from Spain in the 1960s are Eugenia Castro Lago and Constantino Suarez Tobares; between them they have chalked up over 80 years service at Haileybury. Constantino was the last Head Waiter in Dining Hall, Master's Butler and he now works in the Grounds' and Gardens' Department, while Eugenia, is a much loved, matriarchal figure in Trevelyan.*

Our Housemaster, the Reverend W.R. 'Labby' Lloyd (Staff 1911.1–47.2), lived with his family in a house adjoining our accommodation. He was a kind but strict disciplinarian and always a great supporter of the House and its traditions. Hailey traditions included 'House cheering' for School colours, a long walk to the top floor and a song; House Prefects invigilating prep; rounders on Hailey Field on Saturday evening with most participating; last day of term House prayers with *Jerusalem* and the *Vivat*, an emotional time for leavers.

As the 1940s progressed, enemy air raids on London and the areas around meant many nights in the Hailey cellars. The School was only boarders, with many of the parents involved in military and war-time service.

With travel restricted, bicycles were permitted and I recall an eventful journey from Broxbourne station at the start of term with my brother on the handlebars and two cases strapped behind. Its greatest use was on the Ascension Day holiday for a long trip out. The large open-air Swimming Pool was popular, but on one memorable occasion it was closed by the Master following excessive coughing during a long sermon by a visiting preacher 'until the School's cold is better'. Other memories include Deards, the Porter at Lodge in charge of the School Bell, Colin Cobb in charge of the rugger, Major 'Bull' Fair (Staff 1912.3–46.1), HM of Trevelyan, Hank Nurden (Staff 1927.1–65.2), HM of Thomason and R.L. Ashcroft, HM of Allenby. The move to Cheltenham in 1944 of the traditional cricket match against Cheltenham at Lord's, due to the flying bombs, was happily reversed in 1945 as the war in Europe ended.

Memories kept alive by on-going friendship with many Haileyburians who were contemporaries, including Ole Kverndal, (B 1940.3) Bill Tyrwhitt Drake, Neville Smallman (Ha 1941.2), Steve Theobald (E 1937.3) and not least Bill Purkiss (Ha 1936.3), Captain of the House team in my first term in Hailey, who went on to suffer major injuries in the Army during the war. We met again on the beach on holiday in 1953 and thereafter for many years for a cricket match at his Sussex village where he was still playing with artificial legs.

Tony Nunn

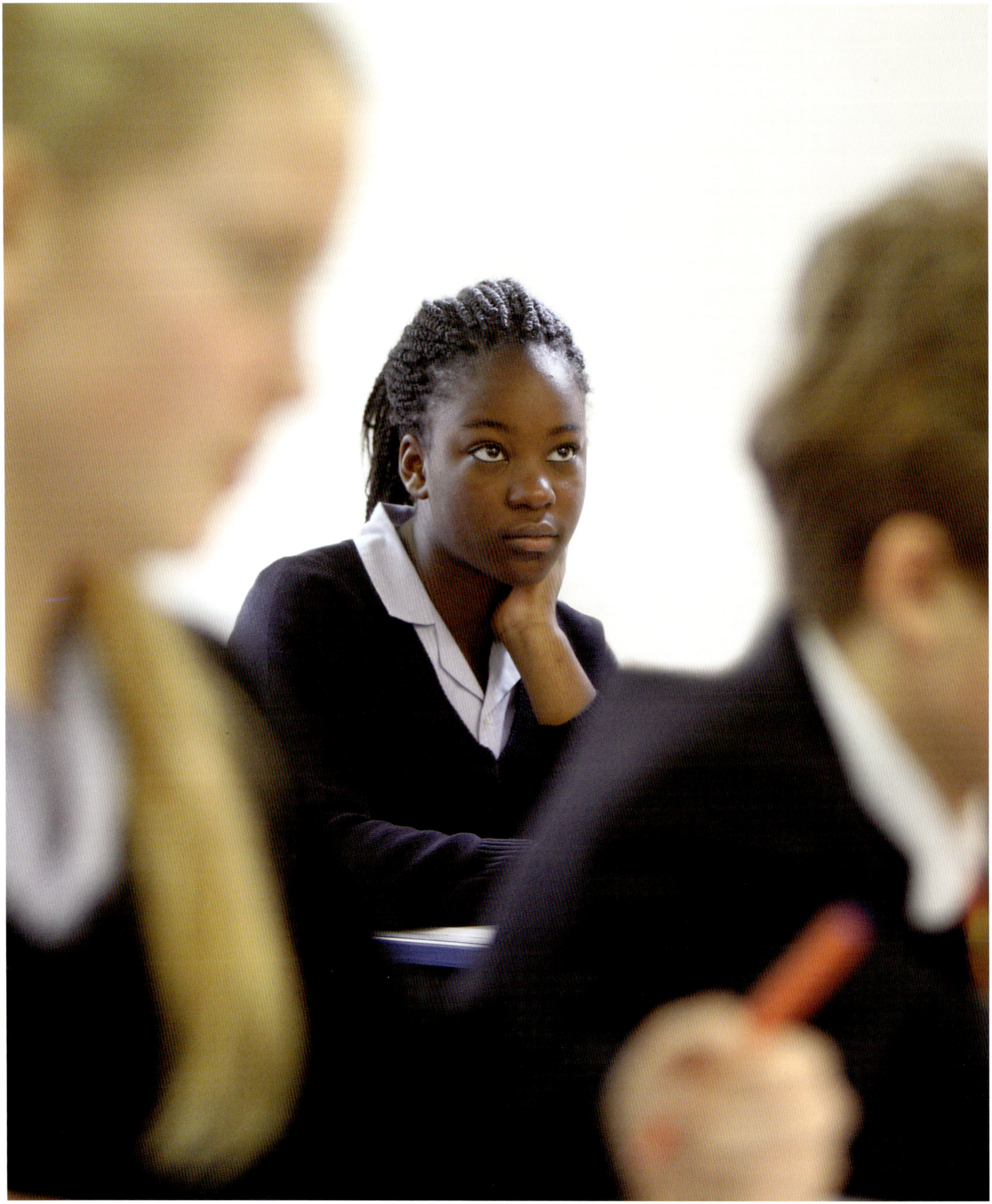

Chapter 8

PROGRESSIVE LEARNING

COMBINED SCIENCE: A NATIONAL EXAMINATION ORIGINATED AT HAILEYBURY

My first 24 hours at Haileybury will be forever etched on my mind as I came to terms with a totally new environment. I met with W.G. Thompson (Staff 1931.3–71.2) who had, with great distinction, led science at Haileybury for longer than anyone could remember. 'Good morning. How are you?' I enquired politely. 'Bloody, thank you!' came the unexpected reply. The next morning I arrived a little late for breakfast in Common Room. I opened the door and witnessed what seemed to be most of the teachers sitting behind their copies of *The Times* around the magnificent table. I was not sure what to do and so, pulling myself to my full height, I said, 'Good morning, gentlemen.' F.R. Thompson (Staff 1928.2–66.2), the formidable President of Common Room, was at the end of the table. He lowered his newspaper, stared at me over his glasses and in an unmistakable schoolmasterly voice said, 'Will you shut up!' Lunch on the Thomason tables was another experience. I sat next to the Head of House and enquired if he found it difficult settling back into school after the long summer holiday. 'Well, sir,' he drawled, 'I do miss the port and cigars in the evening.'

I had only been at Haileybury for a year when W.G. Thompson had a particularly difficult summer holiday and decided he no longer wished to be responsible for Haileybury science. Bill Stewart, the Master, took a risk and offered me, the youngest member of the faculty, the posts of Senior Science Master and Head of the Physics Department. I soon decided that I wanted to do something to try to raise the profile of science in the School. The timetable allowed eight periods of science per week for all pupils up to O-level, with the result that all boys studied physics and chemistry as separate O-level subjects or physics with chemistry as a single O-level subject. Biology was housed in unsatisfactory accommodation as part of Bradby and a relatively small number of boys opted for this subject among the O-level possibilities.

I believed that in order to claim that they had received a good, rounded general education, all pupils should study physics and chemistry and biology to O-level. However, it was obvious that there was no chance of getting 12 periods of compulsory science in the timetable to make this possible. In the days before mobile telephones, a warm bath was an excellent place to have intelligent thoughts as one was unlikely to be interrupted and, for me, this did produce a 'eureka' moment. The only possible solution was to persuade

Below: *Plaque on the Science School.*

the Master that science needed an increase from eight to nine periods per week for everyone. There would be three periods of physics taught by physicists, three periods of chemistry taught by chemists and three periods of biology taught by biologists. The Haileybury scientists would design a new course which would lead to two O-level passes in science. To cut a very long story short, the Master enthusiastically supported this innovation, so chemists Ted Yarnold (Staff 1942.2–71.3) and Harold Hargreaves and biologists Doug Lees (Staff 1952.1–77.2) and Julian Ford-Robertson (Staff 1968.1–93.1) and I set about designing the content of the new syllabus, the Oxford and Cambridge Schools' Examination Board agreed to examine this new double subject, and the Standing Conference of University Entrance Requirements decided that the double O-level would be acceptable to universities which required a science qualification for matriculation. We told other leading schools about the new course and soon Combined Science was established in a range of independent and maintained schools.

The impact on Haileybury science was significant. Suddenly, the prep school scholarship entry had to take compulsory science up to O-level and many of them discovered that they enjoyed the subjects and were rather good at them, with the result that the overall quality of A-level science candidates improved. Haileybury needed new biology laboratories and these were constructed. However, overall, we had been able to ensure that physics and chemistry and biology played their rightful part in the general education of all Haileyburians. We had been able to delay the decisions about 'arts' or 'science' for all Haileyburians until the end of the Fifth form year so that choices about A-level specialisations could be based on knowledge and experience gained from studying the broadest possible range of subjects for as long as possible. This must be of greatest benefit for the general education of all Haileyburians.

It is more than a third of a century since pupils sat the first Combined Science examinations at Haileybury. During this period there have been massive changes in the examination system, but nowadays the most commonly taken GCSE science examination in the UK is a Double Award examination. Haileybury had shown the way!

On a personal note, in 1972 I left Haileybury to become Headmaster of Christ College, Brecon. The scrum half in the Christ College 1st XV was Joe Davies – the current Master of Haileybury. The educational world is very small indeed.

John Cook (Staff 1965.3–72.3)

Practical Fermentation

I taught in a classroom adjacent to the natural history museum full of stuffed birds and other animals and in a glass-walled and roofed laboratory, hellish hot in the summer and freezing in the winter. The desks were on tiered steps and I delivered my lessons below them in university lecture hall style. I won an industry scholarship in 1967 on attachment to Arthur Guinness for a month to learn about the business in order to give careers guidance at Haileybury. I spent the following term brewing Guinness in biology practicals with the boys to learn the practical applications of biology without blowing up or poisoning ourselves. Some brews tasted quite good while others were horrible. Much was learned and biology practical lessons became much more popular.

C.D.A. Cochran

Chapter 8 — PROGRESSIVE LEARNING

Right: *International Baccalaureate Upper Sixth pupils, 2012, who achieved an average of 39 points from a maximum of 45.*

Below right: *Alex Scarborough (K 2002.3) in the Chemistry Dept.*

INTRODUCTION OF THE INTERNATIONAL BACCALAUREATE

I remember it well. Dino's Restaurant in Ware, February 1999. The formidable Barbara Glasmacher, the doyenne of agents sending German pupils to British boarding schools, told us straight: 'You start the IB Diploma: you will have 24 students in September.' To the Master, faced with a steeply declining boarding population, the decision was, as we say now, a 'no-brainer'. And so we embarked on launching an exotic-sounding new examination system just as we also prepared to introduce the revolutionary A-level Curriculum 2000. Were we mad?

There were formidable obstacles. We were trying to do in six months what the IB recommends should take two years. We had to persuade the IB to bend/break their rules. Syllabuses to read and master, schemes of work to write – all at break-neck speed. Within what seemed to be a twinkling of an eye 12 of us were in Vienna being trained in our subjects under the keen eye of our first IB coordinator Rachel Keys (Staff 1998.3–2001.2), who had joined us fresh from the International School of Hamburg. Of the course I remember little, but the memory of a B.B. King concert and singing on

151

PIONEERS OF THE MONSTROUS REGIMENT: GIRLS AT HAILEYBURY

My memory of those dramatic early days following the decision to admit girls at Haileybury is fading rapidly. In fact, the decision was taken before my wife and I arrived at the Master's Lodge in January 1976 ('a cold coming we had of it, just the worst time of the year'); indeed, Council must have been debating the matter back in 1972, or even earlier. The brief entry in Bill Newcombe's impeccable notes on the History of Haileybury and Imperial Service College records: '1973. Twelve senior girls entered the school as pupils; accommodation provided in Red House.' There is no record of the fact that those 12 senior girls had overlapped into Lodge Cottage by the end of 1975, so we enjoyed a handful of them as close neighbours.

Three essential facts must be borne in mind concerning the admission of girls at the School. The first is that a gradual move towards co-education was not necessarily the result of emancipated educational idealism: many boys' schools were facing a numerical challenge as fees grew and the traditional independent school family found it more and more difficult to manage the financial burden. The philosophy tended to follow the practice. This was, of course, greeted with understandable alarm and resentment by the girls' schools, menaced with losing bright pupils at Sixth Form level; and the matter was often handled tactlessly (though it did have the consequent effect of ensuring that many girls' schools put their houses into much better order). The second fact was that Haileybury had been a resolutely male school: Common Room was a stronghold for men only; there were comparatively few women teachers; the Haileybury dormitory hardly suggested the possibility of a girl constituency; rugby epitomised the School's spirit and energy; both literally and metaphorically the School was curtainless. And the third fact was that Red House and Lodge Cottage, admirably overseen as they were by Martin Marriott (Staff 1966.3–76.2) and his wife Judith, were really inadequate for the proper provision of girls' education (though no doubt much fun for the inhabitants, who must have been specially selected as robust personalities in addition to their other attributes).

So, I suppose that the fundamental question was asked early in 1976: do we go ahead with this scheme, or do we turn back the clock? Well, mercifully for Haileybury's future, the answer is plain for all to see. Council elected two significantly wise and experienced members: Betty Clarke, legendary former headmistress of Benenden, and John Buchanan, a true 'wise man', who, with remarkable vision, had led the transformation of Oakham School to complete co-education. We were in good hands, but, of course, development depended on finding suitable accommodation as well as overseeing proper integration in and out of the classroom. The

Left: *Portrait of William 'Bill' Stewart, Master 1963.3–75.1, who oversaw the admission of the first group of girls in 1973, by Juliet Pannett, PS.*

Below: *Alban's House, 1980.*

Chapter 8 — PROGRESSIVE LEARNING

Register records: '*1977. New Sanatorium completed. Alban's (previously the Sanatorium) converted and opened as girls' House.*' So the splendid red brick Sanatorium built in 1867 on a field purchased in 1866 took on a new and colourful life, presided over, brilliantly, by Martin Stephen (Staff 1972.3–83.2) with his wife Jenny (thus launching both their highly distinguished later careers as heads of notable schools). The atmosphere and spirit of this new House – resented no doubt by those in the community who wished for there to be no change in Haileybury's ways – enabled the girls (still at 'senior level') to make a huge contribution to the School's well-being as a forward-looking and dynamic institution.

This was underlined by the next entry in the Register to which I can refer: '*1980. Old "San Flat"* (a perfectly hideous building…) *converted into bedsitters for girl Oxbridge candidates.*' A separate facility for Oxbridge candidates was indeed pretty forward-looking for those far-off days. Such was the success of the operation that the next decisive move became, perhaps sadly, inevitable. Given the demand for girls' places, there was only one possibility which could create geographical coherence for a kind of girls' enclave within the School and that was the transformation of Allenby. So we have the rather bleak entry: '*1983. Allenby House for boys (A) closed down. New House for girls opened temporarily at Highwood (Hw).*' To be followed by: '*1984. Allenby building converted and re-opened as a girls' House (Aby), incorporating the girls from Highwood.*' I must add that this process of transfer, which was painful, was

153

greatly helped by the understanding of Jack Thomas (Housemaster of Allenby for 18 years) and Imogen, and the shrewd inheritance of Philip Stephens (Staff 1978.3–98.2), Housemaster of Allenby, as the second girls' House for 11 years.

Of course, this is not the place for me to rehearse some of the more exciting events of many years ago. Haileybury's first girls have indeed reached a 'senior level' now. I venture to suggest that Haileybury in its present fully co-educational state owes much to those pioneering young ladies who brought such life and talent and fun to the School and changed it irrevocably – and (dare I say it?) much for the better.

David Summerscale

In September 1974 the 2nd battalion of 12 girls joined the original 12 pioneers, moving into Lodge Cottage immediately next door to the Master's Lodge, while the Upper Sixth Form girls moved across Quad to the upper floors of Red House to disturb Dan Hearn's peace and quiet. The Master, William Stewart, kept a personal eye on us new girls to help us settle in, and it was a great shock when he died suddenly during our first year.

On arriving at Haileybury, I relished the musical and dramatic opportunities while missing the established sports of my grammar school and my highly committed dance hobby. Jack Hindmarsh still holds a special place in my memories as one of the Masters who most welcomed and encouraged us – he was delighted to have female sopranos and altos for the Choir.

In some ways we original girls might have been perceived by our male colleagues to 'have it easy', sleeping in bedsitting rooms for two, not dorms, no uniform – I used to clomp around the wooden classroom floors in platform boots then in vogue the first time around. But there were many pressures in those early days. As a former day pupil, I found the myriad little rules which help a boarding school operate smoothly difficult to remember or contrary to common sense, like being unable to use an umbrella when it rained – only College Prefects were permitted to have them, so they became very popular. The most difficult experience for me in the early days was walking into Dining Hall, so few girls amongst 570 or so male pupils and mostly male masters. My colleague Hilary and I sat crammed in on a long Batten table. Coming from a fully co-educational grammar school, I little realised my every move would be watched and commented upon by so many, or that a lack of understanding of girl pupils by some Masters and pupils would create tensions.

We were attached to a boys' House in twos and for House meetings we had to join the whole House in the dormitory, which occasioned a degree of awkwardness both on our part and on that of the male members of the House. In our second year some of us were appointed Dormitory Prefects, somewhat anomalously as the dorms were out of bounds save for House meetings. Often I was the only girl in lessons and in some instances this situation was isolating and uncomfortable. In most subjects, though, we were encouraged and academically challenged to achieve our best. Our combined, most significant achievement is to have assisted in paving the way for full co-education.

Jennifer Parsons (née Van Horne)

As we girls were accommodated in three Houses all over the College grounds and had no specific Housemaster/parent/matron, your boys' House was pretty fundamental to day-to-day existence through contact with the Housemaster, mealtimes, and seating in Chapel or Lists. It was more than just an association. I have heard several stories from 'early girls' about some Masters' apparent

Above: Colvin Upper Sixth prior to the Leavers' Ball, with their housemistress, Lucy Dexter (Staff 2005.3), 2010.

Chapter 8 — PROGRESSIVE LEARNING

lack of understanding and eccentric behaviour towards girls, but I never experienced this personally and mostly felt supported by staff and by Haileyburians in my House and classes. I think I was personally greatly helped by the fact that my father, the Resident Medical Officer, was held in high esteem by the Haileybury community.

In my Upper Sixth year, we girls moved en masse to the old Sanatorium when Alban's was founded. The 'new San' was built next to my family home, Highfield Cottage, with a door through from our hallway. Alban's was a palace compared with the previous accommodation: the study Abbie Webber (M and Alb 1976.3) and I shared in Lodge Cottage was subsequently used as a storage cupboard by the Haileybury Society. Bringing the girls under one roof was a unifying move for friendships, harmony, greater disciplinary control and coordination of the girls.

Four years after leaving Haileybury as a pupil, in 1982 I was half of the first OH wedding to be held in Chapel at Haileybury, having met Doug Everard (BF 1973.2) in the Sixth Form. (Pupil relationships were plentiful at Haileybury in the 1970s, but that's another story.) Our wedding was a true Haileybury event, with an OH best man and ushers, Jack Hindmarsh playing the organ, Jack Thomas the official photographer and Bob Phillips doing the catering. My mother sourced flowers in the exact Haileybury magenta. The cake's top tier was a replica Chapel made from icing. Both our sons were subsequently baptised in Chapel, the younger one just prior to my father's retirement in 1986, with OHs amongst the godparents.

E. Jane Everard (née Etherington) (L and Alb 1976.3)

When my father suggested that we take a slight detour to visit his old school back in the early 1970s, it had an outcome that none of us expected. He was surprised to see girls watching a 1st XV rugby match on the touchline and in characteristic fashion decided to see what they were doing there. It turned out that they were the first girls to arrive at Haileybury and he was so impressed with them that on the way home I was asked if I would be interested in going there for the Sixth Form. Silly question really! I had been living at home and attending an all-girls' convent in Windsor.

The girls lived in Red House, Lodge Cottage and Trevelyan Cottage, and were each attached to a boy's House. I was the only girl in my year in Bartle Frere and was very grateful that their tables were so close to the doors on that first evening when we had to run the gauntlet of all those boys to our tables. I must have had my head in the clouds because I didn't notice all the boys hanging out of open windows in the study blocks summing us all up as we walked by during the first few days. We did not have a uniform, but had a dress code of dark-coloured skirts or trousers and a white or cream shirt and dark jumper in the winter, and floral skirts and plain shirts in the summer, and a dress for church on Sundays. I was only there for two years, but the experience will be with me for a lifetime.

Fiona Illingworth (née Short) (BF and Alb 1976.3)

There were plenty of moments when we were made to feel rather special. In particular I remember the tradition of tea with the Removes – it was very touching as invariably they had gone to great trouble buying cakes and biscuits and for them it was quite an event having 16- and 17-year-old girls visit them. It was a great way to forge a relationship with those younger boys who otherwise would just have faded into the crowd. From time to time we would also be recipients of tokens of affection from those younger boys. I remember I was given by a 13-year-old a piece of wood carved in the shape of a heart engraved with declarations of love. It was very touching.

Sarah Weldon (née Le Huray) (B 1983.3)

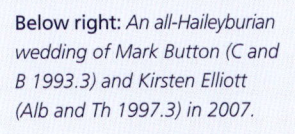

Below right: An all-Haileyburian wedding of Mark Button (C and B 1993.3) and Kirsten Elliott (Alb and Th 1997.3) in 2007.

Below: Ryan Welch (Tr 1999.3) and Laura Swaby (LS and Alb 1998.3) in the Chapel, 2010.

stage with ageing Tamla Motown star Fontella Bass has lingered. And also we were intoxicated by the IB buzz – learning our new trade alongside colleagues from countries ranging from Botswana to Russia via Sweden and Oman. We found out for ourselves what so many others had told us – that IB training is a unique experience, high in quality and truly immersive in an international culture.

And so the grand experiment began. The German pupils, some of them pretty wild, duly arrived. And then that extraordinary second cohort, again almost all German, many of them highly gifted and massively ambitious, helped us quickly to get the programme going. Year three saw the breakthrough when redoubtable Head of School, Beth Bowen (Alb 1998.3) led the charge of indigenous pupils, so that, of nearly 40, well over half were home grown.

The programme is now well established. Why did it work at Haileybury, while other schools have found it more of a struggle? One reason: people. Our staff had the intelligence and broad-mindedness to embrace a new educational concept and deliver an inspiring classroom experience. And our students, especially in those early heady days, were simply outstanding, enabling us to march rapidly towards a mid-30-point average, which was vital to long-term success. And our parents were patient. There were many teething problems, handled superbly in those first two years by Rachel Keys. And in our third coordinator, James Kazi (Staff 2000.3–08.2), we had an educationalist who has now established himself as a national figure in the IB movement.

The road has not always been easy and native pupils remain questioning of the value of the IB, when it involves so much more work than A-levels. To them I would say: look at the independent research, which clearly shows that the IB prepares you brilliantly for university, and take note of the regular pleas from employers who despair that so few British graduates have an international outlook in our interconnected world.

Tim Woffenden (Staff 1990.3–2004.3)

THE RED BOOK

One of Haileybury's oldest institutions, the *Red Book*, ended in 2009 after 136 years of publication, now existing only as an internal document of very restricted circulation. Known as the *Universal Biography* in the 19th century it was an alphabetical listing of all of the pupils, first published on 7 April 1874. School numbers, House lists, dates of birth, parental addresses and an arcane system for numbering Smijths, Smiths and Smyths were all included between the covers of the publication. There were three editions a year and it acted as a way for the average Haileyburian to learn something about his contemporaries, especially if they were in a different House. The other information the book contained was a list of beaks arranged in 'Red Book order', a form of precedence based solely on the date of the teacher's appointment. While the *Red Book* is now essentially extinct, 'Red Book order' still exists within the confines of the Common Room. Named after its red covers, it partnered the *Blue Book*, which was the repository of academic information needed for the following term and gave information about dealing with your luggage.

The *White Book*, a grey paper-covered list of pupils, replaced in 1866 the examination lists, which were sent home to parents, and in 1867 its cover was changed to blue and form lists placed every pupil in strict order of academic success.

ATMP

Opposite: *The piece of wood from Erskine Childers' yacht,* The Vixen, *a 30ft former lifeboat that was sailed by Childers and William Le Fanu (Tr 1875.3) in 1897. This voyage helped to inspire Childers' thriller* Riddle of the Sands *with the boat described as* The Dulcibella.

Below: *The Library, 2012, and opposite, 1932.*

Chapter 8 ~ PROGRESSIVE LEARNING

THE LIBRARY

The original library of the East India College occupied plum position in the centre of Wilkins' great Terrace. It was flanked by the Committee Room and Chapel, and bore a suitably grand frontage for a library that was described by Wilfrid Blunt in his book *The Haileybury Buildings* as being 'famous throughout England'. The closure of the College in 1858 saw the contents removed to Leadenhall Street, apart from a few, now cherished, volumes that escaped the general dispersal of College contents.

The new Haileybury College grew fast and it was overcrowding that forced a major rethink. Chapel and Library, broadly speaking, changed places. The old Library facade was moved to front the new Big School where it remained until 1912, when it was replaced by the present enlarged Big School, with its greatly embellished Ionic frontage. A new chapel was built and the old chapel, with the addition of rows of bookcases, was converted into the new Library, where it has remained since it opened in 1880.

The New Guv'nor of 1880, looking around today, would see much that would be familiar: the handsome Victorian bookcases, the magnificent vaulted ceiling with its mouldings, elegant Georgian windows and double entrance doors. Much would be unfamiliar: the V.C. honours boards erected at the far end, the spiral staircase leading to the gallery, the electronic innovations in the form of computers and their peripherals. Doubtless he would be struck by the huge increase in the number of books and by the luxury of wall-to-wall carpets.

The sharp-eyed observer will find much of interest. A large oil painting by former Head of Art J.D. Higgins, a copy of *The Last Sleep of the Brave* by Alphonse de Neuville, shows the bodies of Melvill and Coghill after the Battle of Isandlwana.

Wilfrid Blunt painted *A View from my Room, Haileybury* in 1927 and it was given to the Library, where it has hung ever since. The outlook from his flat at the top of Big School, looking over a frosty Quad towards the Porter's Lodge, has changed little since then. A bust of William Wilkins, bearing a remarkable resemblance to Michael Caine, was bought at auction by Alistair Macpherson (Tr 1934.2), Haileybury's first Honorary Archivist, and placed in the Library. The curious lump of wood mounted on a small plinth and bearing a brass plaque is a piece of the *Dulcibella*, the boat belonging to Erskine Childers (Tr 1883.3), which features in his famous novel *The Riddle of the Sands*. When Childers met his end by firing squad, the boat fell into disrepair and a small piece was sent to his alma mater by fellow Haileyburian G.M. Knocker (C 1913.1). Underneath in neat copperplate is the legend *'She fell to pieces in the slipway yard at Lymington, Hants, September 1948'*.

Transferred to the Library in the 1980s from the Chemistry Department, where rather curiously it had found a home, is the original brass nameplate from the 'V' Class *(the School's Class)* locomotive, No. 30924, bearing the 'Haileybury' name. The locomotive was broken up in 1962 and the engine plate donated to the School.

The most recent addition is a framed facsimile of the 'Changi menu' celebrating the OH reunion in Changi POW camp on 18 August 1945. Four English

157

and two Australian Haileyburians shared the feast of a tin of beans and a tin of dripping that had been hoarded for three years. Close by are two prints by Bruce Bairnsfather (USC 1898.2), the celebrated First World War cartoonist and creator of 'Old Bill'.

In many ways, the libraries of our great public schools are unique. In addition to their educational role as supporters of the curriculum, they are a repository of many unsung and often unseen treasures. A public school librarian's role is more than just that of organiser and provider of information, it is also one of conservator and curator, and one who preserves the contributions from the past and values their links with the present. What do we know of these librarians of the past? There is surprisingly little on record.

Albert Charles Clark was the first Haileybury Librarian from 1863 to 1887. He was followed by Wardlaw Kennedy (Staff 1883.2–1919.2), who served as Librarian for 30 years until 1918. A remarkable character, described by Carrington as *a man of extraordinary accomplishments and unexpected hobbies, naturalist and man-of-letters, he seemed to know every book in the world*. His book, *Thumbnail Studies in Pets*, is wonderful for the sheer dottiness of the photographs of him in Quad, clad in blazer and boater, supervising his pet armadillo harnessed to a small cart with a pet rat as a passenger. A mongoose is curled up in front of the fire in his rooms, and various exotics from meerkats to alligators lived out their lives in his loving care and took their exercise on the hallowed turf of Quad.

Not much is known of the Reverend Charles Henry Brown (Staff 1907.2–37.2), who was employed in 1907 and whose dates suggest that he would have succeeded Kennedy. Described as a 'middle-aged clergyman', he handed over to the distinguished Charles Carrington, who was Librarian from 1922 to 1924. Under him the Library, by now numbering approximately 15,000 volumes, thrived, and his diligence helped to ensure that the growing collection was comprehensively catalogued. Carrington's brother-in-law, Edgar Matthews, was the next incumbent, from 1924, and seems, from sketchy records, to have handed over to Bernard Theodore Hebert, who was on the staff from 1919 to 1939. We know that the next two Librarians were Lionel Gough (Staff 1930.3–6.2), described by Wilfrid Blunt in a letter to the *Haileyburian* of March 1975 as having made a very valuable contribution, and John Hampden Jackson (Staff 1929.3–38.2), the author of many history books, six of which are still in the Haileybury collection.

Charles Wilfrid Adams (Staff 1910.2–43.1) left Haileybury in 1943 after 33 years, most of which he seems to have spent in the Library. Ashcroft described him as 'one of the last of the true eccentrics ... devoted to indexing and cross-indexing the books'. The next 33 years saw Francis William Manning (Staff 1939.3–75.2) at the helm as the College's longest-serving Librarian. Fittingly it was FWM who was photographed with a young Queen Elizabeth in the Library on the occasion of her visit to mark the College's centenary in 1962.

He was followed in 1975 by David Wright, who, on being handed a bank book showing a balance of £36, was warned that most requests to purchase new books were to be discouraged. In 1989 Elspeth Harvey was appointed as the first full-time Librarian, with the brief of updating the Library to meet all the needs of the rapidly changing pupil body. The age of

Wardlaw Kennedy, Librarian, with his armadillo 'Pig' (above) *and 'Rikki', his mongoose* (inset), *1890s.*

Chapter 8 — PROGRESSIVE LEARNING

the computer had dawned and many of the older valuable books had to be sold. Any books written by anyone associated with Haileybury, or indeed the EIC, ISC or USC, were kept, as was anything about these schools, or old Indian or local history.

This century sees the Library facing a new challenge. The age of the electronic book is gathering pace, although it is too early to tell what the effect will be on traditional libraries. By adapting and ensuring that it is able to meet the needs of future generations of Haileyburians, it is to be hoped that the Library will remain at the heart of the School for many years to come.

Many books in the Haileybury collection are faded and worn, pages foxed, covers unappealing, but there is a good reason why they are not replaced with newer editions or cleaner copies. Open them and they reveal the handwritten dedications, the notes and messages from one generation to another, and it is this that makes a book so much more than the sum of its parts.

Songs of a Strolling Player by Robert George Legge (L 1878.3) is a flimsy and battered collection of verse published in 1893. I suspect it had a limited print run and this copy may well be one of a very few still in existence. Inside is this handwritten poem:

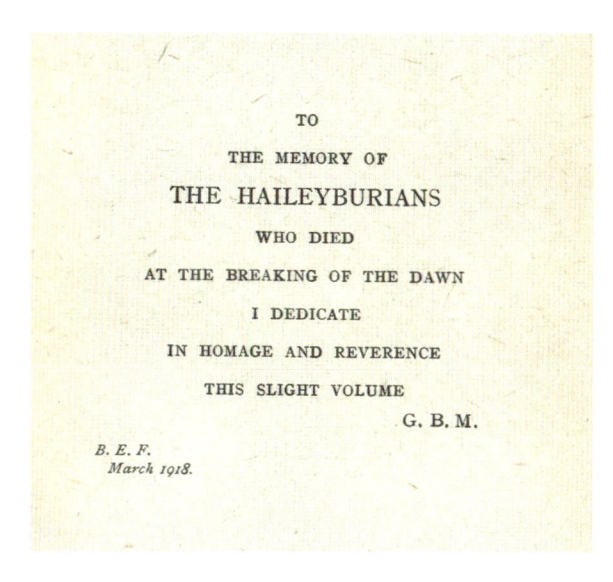

To Haileybury
Whatever our fortune and our fate
Wherever we wander, soon or late
We turn, as men turn to their home,
To the old school beneath the dome
And thank her with our hearts laid bare
For manliness implanted there.

Inevitably dozens of dedications reflect the loss suffered by so many families during the turmoil of the last century. *If We Return: Letters of a Soldier of Kitchener's Army* by G.B. Manwaring (Geoffrey Manwaring Brown, Tr 1905.1) was published by John Lane in 1918.

In contrast, *These for Remembrance: Memoirs of 6 Friends Killed in the Great War* by John Buchan with an introduction by Peter Vansittart (B 1934.3) was presented to the Library by H.E.A.H. Stewart (Ha 1985.3) in memory of his great-grandfather, John Buchan.

The Library has favourable mention on page 40 of Robert Speaight's *The Property Basket*: *My favourite corner of Haileybury was the School Library. Here I would spend whatever time I could spare, poring over rather old-fashioned editions of Shakespeare.* Speaight was author of more than 30 books, as well as a successful Shakespearean actor.

Elspeth Harvey (Staff 1989.3–)

159

FIELD TRIPS

Trips away from the School have long been an integral part of the added value that Haileybury has aimed to provide. Ranging from the theatre tours to North America and the Low Countries, to the tours under successive Directors of Music to Austria and Italy, to numerous sports tours as far afield as Australia, New Zealand, South Africa, Himalayas, Morocco and the West Indies, to geography trips to Iceland and religious studies visits to India, the breadth of activity is little short of astonishing.

Less spectacular in terms of destination, but far more regularly visited and by far larger numbers of Haileyburians, has been Woolacombe, where for 40 years Sixth Form biologists have gone to study coastal ecology. With its marvellous beach on the North Devon coast, in an outstanding area of natural beauty, the village lies on the edge of the sea and of tackiness, with surfing now its main *raison d'être*. Yet the tidal rise and fall is spectacular and many generations of A-level and IB pupils have come to know the dunes and rocky shore there and at nearby Lee Bay very well indeed.

Eyes have been opened to the natural world in a way that simply cannot be achieved in a laboratory or on film. To the untutored eye, little changes year on year on the shores and in the dunes, but the fascination of 'hands-on' discovery of lives at one's feet comes new to everyone, as does the chance to glimpse how 'the birth and the death of unseen generations are interdependent in vast orchestration'. Not only better understanding of scientific principles results but, and in many ways more importantly, field trips help to promote a better understanding by pupils of themselves, their colleagues and their teachers.

PRW

Below: *Biology field trip to North Devon, 2011.*

Below left: *Zayna Khan (M 2010.3) and Carmen Hartnigk (M 2010.3).*

ATTLEE LECTURES AND THE POLITICAL SOCIETY

Attlee was proud to be a Haileyburian and it was not unusual for him to wear the magenta, silver and black tie when he presided over the cabinet. He loved Haileyburians just as Baldwin loved Harrovians, and was delighted to find places for them in his post-war government. Among these were Sir Lynn Ungoed-Thomas (Tr 1918.3) (Solicitor General), Geoffrey de Freitas (C 1927.2) (PPS to the Prime Minister and Under Secretary for Air), Julian Snow (B 1923.3), later Lord Burntwood (Government Whip) and Lord Mayhew (M 1929.1) (Under Secretary at the Foreign Office). Attlee was proud to have occupied the same space at School as the great Viceroy, Lord Lawrence, and he remembered the names of his contemporaries to his dying day. In retirement he enjoyed watching cricket matches on Pavilion and was a regular spectator

Chapter 8 — PROGRESSIVE LEARNING

Above: *David Owen with the Master, David Jewell (1987.2–97.2), Dan Hearn (standing, right) and members of the Political Society, 1990.*

Above right: *The Political Society Visitors Book, 1989, signed by Attlee lecturers, Lord Hailsham and Ian Stewart.*

Right: *Lord Wilson of Rievaulx, who delivered the inaugural Attlee lecture in 1987, with Dan Hearn.*

Far right: *Former Prime Minister, Sir Edward Heath, 1988.*

at Lord's for the annual Cheltenham vs Haileybury match. He also attended School plays, when he met the cast members, and formally opened the new Art School in 1965, his last visit. He never questioned the right of a Labour Party member to send a child to a private school, though his own son, needing specialist care with dyslexia, did not go to Haileybury. He bequeathed his Garter banner to the School.

As a new beak it struck me as slightly odd that Attlee was only mildly embraced by the School. On questioning this I was reminded by a very senior member of the Common Room that our former Prime Minister was 'a socialist'. Indeed, it is said that when Attlee, as Prime Minister, came as guest on Speech Day, two Housemasters were conspicuous by their absence. To rectify this, the Political Society hosted in 1987 the first Attlee Memorial Lecture. The inaugural lecture was given by the Rt Hon. Lord Wilson of Rievaulx, who had been a member of Attlee's 1947 cabinet. Wilson was gracious in manner, but he became agitated at dinner by the refusal of the President of the Common Room to bring forward the

HAILEYBURY — A 150th Anniversary Portrait

loyal toast so that 'gentlemen may smoke'. The former Prime Minister was mollified by a huge Havana cigar.

Police security was much in evidence in 1988 for the visit of another former Prime Minister, Edward Heath, who had to be provided with a 'safe room' (in Hailey) in case of an attack. Heath enjoyed our hospitality and stayed on until after midnight. Sniffer dogs and police were on patrol again for the visit of Enoch Powell, who was a most compelling speaker, holding the attention of the audience for 39½ unscripted minutes (having been asked to speak for 40 minutes). He was somewhat waspish during question time, but we reduced him to tears with the gift of a leather-bound 18th-century *New Testament*. The loquacious polymath, Roy Jenkins, alas, spoke a little above the audience's understanding in 1989. He mellowed when presented with the Common Room's finest claret. Lord Hailsham delighted us with anecdotes of meeting the political heavyweights of the 20th century, from Stalin to Thatcher. So physically incapacitated was the great man that he spoke to a restricted audience in the Master's Lodge.

'An empty taxi drew up at No. 10 and out stepped Clement Attlee.' Churchill's cruel aside is not accepted by political historians. The respect that he now holds encourages visitors to come to Haileybury and speak under the umbrella of his name. In 1995, to mark the 50th anniversary of Attlee's arrival at No.10, it was decided to involve the whole school in an 'Attlee Day'. The day opened with a service of thanksgiving. The hymns, readings, prayers were all the choice of Attlee when a similar service was held after his death in 1967. The School and Choir responded as only Haileyburians can. Kenneth Harris, the author of the first Attlee biography, remarked, 'You had to have a heart of stone not to be moved by that service.' The Attlee Oak was planted, the Attlee Room named (by Lord Tonypandy), an Attlee Lecture given (by Professor Peter Hennessy) and a 1945 lunch menu of bangers and mash, spotted dick and Camp Coffee was eaten, as then, by the whole School on House tables.

The Political Society also sought to rectify this early lack of appreciation by inviting Kenneth Harris to speak. Later Francis Beckett, a more recent biographer, was a guest of the Society and in 2007 David Howell, a recent biographer, gave a lecture to the Society. Felicity Harwood, Attlee's daughter, came to talk about 'A daughter's view of a PM'.

Military men and their political masters have been welcome visitors to the Political Society. Lord Trenchard, son of the founder of the RAF and Minister of State for Defence, was followed by General Sir Michael Rose, who spoke about his role as an SAS operator in the recovery of the Iranian Embassy in London and later returned to speak on 'Leadership', having just retired in 1997 and having been Commander-in-Chief in Bosnia. In October 1993 Colonel Bob Stewart, something of a TV pundit, spoke on 'The politics of Bosnia'.

On 3 November 1983 David Butler, a psephologist and TV election commentator, spoke on 'Post-war elections'. His grandfather, A.G. Butler, had been the first Master of Haileybury. Two prolific, best-selling authors, both right wingers, Frederick Forsyth and Jeffrey Archer, proved extremely popular speakers, as did Matthew Parris, columnist for *The Times*, who gave two witty speeches in the 1990s.

No OH has been more supportive of the Political Society than Chris Lowe (L 1962.3), a familiar newsreader for the BBC over many years. In 1967, while Head of Lawrence, he read a lesson at the funeral of Clement Attlee and again at the Service of Dedication on 'Attlee Day' in 1995. His talk on 'Politics and the media' was full of insight. Two other prominent journalists cut their teeth while boys at Haileybury. In

Cartoon by Govind Dhar (BF 1997.3).

162

Chapter 8 — PROGRESSIVE LEARNING

Above: *Erskine Childers and his wife Molly sailing in the Baltic aboard their yacht the* Asgard *in 1905. This was the boat he used for gun-running in support of Irish Home Rule in 1914. He served in the RNAS and RAF with distinction during the First World War but became a vital figure in the Irish Struggle for Independence. When he was arrested for possession of firearms under the 1922 Emergency Act, in that year, Winston Churchill said, 'I have seen with satisfaction that the mischief-making, murderous renegade has been captured'. Fourteen days later, with his appeal still pending, he was executed, thus removing one of the most important figures in the IRA at that time.*

1969 Simon Carr (K 1966.2), now a political sketch-writer for the *Independent* and one-time speech writer for the New Zealand Prime Minister David Lange, read a paper on the 'Voting system and PR'. Quentin Letts (H 1976.3), feature writer for the *Daily Mail* and the *Sunday Telegraph* and once 'Peterborough' in the *Daily Telegraph*, was an enthusiastic member of the Political Society while at school.

Parents have also given their time. Lord Parkinson (Chairman of the Conservative Party and MP), who regarded Attlee as one of the two greatest post-war Prime Ministers, and Chief Emeka Anyaoku (Commonwealth Secretary General) have both spoken at meetings of the Society.

After 334 meetings of the Society my last association was a formal dinner at the East India Club on 23 February 2000 and a relaxed farewell party on 23 June. We had moved from a handful of members to more than 80, from drawing room talks to large meetings in Big School. Talks have been given by pupils and by distinguished national figures. There have been high moments aplenty and the odd dull meeting and I have loved every moment because of the overwhelming support, affection and enthusiasm of countless Haileyburians. Attlee's name is now more planted and respected in the minds of Haileyburians past and present. So, in time, will two other names be given due regard: the political scientist, the Reverend T.R. Malthus, a one-time resident of Hailey House, and, more controversially, Erskine Childers.

Dan Hearn

Soon after my appointment to succeed Dan Hearn as Head of Politics at Haileybury, I was invited as a special guest to the 12 Attlee Memorial Lecture, delivered by the Rt Hon. Michael Howard MP. The grandeur and significance of the event were impressed upon me and I have striven in the years since to match the speaker invited to the prestige of the occasion.

In March 2001, Lord Mayhew – who as Sir Patrick Mayhew served as Secretary of State for Northern Ireland for five years – as the 13th lecturer delivered a measured and insightful address on the issues and challenges of leadership in the context of the difficulties presented by a society riven by deep cultural, social and political divisions. Lord Cranborne spoke about the Cecil family's long history of political service and then of his famous deal with Prime Minister Tony Blair on Lords' reform. The 15th Lecture was delivered by Clare Short in November 2003. Ms Short thus became the first – and thus far the only –- female lecturer, speaking passionately about her beliefs as a conviction politician and how she had been inspired by the example of Clement Attlee. She was followed in March 2005 by Dr Tim Hames, who, as a leading journalist and parliamentary sketch-writer with *The Times*, was able to give us fascinating insights into the power and influence of the media on both the politics of the day and on leadership in society.

The 2008, lecture saw Lord Tebbit deliver a composed and deeply personal account of his years – as Norman Tebbit MP – of working closely with Margaret Thatcher and included the horrific events surrounding the Brighton bombing of 1984. He was followed in October 2009 by the Reverend Ian Paisley, who likewise gave a passionate account of his long struggles with the seemingly unconquerable problems of Northern Ireland which yet led to the Good Friday Peace Agreement and his sharing of Unionist power with Sinn Fein. Frank Field MP spoke in 2010, recounting his appointment as Welfare Reform Minister in Tony Blair's first government and how the blight of welfare dependency remained an issue essentially beyond party politics.

The rich mix of people who have addressed us over the years is testimony to the appeal of both Haileybury and the legacy of Clement Attlee. Generations of Haileyburians speak highly of the opportunities they have had to hear such prominent people relate their experiences and link them to the character they developed whilst at schools such as ours.

Michael Perrins (Staff 2000.3–)

HAILEYBURY — A 150th Anniversary Portrait

A BRIEF HISTORY OF THE HAILEYBURY DEBATING SOCIETY: *MUSAS AMAT IMPARES*

Early Years

The Society was set up for 'the promotion of the general welfare of Haileybury and the culture of its members in particular'. Initially called the Senior Literary Society, the very first meeting was in the open air of Hailey Field. While the Society debated the most important issues of the day, it was an elite group which took the first steps in the history of Haileybury debating. Membership was by election and was highly sought after. The intricacies of membership and the seemingly endless changes in criteria, especially the number of boys from the Classical and Modern Sides who could be admitted, could easily fill a small volume. Suffice it to say that the Modern Side was seen to be in need of 'missionary work' and the members themselves considered it the 'aristocratic society'.

Back then, the House voted against women's suffrage, for women smoking, for socialism in Russia, against Gladstone and against republicanism. The House today is more tolerant of women, but less so of socialism. The Debating Society, as it became known, seems to have been a very lively environment, especially given that the minutes of a debate in 1883 record that 'certain revelations were of so serious a nature that the minutes had to be destroyed'. Let us also bear in mind that everything in those days was pupil-run.

Senior Literary and Debating Society

In 1928 the Society reinstated its original name and became the Senior Literary and Debating Society. This desire to recapture the glorious past always burns brightly in debating societies and indeed today's Debating Society now has, as they did in the 19th century, a 'Convivium' and a 'Founder's Cup'. What is particularly striking about the minutes is their complete honesty and frequent acerbity. In 1915 it was noted that the recently elected 'junior member for Batten had been a great disappointment'.

The 626th meeting defeated the motion 'This House believes coalition to be the best form of government'. Although there were Conservative majorities on many issues, the same cannot be said

Above: EXTRA *magazine of the Senior Literary and Debating Society that existed between 1934 and 1948.*

Left: *Molly Mendoza (C 2007.3), Serjeant-at-Arms of the Debating Society 2011–12.*

164

Chapter 8 — PROGRESSIVE LEARNING

'MUN'

Model United Nations (or 'MUN') is a major co-curricular activity at Haileybury. The Haileybury MUN Conference, held annually over the last weekend of the Easter Term, attracts entrants from across the UK, in addition to a very healthy (and growing) number of overseas visitors, ranging from the USA, to Africa, to Continental Europe and the Middle East. The Conference now caters for around 750 delegates and over 100 staff, with a large contingent of committed Haileyburians deployed to service and run the event. The pupil Secretariat Team appointed annually runs not only our conference, but also a year-long programme of MUN Development and Preparation for all age groups and at various times each week, supported by an enthusiastic group of staff. Haileyburians attend other conferences, both in the UK and overseas in ever-increasing numbers, with regular attendance at the prestigious THIMUN Event in The Hague each January being a particular highlight.

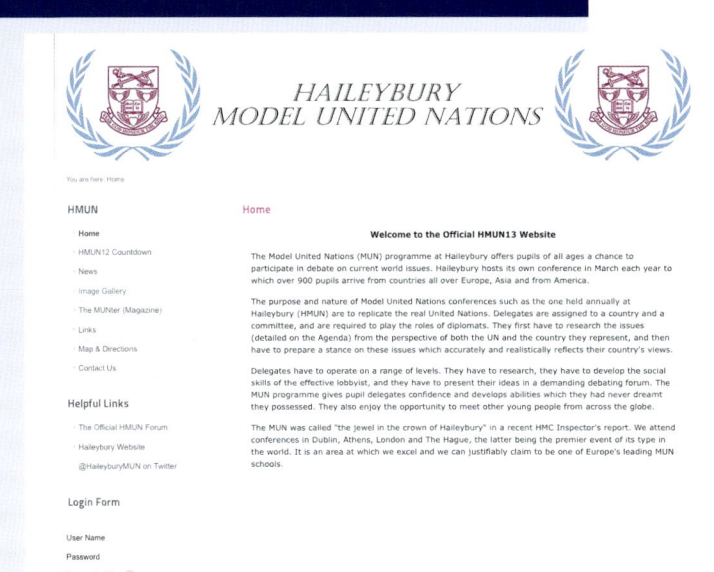

Below: *R.H. Barton (B 1919.2) speaking from his study on 7 February 1924 as the Conservative candidate during the rag election, organised by the Senior Literary and Debating Society, 1924. The result was 390 Conservative, 129 Labour and 43 Liberals.*

for the debate in 1931 disapproving of Mickey Mouse (although in 2010 it was decided Santa Claus should be shot). The debating society of this time seemed to have great peaks and troughs of attendance and seriousness, with membership always around 30. S.M. Toyne (the author of the 1912 work *History of The Haileybury College Debating Society* and twice its President) frequently returned, notably for the 1,000th debate in 1949. The debates around this time were less political and the literary element was still important, including poetry readings and performances of original dramatic works.

By the late 1950s, there was still a strong debating presence, the Society engaging in a debate against Felsted and achieving the honour of being criticised in the *Haileyburian* for being 'very silly'. The attendances at these debates seems to have been fairly low and in 1963, the House voted for state control of all education. It was still described as being in the 'big four' societies, but also 'uninspiring and [with] speaking poor'.

Fall and Rise

In 1965 the *Haileyburian* reports an open debate and 81 members. By 1972 it reports, in the 'Fringe Interests' section, that the Senior Literary and Debating Society 'remains, perhaps regrettably, the most elite society' and was 'not especially ambitious'. It would be 33 years before debating would be reported in the *Haileyburian* again, hardly featuring in School life in that time.

In recent years Haileybury debaters have entered competitions for the first time, such as the ESU Mace and the Oxford and Cambridge Schools competitions, with success for Oliver Winters (LS and L 2002.3), Amy Gandon (LS and H 2002.3) and Rupert Flint Cahan (LS and K 2002.3). Over the next three years, the foundations for high-quality debating, both within and without the School, were laid. In 2008, Jessica Kaye (Staff 2008.3–10.2) and Ben Sandell (Staff 2008.3–10.2) took over, Common Room vs Pupil debates became increasingly popular, and a junior House debating competition was introduced.

The Present and the Future

Today we enter all the major debating competitions and have been East of England ESU Mace Finalists

Chapter 8 — PROGRESSIVE LEARNING

Opposite: *Dalia Frontini.*

Below: *André Libeaux (BF 2011.3).*

several times. In 2012 a debating tour to Wales took place. Moreover, we have a wide variety of internal competitions, open to all pupils.

In many ways, debating at Haileybury has come full circle: we have come back to a pupil-run society with elected officers (now headed again by a President), with public debates for the School and wider community as our bread and butter. Are we still elite? No, in that all our debates and training sessions are open to all. Perhaps we are still elite in that all our debaters have to think, both for themselves and from someone else's perspective. They have to tackle the major political, moral, economic and social issues of the day in an intellectually vigorous way, while entertaining the audience and working as a team. Over the next 150 years, I am sure debating will bring these qualities to as many people as possible.

Peter Blair (Staff 2009.3–)

167

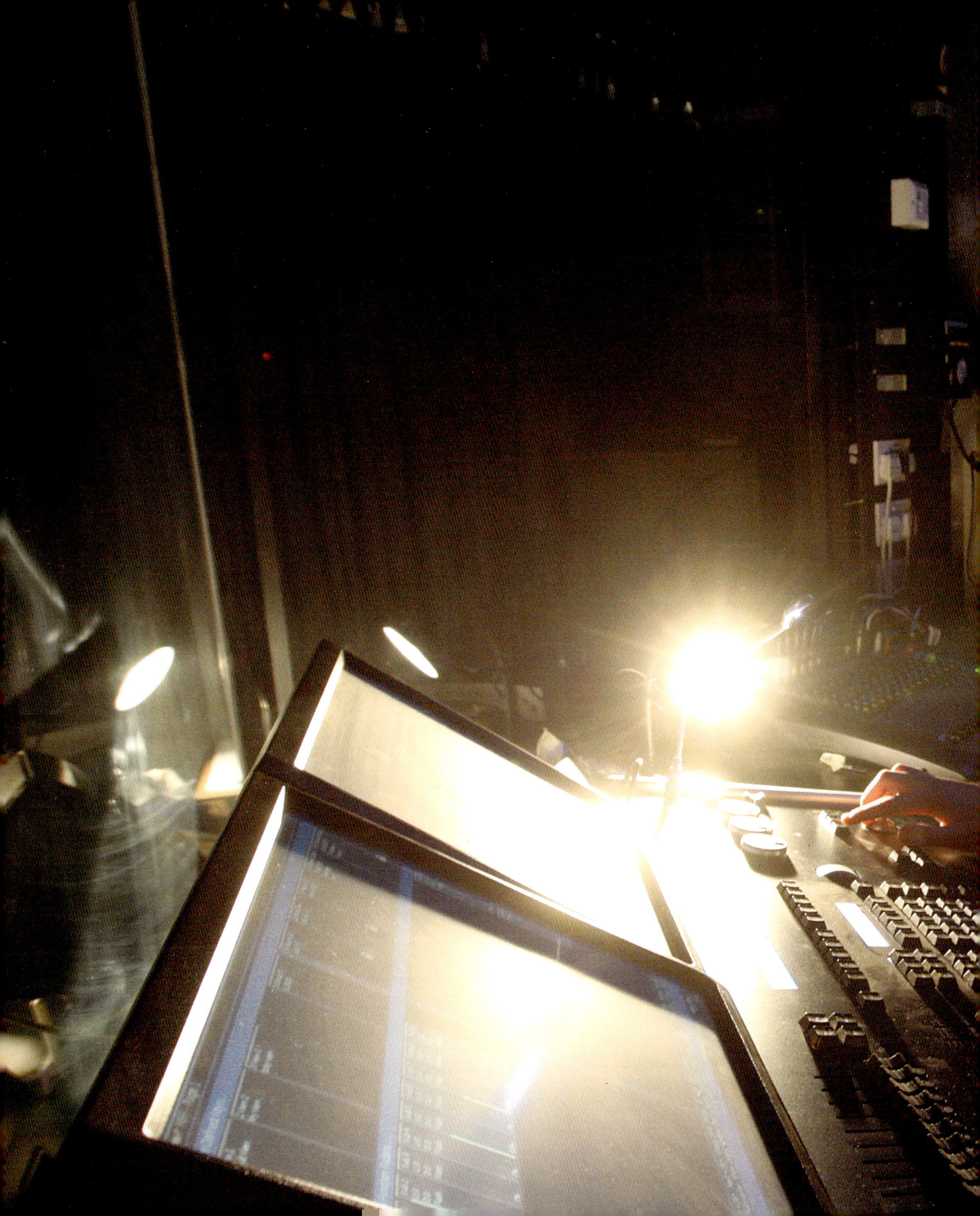

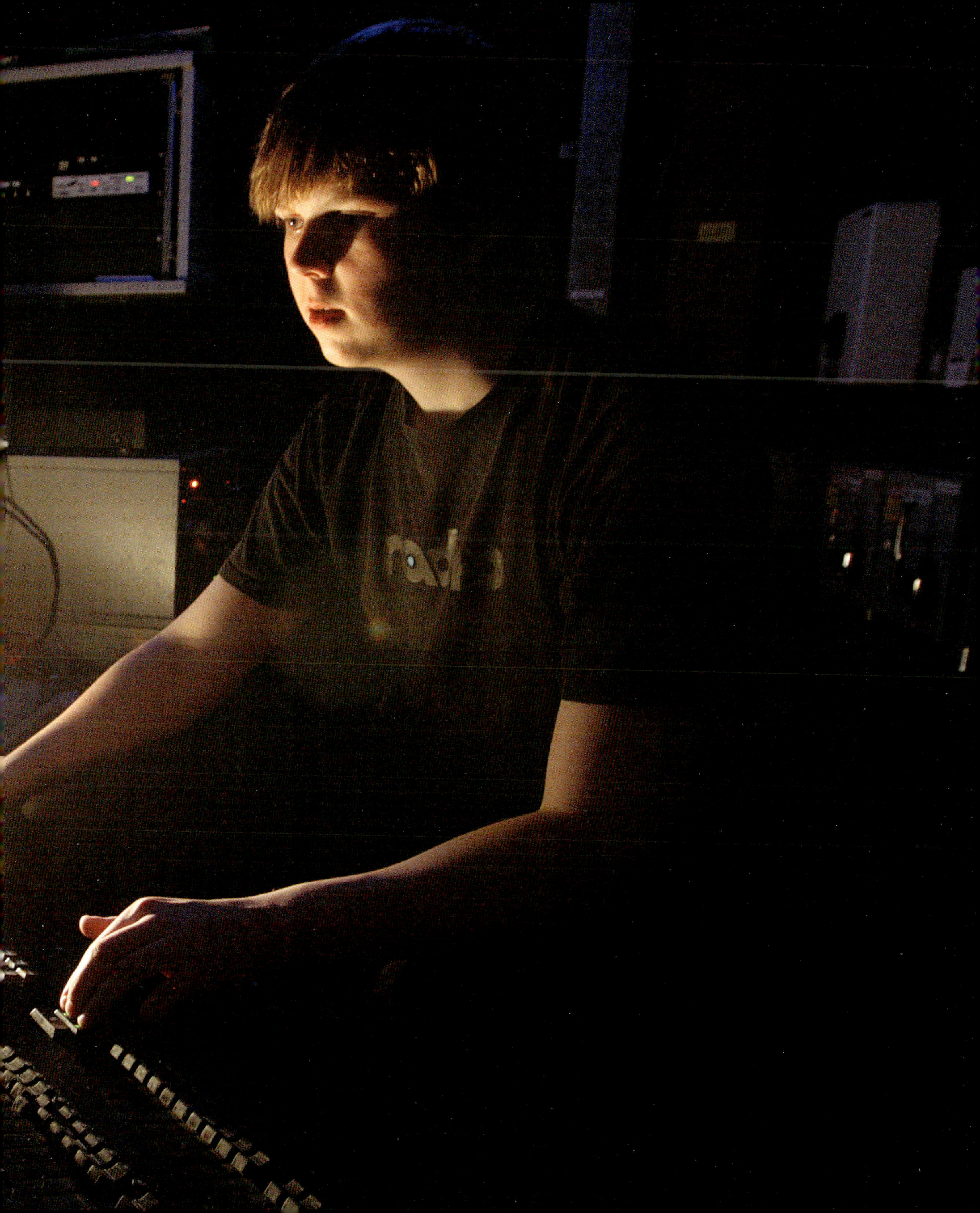

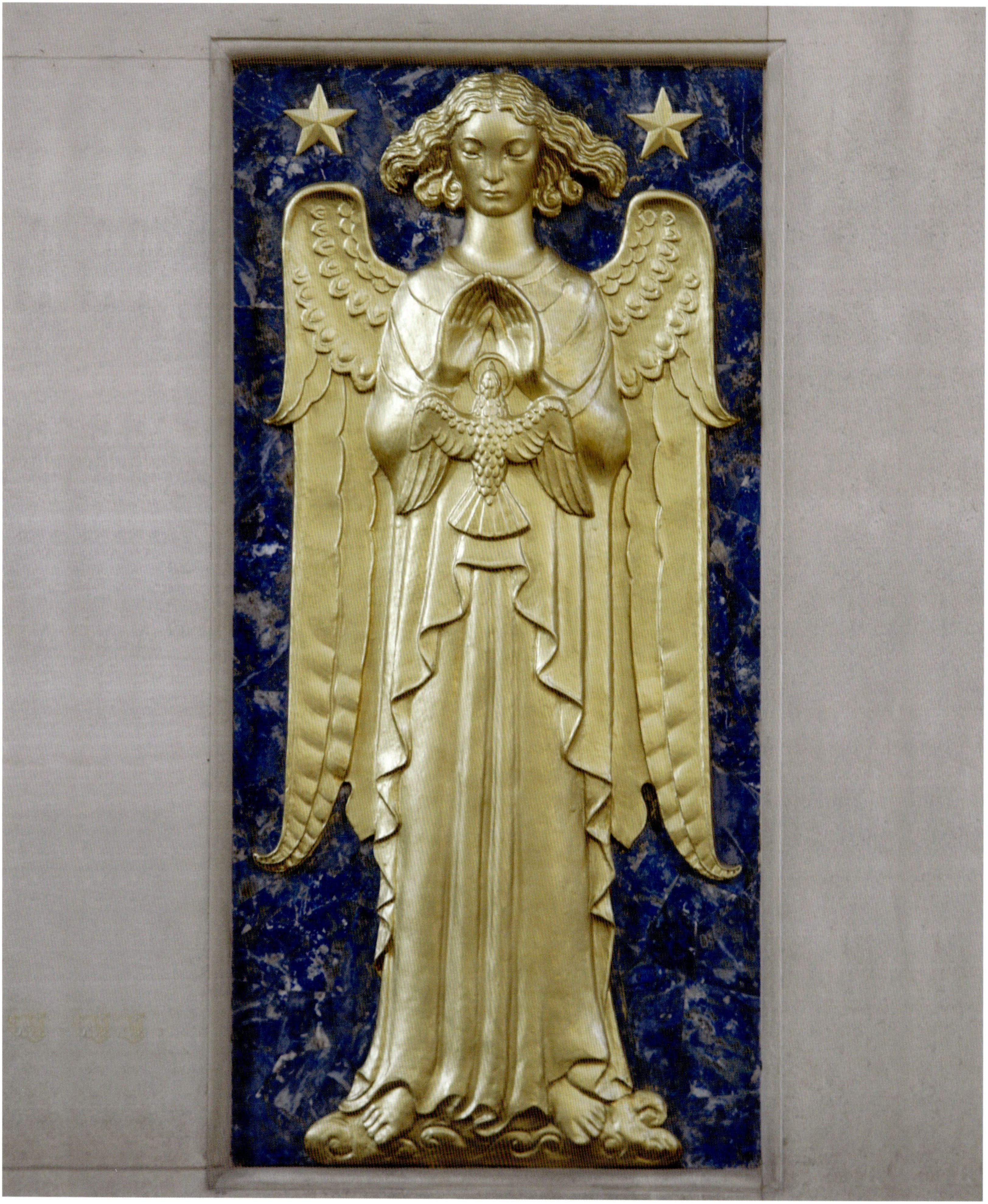

Chapter 9

THE DIVINE SCHEME

Right: Chris Briggs speaking to the School at a daily service during 2012.

A STRANGE PARISH

Being a parish priest at heart, Haileybury can sometimes feel like a very strange parish. All of the elements are there: the people; the hatches, matches and despatches; the times and seasons; and bells that ring for Lists, for Chapel, and for Physics, lesson 4, week B.

There are surprises, like the unexpected visit from one of the members of the Clerk of Works Department whose baby grandson was sick with meningitis and was not expected to live. 'Would you go and baptise him? He's in Leicester Royal Infirmary.'

There is the regularity. The Eucharist, early on Tuesday, Thursday and Sunday mornings. Never a great crowd, but part of the regular heartbeat of prayer; the rhythm of worship.

There is the daily routine. Meeting with sometimes very nervous Chapel readers, who hope that they won't 'stack it on the stairs' and make a fool of themselves. It is a great joy to see how serious they are. It is important for them to get it right, and it is a small step on the road to confident public speaking; maybe one day as the chairman of the board.

There is the ever-changing culture. Thirty-eight candidates for confirmation may not seem a great number when compared with the 107 who were confirmed in the November of 1961. 'New Guvs' now represent many countries and faith traditions. They may not be confirmed any longer as a whole year group, but you can be sure that those who are have chosen it and are committed to it.

HAILEYBURY ~ *A 150th Anniversary Portrait*

The Chapel, and what it stands for, is at the heart of Haileybury. When Old Haileyburians return they naturally come to sit for a while in the Chapel. They remember where they used to sit and the hymns they liked to sing: *Lift up your hearts*; *I vow to thee*; *And did those feet, in ancient times*. There was the time when a small group of septuagenarian OHs came into Chapel early for a reunion service. They pushed and prodded each other like new Removes. One was a knight of the realm and they teased him about which memorial plaque would be inscribed with his name.

Of course, some of the old ways have been lost. Now the regular pattern of exeats is punctuated by an in-weekend and School Service every half term. A 9pm service on most other Sundays provides a liturgical 'welcome back' in readiness for the demands of a new week. Perhaps there is still some scope for a regular Sunday morning service, with everything that goes with that, including a Sunday School for staff children.

One thing that has not changed, unlike many other schools, is the gathering of the community for morning chapel. From Tuesday to Friday we have ten inclusive but predominantly Christian minutes of singing, reading, reflection and prayer. In this time we explore matters of faith, morality, friendship and integrity in a way that is tolerant of and sensitive to those of every faith and none. We are a school, after all, and Chapel is an opportunity for us to listen to God, and to each other.

How fortunate we are that in the 1870s there was the will to build such a magnificent Chapel to cope with the needs of a growing school. It still manages to accommodate the 13+ community of pupils and staff in numbers that would have been unthinkable for our founders. It is a church that can cope equally with a triumphant gathering of 700, and the intimate service of ten or so for an adult baptism. It just works.

The Chapel embodies the motto, '*Sursum Corda*', 'Lift up your hearts', and in the preface to the 2006 *Service Book and Hymnal* we read, *This book is designed to assist the lifting of hearts to God in times of celebration, private reflection and in the simple daily rhythm of prayer and song in Chapel worship. In an increasingly busy world these moments of reflection and prayer remind us that our ultimate value lies in our 'being' rather than our 'doing'.*

Chris Briggs (Chaplain 2000.3–)

Above: *Watercolour by Francis Phillip Barraud of the interior of the Chapel, showing Campbell, Smith & Co.'s 1879 decorative scheme, with the pews facing inwards. This replaced the original interior decoration which was destroyed by the disastrous fire of 1878. In 1936 Sir Herbert Baker redesigned the interior, moving the organ, re-orientating the pews and constructed a second dome (pierced) on the inside. He also replaced the polygonal apse with a semicircular one lit by five stained-glass windows and painted the whole interior with a cream wash.*

Chapter 9 — THE DIVINE SCHEME

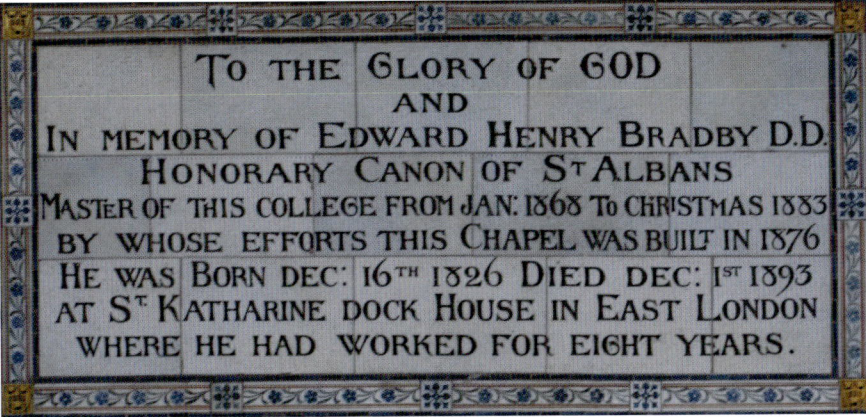

> TO THE GLORY OF GOD
> AND
> IN MEMORY OF EDWARD HENRY BRADBY D.D.
> HONORARY CANON OF ST ALBANS
> MASTER OF THIS COLLEGE FROM JAN: 1868 TO CHRISTMAS 1883
> BY WHOSE EFFORTS THIS CHAPEL WAS BUILT IN 1876
> HE WAS BORN DEC: 16TH 1826 DIED DEC: 1ST 1893
> AT ST KATHARINE DOCK HOUSE IN EAST LONDON
> WHERE HE HAD WORKED FOR EIGHT YEARS.

Among the memorable occasions during my nine years as Chaplain at Haileybury, I remember particularly the service held in 1991 to celebrate the release of John McCarthy (B 1970.2), who had been held hostage in Lebanon for five years. I recall the thanksgiving service prior to the opening of the Attlee Room, funerals with tangible feelings of sadness, and baptisms and weddings which were times of great rejoicing.

However, for me the most important times were those when very few people were present. Twice a week at 7.20am and on Sundays at 8am we would celebrate the Holy Eucharist. Usually there were only one or two people present: Father Jim Pullen (Staff 1975.3–2001.2), David Wright, David Jewell or Lloyd Bookless (Staff 1969.3–2005.2) perhaps, and a small number of boys and girls. In the summer exam season, the pupil numbers would mysteriously increase with the levels of anxiety. But it was good if, for whatever reason, individuals felt it right to bring their concerns 'before the Lord'. There were also moments when I would enter Chapel to find boys and girls sitting quietly, enjoying a small oasis of silence in the noise and bustle of School life. Tragedies, joys, loneliness and thanksgivings had led them to sit quietly for a moment to help make sense of human life. I hope that Chapel, in this respect at least, serves a purpose and remains a source of help and encouragement in times of need.

Martin Beaumont (Chaplain 1992.1–2000.2)

ORGANS OF HAILEYBURY

When the School opened in 1862, the Chapel (now the Library) was next to the Master's Lodge. The pews faced across the Chapel collegiate style and a harmonium provided the musical accompaniment. As numbers grew, a new chapel was needed. Arthur Blomfield, the School's architect, designed a building with a large Byzantine-style dome. Work began in 1876 and the new Chapel was consecrated on 27 June 1877. Initially the harmonium from the old Chapel was used, although an organ had always been included in the plans. In the middle of 1879 an organ, designed by Arthur Blomfield and built by J.W. Walker, was installed on the north side of the nave. The instrument had two manuals (12 stops) and a single 16' Bourdon on the pedal. Further pipes were added in 1880 and the organ completed the following year. The instrument was typical of the organs one might come across in a modest parish church.

Canon Edward Lyttelton succeeded Bradby as Master in 1890. His two passions were cricket and music. It can be assumed Lyttelton considered the Walker organ too small for its role. He used Speech Day 1900 as the occasion to launch an appeal for a new organ. A contract was agreed with Norman & Beard in 1901 (cost £2,192). The design for the new instrument in a gallery at the west end of the Chapel was by Reginald Blomfield, nephew of Arthur Blomfield. The organ had 42 speaking stops arranged over three manuals and pedals, the size of instrument one might come across in a cathedral. Although the instrument looked and sounded magnificent, there were faults. A gas blower was chosen to supply the wind. Sadly this type of blower was both unreliable and dirty, often supplying soot and fumes to the organ along with the wind. Norman & Beard dismantled the organ in 1916 for cleaning and proposed another rebuild in 1925. However, Bruce Hylton-Stewart (Staff 1916.1–1933.3), Director of Music, decided to seek other opinions. Solutions were proposed by three other organ builders, Willis, Rushworth & Dreaper and Harrison & Harrison, the preferred choice of Hylton-Stewart. The Council meeting of March 1926 confirmed the project could go ahead and Harrison & Harrison was asked to prepare a

Opposite: *The Klais organ in action, 2012.*

Left: *The first organ.*

Below: *Design for the 1901 organ by Reginald Blomfield.*

Chapter 9 — THE DIVINE SCHEME

contract. However, 1926 was an unfortunate time to be asking for donations and the project was postponed. In time the original builders managed to win favour with Hylton-Stewart and in 1929 rebuilt the organ.

When Canon Bonhote became Master in 1934, one of his first projects was to redesign the Chapel. In his opinion most of the congregation could neither hear nor see what was happening. Sir Herbert Baker was engaged as architect. He proposed turning the pews to face the altar, dividing the organ and placing it in rooms on either side of the Chapel, moving the console into the gallery and adding extra seating for the congregation. Director of Music Henry Havergal (Staff 1934.1–36.3) was strongly against the plan. However, he acquiesced to the Master and in January 1935 suggested four organ builders to offer schemes for the revised Chapel. Harrison & Harrison (Havergal's first choice) refused outright to move the organ into chambers. Consequently, proposals by Rushworth & Dreaper were accepted and the organ was rebuilt according to Baker's plans (54 stops) at a cost of £3,000.

By 1990 the action was once more unreliable. This, coupled with water damage from leaking roofs and water pipes, meant further restoration was unavoidable. Alexander Anderson, Director of Music from 1989, entered discussions with the Master and Council accepted advice offered by numerous authorities to build a new instrument. David Sanger was appointed consultant and six builders were invited in 1991 to tender for the new project. Having considered the various proposals, Johannes Klais of Bonn was selected as the preferred choice. The scheme underwent extensive development (four designs) by Klais before the current instrument was finalised. The instrument has 30 stops arranged over two manuals and pedals. Visually (and quite coincidently) there are echoes of Reginald Blomfield's design of 1901. The divisions of the organ are plain to see, with the Swell division placed above the Great division and the Pedal pipes placed against the back wall. To my mind it is a magnificent instrument that enhances both the architecture, music and worship in the Chapel to great effect.

Derek Longman

THE SESQUICENTENNIAL WINDOWS

The two Sesquicentennial Windows were donated by the Haileybury Society. They are the first major addition to the Chapel since the installation of the Klais organ in 1992. The two new panels flank a depiction of the Ascension by Herbert Bryans (E 1870.3), dedicated to the memory of Major General Sir Thompson Capper (Ha and Th 1876.1), who died of wounds on 27 September 1915.

The scheme for the windows was devised so that all three windows in the western transept form a coherent narrative as well as each panel having its own message. As a triptych the theme is taken from the Mystery of Faith declared in the Eucharist service, Christ has died, Christ has risen, and Christ will come again. In the first panel, the gifts of the Holy Spirit are symbolised by the angels carrying columbines. The gifts of the Holy Spirit being wisdom, knowledge, discernment, faith, healing, the working of miracles, prophecy, tongues and the interpretation of tongues; gifts which are given to all. In the second new window the angels bear symbols representing the nine fruits of the Holy Spirit. The fruits were chosen as the theme for this window because they symbolise what can be attained through a Christian education. The extract from *Isaiah 11* reinforces the symbolism of the two windows and has a strong educational as well as spiritual message, while the background of the window is powdered with representations of the House badges and heraldry to mark the history of the School.

The Form Room Block and the South African War Memorial were included in the panels because they are the first and last parts of Haileybury that pupils see when they enter or leave the School through the main entrance.

ATMP

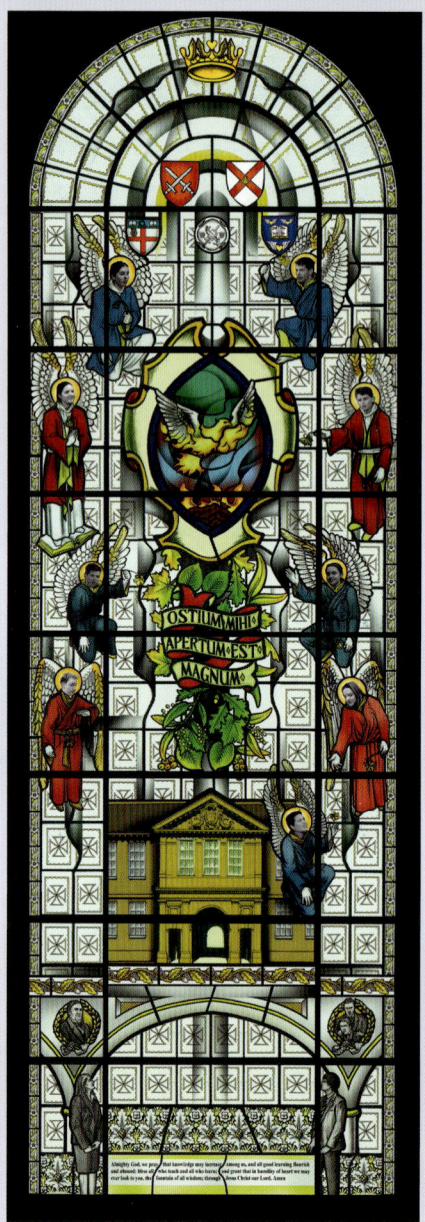

Above: *Designs for the sesquicentennial windows being painted and constructed by Petri Anderson, Mongoose Studios.*

Left: *Construction of the windows.*

Chapter 9 — THE DIVINE SCHEME

Right: *Part of the East India College communion plate. The two chalices and flagon were stolen in 1996 and retrieved in 2011.*

Below right: *Haileyburian bishops at the Lambeth Conference, 1930. Standing (l to r): H. Gresford Jones (Tr 1883.3), Bishop of Warrington, E. Chatterton (Th 1876.2), Bishop of Uganda, A.B. Karney (BF 1888.2), Bishop of Johannesberg; seated: St J.B. Wynne-Willson, (Fifth Master of Haileybury), Bishop of Bath and Wells, J.A. Kempthorne (Tr 1878.3), Bishop of Lichfield, H.F. Le Fanu (Tr 1884.2), Archbishop of Perth and Primate of Australia, A.W.T. Perowne (L 1880.2), Bishop of Worcester, N.S. Talbot (Th 1893.1), Bishop of Pretoria.*

WANDERING COMMUNION PLATE

On 24 June 1996, after a special thanksgiving Eucharist for David Jewell, part of the East India College communion plate was stolen and, despite a large amount of publicity at the time, the pieces were not recovered. In 2011 the three missing pieces, a large flagon and two tulip-shaped chalices made by William Pitts, were returned to the School after appearing in a catalogue for a silver sale. This was not, however, its first peregrination.

The history of the communion plate is a fascinating one, linking the East India College and the School closely together. On 5 September 1815, Joseph Batten, the second Principal of the East India College, wrote to the Chairman of the Committee of College and submitted an estimate for the cost of commissioning communion plate for the Chapel. Batten wanted 'one flagon, two cups, two plates for bread and one collecting plate' and suggested that this was the very least he needed. The Grecian motifs of the silver plate was designed to reflect the decoration that Wilkins had used in the Chapel in 1809. The East India Company paid for the communion plate, buying it from the exclusive goldsmiths, Rundell, Bridge and Rundell, at the cost of just over £109.

When the College closed in 1858 the plate made its way to the India Office, where it remained, locked away, until 1874 when it was sent to the Royal Indian Engineering College at Cooper's Hill, Surrey. Cooper's Hill closed 30 years later, in October 1906, and it was suggested to the School that it should apply for the communion plate. The Master, Reverend Basil Wynne-Willson's (1905.3–11.2) petition for the set was accepted by the Secretary of State for India and he presented it, for the use of Haileybury College, in view of the fact that 'this plate was formally used at Haileybury College in the time of the East India College'. In February 1907 the set was returned to the School and the plate remained there until 1996 when the chalices and the flagon were stolen.

ATMP

SOME MEMORABLE CLERICS

Jelly Belly, Jelly Belly,
he's our jolly Jelly Belly
he plays the accordion
and knows the songs to make us merry.

The song was sung in the slums of Somers Town around St Pancras station in the 1920s. 'Jelly Belly' was Father Basil Jellicoe (BF 1912.3), whose work to establish the first housing association and clear the slums transformed the lives of tens of thousands of people. Jellicoe was a great saint who died young, having burned himself out in the service of his vision of the Heavenly City.

Others serve in other ways. When Roy Sinker (BF 1922.3), then Archdeacon of Stow, came to the clergy wives' meeting in my parents' house, his wife told my mother that strawberries would be bad for her as she was nursing me. In reparation Mother always made sure I had strawberries on my birthday.

It is the fault of another OH archdeacon that since 1980 the Ripon Cathedral manuscripts have been deposited in the Leeds University Library. Donald Bartlett (B 1887.2) was Archdeacon of Ripon and then Canon of the Cathedral responsible for the library. Bartlett is described as an 'unsuspicious person' and would put the key to the safe away in a cupboard without concealment. This resulted in a theft in 1964 of a *Book of Hours* and one of only six copies of a very rare Caxton printing. He remarked that like a lady who lost a pearl necklace, 'I may have lost my necklace, but I do not intend to lose my peace of mind'. The books proved to be so rare as to be unsaleable and were returned in the post a few months later.

Clergy are a mixed lot, and that is true of OH clergy. We have our scholars: John Burnaby (BF 1905.1), whose contribution to the study of St Augustine remains seminal, and W.H.C. Frend (Th 1929.1), a leading light in the study of the early church. Reverend Sir Edwyn Hoskyns Bt (Tr 1897.3), whose work transformed the way the text of the Bible is approached, was the son of the OH Bishop of Southwell. The tradition continues to this day: Luke Bretherton (L 1982.3) is a contemporary theologian who is leading the Church of England in reflection on the nature of society.

Bishop John Jameson Willis (M 1887.1) was accused of heresy. Frank Weston, the saintly and determined Bishop of Zanzibar, was outraged when

Below: *Luke Miller (Ha 1979.3), Archdeacon of Hampstead and President of the Haileybury Society 2010–11.*

Below left: Jellicoe the Musical, *premiered at the Shaw Theatre, 2003. Father Basil Jellicoe may be the only OH to have a musical written about him.*

Chapter 9 — THE DIVINE SCHEME

Our most senior clerics have been Henry Le Fanu, Primate of Australia, and Richard Wimbush (M 1923.1), Primus of the Episcopal Church of Scotland. Emma Loveridge (Alb, A and Th 1981.3) became the first OH woman priest when she was ordained in 2000 while Paul Collier (Th 1976.3) is our first openly gay priest and has campaigned on behalf of same-sex unions.

Gerard Irvine's (E 1934.1) obituary in *The Daily Telegraph* described his ministry at St Margaret's Westminster: *A food-stained cassock indicated that he had not troubled to remove this garment at lunchtime, neither had he found opportunity to do so before serving tea in his clergy house to Rose Macaulay or John Betjeman. The house was described by Anthony Powell in his journals as 'somewhere between a Firbank novel and Cruikshank's illustrations of the Old Curiosity Shop'.*

Irvine was also noted as a great pastor and serious priest, and that is true of the hundreds of OHs whose ministry has been in parishes and missions across, up and down this country and round the world.

Nothing has been said of the clergy of denominations other than Anglican, nor of those who profess other faiths, simply to note that the spirituality of Haileyburians is not confined to the established church.

Luke Miller

Above: *The Lyon Window. A memorial to John Lyon (Tr 1905.2), youngest of the five Lyon brothers who attended the School. John died of leukaemia in the Sanitorium on 2 December 1907. The window was by Herbert Bryans.*

Willis, together with the Bishop of Mombassa, celebrated Holy Communion at a gathering of missionaries of many different denominations at which all the delegates except those from the Society of Friends were communicated. This was in 1914, long before any idea of intercommunion was accepted, and Bishop Weston protested to the Archbishop of Canterbury in the strongest terms. There was a national ferment in ecclesiastical circles and a heresy trial threatened.

LIGHTING THE WAY

There were often funny times in Chapel. During one Candlemas service, we were up in the choir stalls singing and holding candles by which to read the music when one of the chorister's sheet music caught alight. We did our best to carry on singing and not laugh as he frantically tried to put the flames out. Another was when I was doing a reading during the Carol Service. Chapel was so full that there were people sitting all the way up the steps and down the side aisles at the back, so I had to climb over people to get down from the choir and then was faced with having to go out the back door and run around the Library, fight my way in through the side door and up to the lectern. *Good King Wenceslas* is only five verses long and I nearly didn't get there in time! It was difficult not to arrive puffing and panting to do the reading and then I had to do the whole thing in reverse to get back to sing in the Choir again.

Fiona Illingworth (née Short) (BF and Alb 1976.3)

HAILEYBURY ~ *A 150th Anniversary Portrait*

Below: Richard Rhodes-James, who was a member of Common Room for 34 years and Housemaster of Melvill for 21 of them.

RICHARD RHODES-JAMES

One of my most significant memories of Haileybury is crowding into Richard Rhodes-James's flat after Chapel on a Sunday morning with up to 80 or 90 boys to hear gifted Christian speakers such as E.J.H. 'Bash' Nash or David Watson. In fact, I look back on Haileybury as the place where one of the most important foundations of my life was laid, that of coming to a personal faith in Jesus Christ. This goes back partly to the excellent Lent Missions laid on in Chapel, but even more to 'Rhodie's ministry' which flourished in an amazing way during my time there.

I had been invited by a friend to come along to the meeting for some time, but resisted on the grounds that I had better things to do. But one day (probably in about 1970) I ran out of excuses and agreed to go along. What happened that day changed my life for ever. Twenty years later I was ordained into the Anglican ministry and here I am now about to embark on a new journey with my wife, working with the church-planting organisation, France Mission, in Châteauroux.

I owe so much to Haileybury and, in particular to that group meeting in 'Rhodie's' flat. I could never have dreamed where it might lead.

Paul Dowling (Th 1968.1)

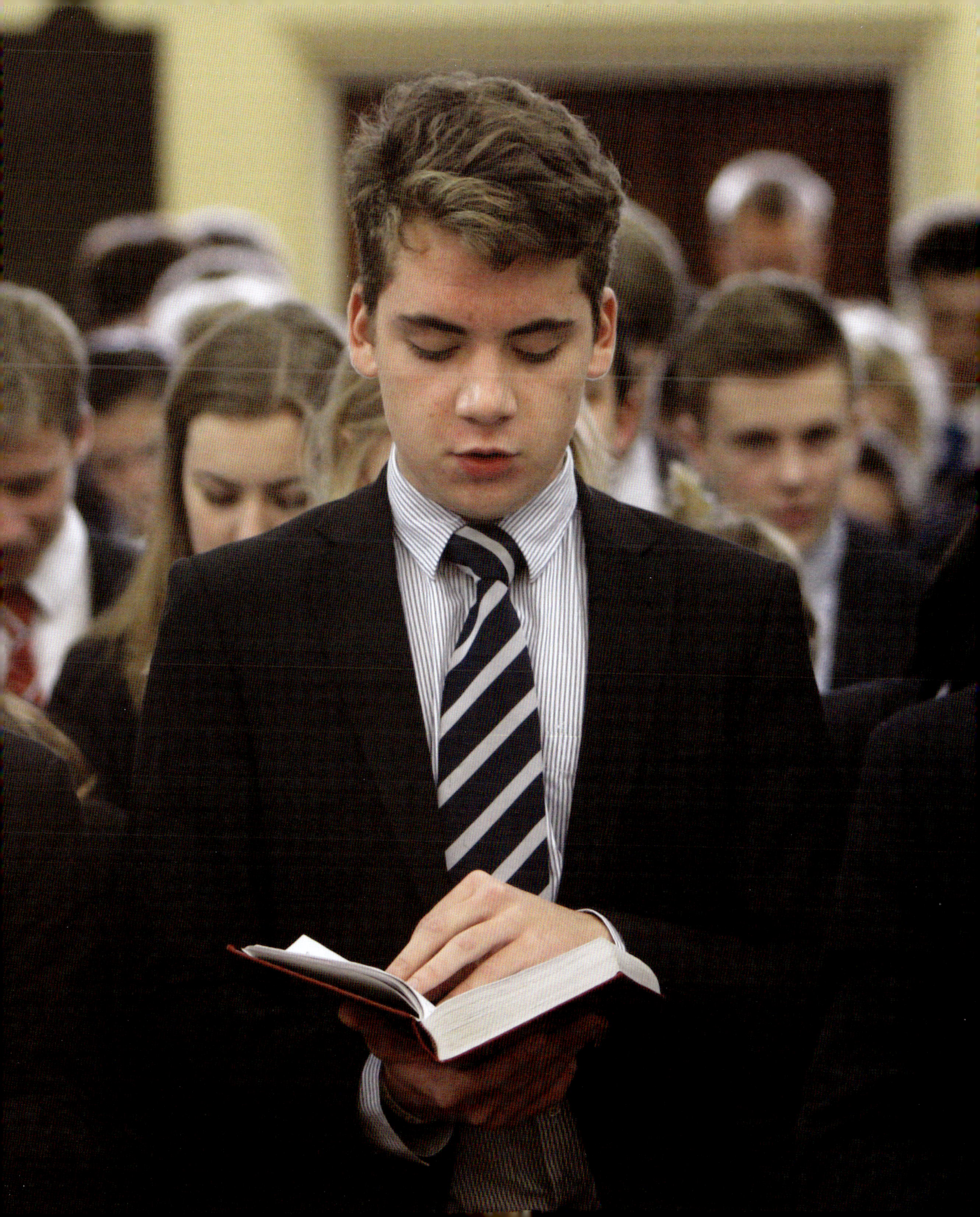

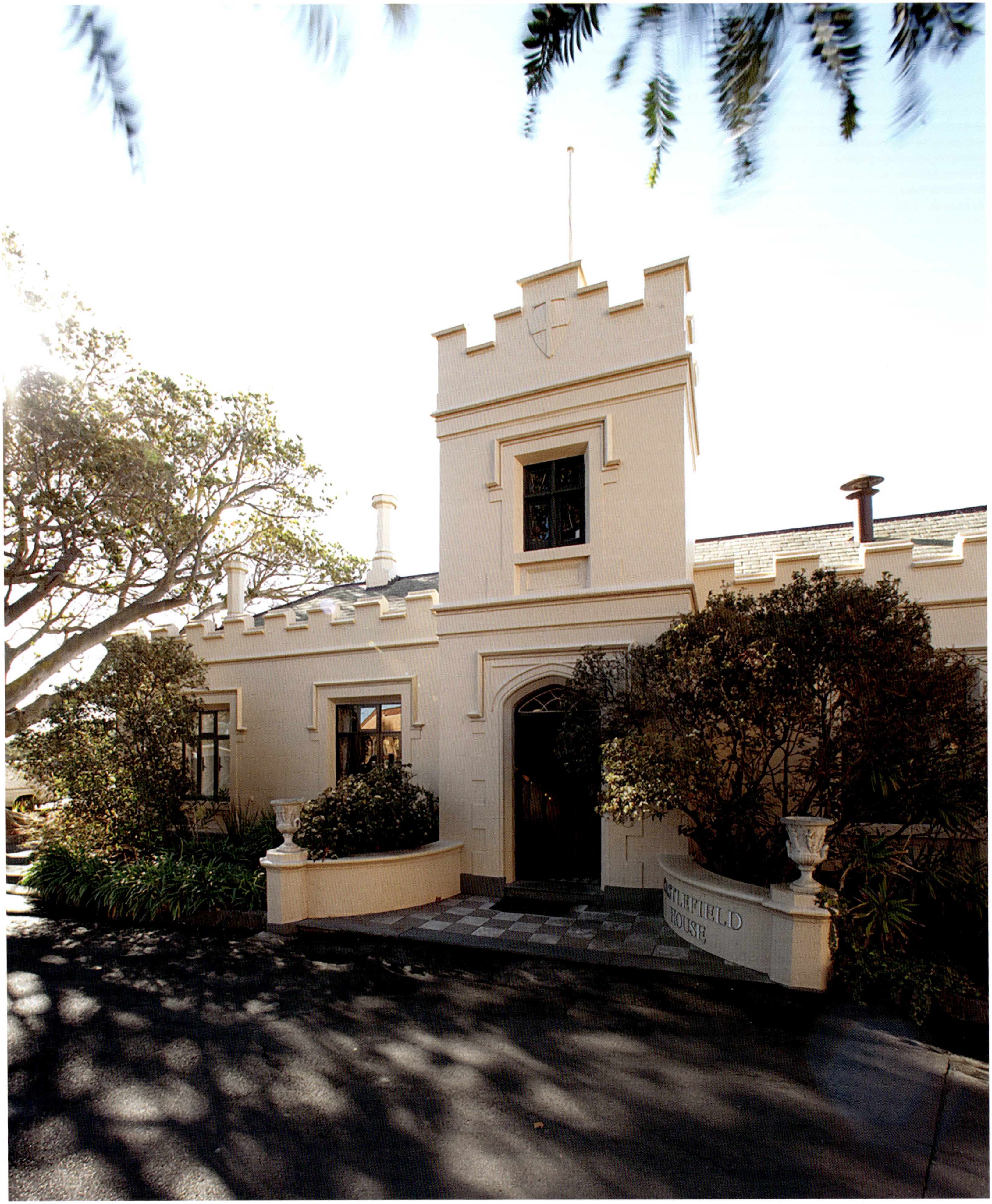
HOUSE

Chapter 10

THE WIDER WORLD

HAILEYBURY MELBOURNE

Charles Rendall left Thomason House in 1873. Just under 20 years later, in 1892, he founded his own school, named after his alma mater, in the old Brighton Coffee Palace on the corner of New Street in Brighton Beach, Melbourne, Australia. From an initial roll of 17 pupils, the school grew to 100 pupils by the time of his retirement in 1914. It has continued to grow, passing into the trust of the Presbyterian Church at the start of the Second World War, acquiring more property and opening both a junior school and a girls' school. It is now one of the leading independent schools in the Asia-Pacific region, with three campuses and over 3,000 pupils, and exchange students once more wing their way between Melbourne and Haileybury.

In 1961 I went to Haileybury Melbourne for two terms. This came about because the Headmaster of Haileybury Melbourne, David Bradshaw, came to Haileybury England Speech Day in 1960 and offered what was expected to be an exchange scholarship. I was 17 and had already taken my A-levels and had a place at university to read Medicine. If I left Haileybury at Christmas I would miss the hockey and swimming seasons, but I could see the world for free. No contest, really.

On the boat out was Tony Sleight (Ha 1955.3), a year above me at School and also bound for Cambridge. He was off to be a jackaroo on a sheep station, I was going to school. Had I got it wrong, somehow?

Haileybury Melbourne had recently been invited to join the Associated Public Schools of Victoria which had expanded from six to 11 schools. This was promotion from the second rank of Associated Grammar Schools; they were very proud of it and anxious to make their mark. The School was then at Brighton on the east coast of Port Phillip Bay. The boarding house was Rendall, after the OH founder, with about 50 boys accommodated in huts of varying

Assembly in the School Hall, Haileybury Melbourne in the 1960s (right) and the Castlefield campus today (opposite). In 1960, this formed the entrance to the boarding house.

sizes. I shared a study with the Head of House for the next two terms.

I arrived in January. For the first week the temperature was over 100°F every day; I wasn't sure I was going to survive. The boarders, a close-knit bunch, were allowed down to Brighton Beach, about half a mile away, before breakfast for a swim in the sea, which just about got us through the day. I was immediately impressed that the senior boys were much friendlier with the juniors than in England. In England I hardly spoke to my brother, only two years older than me, from beginning of term to end; it just wasn't done to be seen talking to a senior even if he was your brother. But in Melbourne there were 50 boarders against several hundred day boys; furthermore, the boarders were regarded as country boys whether their fathers were farmers or pillars of country towns, and they stuck together.

January was cricket season. I had never been much good at cricket at home, being more of a swimmer; but the standard of swimming there was sky high. I rapidly realised I would never get a look-in, so down to the nets. 'Weary' Clarke (one of those impenetrable Australian nicknames) was master i/c and must have seen something that eluded them in England as I was picked for the 2nd XI, made a couple of decent scores and was picked for the 1sts. This proved to be the zenith of my cricket career. I still have a newspaper cutting. Geelong Grammar beat us by an innings in a two-day match. I don't think I scored any runs but in desperation the skipper tossed me the ball and I took none for 36 from three overs. Still, I spent the rest of the season in the 2nds, made a lot of friends from non-boarding houses, and got to know some of the geography of Melbourne visiting other schools.

Meanwhile, I had elected to take English Literature and French Language as my subjects. *Père Goriot* was the French text and the teacher was first class. Naturally, he had spent time in France, which meant that his French accent was perfect if you were Australian, but to me he sounded like a Frenchman speaking French with an Australian accent. Of course, there was no exam at the end of it for me, but I thoroughly enjoyed the discipline and if my holiday French is slightly better than the average Brit's then I have Haileybury Melbourne to thank.

English Literature was good, too: *Wuthering Heights*, along with a bit of Shakespeare. I loved it. Much less precise than the Biology, Physics and Chemistry A-levels I had had to do for Medicine. Came the Easter holidays and an English OH called Owen Fowler (Ha 1906.3) had arranged a few days' stay on a massive sheep station for me.

The next term's sport was 'footy', or Australian Rules Football. I was dying to have a go. Being a completely new game to me I was never going to make the 1st team, but at 18-a-side I thought I might have a crack at the 2nds, and scraped in. Footy also led to a shameful episode. My friend Ron insisted I

Above: *Pupils at Haileybury Melbourne today.*

Chapter 10 — THE WIDER WORLD

accompany him one Saturday to watch the Brighton Tigers, the local premiership team. Australian beer is very strong, and although drunk from small glasses called schooners, it is very cold so that it is all too easy to drink too many before you know it. I was spotted rolling rather unsteadily back into school and was sentenced by my Housemaster, a nice man called Hansen, to write an essay on *The Waste Land* by T.S. Eliot. I suppose today I would Google it and get a few clues, but there was no internet then and I imagine my effort was as much double Dutch to Mr Hansen as T.S. Eliot was to me, though I was filled with remorse and did try very hard.

At the end I felt I had achieved something that would stand me in good stead for life. Haileybury Melbourne has gone from strength to strength, moved south in Melbourne to a huge campus including an 8-lane 50m Olympic-sized swimming pool. The Brighton site is now just one of several satellite campuses.

Richard Young (M 1956.3)

Below right: Sir George Edmonstone, Lieutenant Governor of the North West Province (third from right) with his advisors, c.1862.

Below: Edmonstone House Common Room, 2012 with the portrait of Sir George Edmonstone.

A SOUTH AFRICAN NOMAD

From our approach up Hailey Lane, a dome pointing out of the landscape was my first view of Haileybury. Over the previous day I had exchanged the swelter of a sugar farm in Natal for the chill of England in January. How the past is another country was reflected in my flight: Durban, Johannesburg, Salisbury in Rhodesia, Luanda in the Portuguese colony of Angola, and then northwards into the winter hemisphere. Also aboard were Andrew du Toit (Ha 1973.1), the Rhodesian Nomad Scholar, and Dan Hearn, the Haileybury Master and rugby coach who was to be our guardian for the year ahead.

Compared with the white, Cape Dutch buildings of Hilton College near Pietermaritzburg, where a month before I had completed my South African schooling, Haileybury had an austere and elemental beauty. Dominant was the majestic sweep of Terrace, with its great dome looming above it, but notable too were the Chapel and Dining Hall and classrooms. The Edmonstone dormitory, as I soon discovered, was an elongated chamber of low-walled partitions, in which the position of each occupant's bed was a reflection of his status. On the wall at the hallowed end was the portrait of Sir George Edmonstone, a provincial governor in the Raj, whom the House's name commemorated.

If I cast my mind back over nearly 40 years, I remember hurrying to breakfast on cold mornings,

185

subscribing to *The Times* and *Melody Maker*, listening to Fairport Convention and Roxy Music in my study, which each term I shared with a different Housemate, fencing in the Gym and running in athletics meetings. Another memory is the extraordinary vigour of spring, and the balmy summer days with the drone of lawnmowers and the sounds of cricket. In the classroom, I recall a moving recitation of Kipling's *Gunga Din*, by 'Chalky' White (Staff 1968.3–77.2), a Master who had lived in India. As my main sport was rugby, I remember the exhilaration and the mud, and how the XV trounced Stowe in the opening game and then later in the season stumbled, losing to several teams. That we prepared ourselves mentally before each game by listening to the Rolling Stones' song *Angie* on a cassette recorder seems now to me odd. And then I flew southwards again, into another sub-tropical summer.

Haileybury's past has many imperial resonances, which for some may be uncomfortable. But for me, an offshoot of English culture sown far from the centre, they are my heritage.

John Conyngham (E 1973.1)

AN AMERICAN AT HAILEYBURY: A CROSS-CULTURAL EXPERIENCE

When I arrived at Haileybury to spend a year in the autumn of 1976, I thought that I knew all there was to know about public schools. After all, I had grown up at such a school in the United States where my father was a teacher. What could be different? I would soon discover how wrong I could be.

First off, there was the peculiar vocabulary: 'New Guvs', 'Plebs', 'Dates', to have an 'Out'. My Housemates had helpfully collected a lot of 'drapes' for my study. I couldn't grasp why I would need so many curtains when there was only a single window. With the limited heat available in the KBM study block, pupils lined the walls of their studies from floor to ceiling with fabric, in an effort to keep warm. This was back in the days when the Houses were vast, single rooms, with 40 or 50 boys sleeping in lines of beds with identical reddish blankets. To my eyes, Kipling House resembled an enormous stable, with stalls for boys instead of horses.

Compared with my school in the States, Haileybury was quite hierarchical. One's place in the system was made plain for all to see by a dizzying array of neckties, each indicating House affiliation, success on the playing fields, or status as a Prefect. On my trip back to the States I was amazed to be queried by a fellow passenger, 'Excuse me, but isn't that a minor sports tie you're wearing?' It was, of course.

In 1976 there were about 600 pupils, of whom 30 were girls, present in the Sixth Form only. One couldn't help but feel sympathy for these intrepid young women, who could no sooner step onto the Quad before an eager male escort or two would appear on each side, competing for their attention.

There were other cultural differences. I was once upbraided by Kipling Housemaster Hugh Sawbridge for being disrespectful to him. Who knew that in the UK it was considered impolite to speak to a Master with your hands in your pockets? Then of course there were the differences in British and American English. As Hugh Sawbridge was fond of repeating, 'The difference between we English and you Americans is that you put your boots in the trunk, while we put our trunks in the boot.' And there was the embarrassing instance when I complimented a girl on her 'pants', which means 'trousers' in the States.

But my time spent at Haileybury proved to be invaluable to me in my profession as an English language teacher. I became fluent in both British and American English, which are both taught around the world today. My exposure to life at Haileybury spurred my interest in language and in inter-cultural communication. For a year at Haileybury was certainly a cross-cultural experience for me.

Joe McVeigh (K 1976.3)

A SPIRIT OF ADVENTURE

Many of the pupils who arrived at Haileybury in that vital first year of 1862 went off to serve and explore in India, the Transvaal, Griqualand, Canada, Ceylon, Afghanistan, Australia, Lapland and Brazil. While George Hoste had the honour of being the first pupil to be admitted to the School on its first day (the Mitchell brothers arrived a day early), his cousin Henry 'Skipper' Hoste (Th 1863.2) was perhaps Haileybury's first real adventurer. At the age of 24 he took leave from his employer to join an expedition to explore an area that now includes Malawi, Tanzania and Mozambique, and suppress the slave trade. 'Skipper' later became second in command to the famous big game hunter and Rugbeian, Frederick

Chapter 10 — THE WIDER WORLD

Opposite: *Platycerium coronarium, discovered by Henry Nicholas Ridley FRS, first Director of the Singapore Botanical Gardens, after whom more than 100 species of flora and fauna have been named.*

Below: *Sir Alfred Sharpe (centre), first Governor of Nyasaland, with the Legislative Council of Nyasaland, 1910.*

Right: *Sharpe's grysbok.*

Courtney Selous, in an exploration for the British South African Company into Mashonaland.

By the time Jules Verne's Philias Fogg set out from the Travellers Club, Pall Mall, on 2 October 1872, Haileyburians were already spread across the world, working in many different capacities, and one beak, Arthur Carlisle (Staff 1872.2–1907.2), had already travelled round the world in 1870. Exploration had clearly captured many boys' imagination, hardly surprising when the Library was filled with reports and books that charted the discovery of unusual and faraway places. Henry Nicholas Ridley (BF 1868.2) took part in botanical expeditions to Christmas Island, Java, Sumatra, Borneo, the Malay Peninsula, Jamaica and South America. From Lawrence House, Thomas Simcox Lea (1869.1) travelled through Australia and the Hawaiian Islands collecting plants for the British Museum and he also served on the British Museum expedition to Fernando de Noronha under Henry Ridley in 1887. From Lawrence, Phillip Henry Gosse (L 1892.3) explored the Chilean Andes, discovering huge spiders which chilled the blood of the expedition members.

Sir Alfred Sharpe (Hi 1867.3) was perhaps the Haileyburian who made the greatest impact in Africa. After a short time as a colonial officer in Fiji, he moved to south-eastern Africa to start out as an elephant hunter. When in 1888 the Arabs revolted against the British control of Nyasaland, Sharpe became a volunteer serving under Sir Frederick Lugard and seven years later he came to fame as the man who destroyed the slave-raiding tribes around Lake Nyasa. Spending a considerable amount of time exploring the Zambezi between 1890 and 1894, Sharpe was made Vice-Consul for territories under British influence north of the Zambezi. He found that exploration had changed very little since Livingstone's time and Katanga was a difficult destination to reach when all of your porters had been frightened off by angry tribesmen and supplies were stuck thousands of miles away because of a smallpox epidemic.

On one of his expeditions Sharpe discovered a small antelope at the southern end of Lake Nyasa, which was named after him, Sharpe's grysbok (*Raphicerus sharpei*). After 30 years of exploring Nyasaland and the Congo, three journeys following the Nile, surviving two shipwrecks, helping to plan the Cape to Cairo railway with Cecil Rhodes and becoming the first Governor of Nyasaland, Sharpe retired for a time for the peace of the countryside around Haileybury. Even though Sharpe was a big game hunter he understood the importance of the conservation of species and he set up an elephant reserve to protect them from over-hunting in his last year as Governor.

On another continent Haileyburians were combining soldiering and exploration to help understand the borders they were protecting. Captain Robert Otter-Barry (E 1893.3), a fluent Chinese speaker, spent time exploring the vastness of Mongolia while keeping an eye on the Russian involvement in the region, publishing a fascinating book on the subject called *With the Russians in Mongolia* in 1913. A few years earlier, Major Clarence Dalrymple Bruce (Th 1876.2), while commanding the Chinese regiment Wei-Hai-Wei, left Peking, crossed the Gobi desert alone and ended his journey in London. Bruce then spent a significant amount of time travelling in the Caucasus, watching Russians in 1902. He wrote *In the Footsteps of Marco Polo* about his last major expedition, which started in 1905, a journey from Shimla to Peking, taking ten months. Kynard Hawdon (M 1891.3) in the same year took rather less time to accomplish his task when he travelled from London to Quetta overland in a record-breaking 37 days. The information Hawdon gleaned on this journey about the Russian movements in the region led Sir Henry Campbell-Bannerman to praise the young officer's gallantry in his *Defence of India* speech. While Hawdon undertook his expedition because of his concerns about the Russians, when George Rawlins (Ha and L 1875.3) in 1906 rode back to rejoin his regiment at Bannu from leave in Bombay, he went via Persia to prevent the onset of boredom.

In 1912 Alexander Mitchell-Carruthers (L 1896.2) was awarded the Royal Geographical Society's Patron's Medal in recognition of his work in Mongolia and Central Asia. Carruther's first expedition, in 1908, was with the British Museum to the Ruwenzori mountain range on the Ugandan border and there is a mountain squirrel and a small bird, a cisticola, named after him. In 1909 Carruthers explored Northern Arabia, surveying 700 miles of uncharted desert, and during the First World War was employed to compile maps of the Middle East for the War Office. Carruthers used his skills after the war to provide support for other explorers and travellers, winning the Sykes Medal of the Royal Central Asian Society in 1956.

ATMP

Left: *Carruthers's Cisticola* (Cisticola carruthersi).

FRIED EGGS AND THICK-CUT CHIPS

Having spent my first 13 years in Hong Kong, I set out for Haileybury in 1986 without really knowing what to expect. I knew I was going abroad for a UK boarding school education, but I was too young and naive to think too much ahead of what it meant. The five years at Haileybury turned out to be one of the best times of my life, and the experiences and friendships I gained there are still with me today.

There are many memories to recall, from my first dinner of fried eggs and thick-cut chips seated on the long benches; to the New Guv'nors' test; the times we spent chatting and hanging out on the roof of the 'bogs'; the skills I got playing pool and table tennis in the common room; very useful today!

I always appreciate the sports we did then, so much that I am still drawing my fitness credits today from those times: from getting hit by the first rugby tackle when I had no idea of the game, to playing with the Hogs in the final years; playing soccer on XX Acre in the freezing Easter term; captaining the School badminton team, with over half the players being Asian. My fondest memories are of the swimming team, in which I am very proud to have competed for the School every year, winning inter-House swimming as House Captain and earning my Wings tie.

Other activities such as doing the weekly Corps training with the Army, waxing our boots, rifle shooting with the Special Shooting Squad, and the 'bootcamp' are all good stories to tell. Those Oxford and Cambridge writing pads, Parker ink pens and the Bic-4 pens – I went through so many over the years. I cannot forget the life-saving Grubber for the ever-hungry teenager, especially the cheese-on-toast.

I was inspired by Mr Higgins's eye for art and Ms Golden's (Staff 1986.3–88.3) knowledge of printing and photography. Mr Bartlett equipped me with the drawing techniques which became core skills in my study of architecture.

Edward Chi Kim Tsui (Ha 1986.3)

Chapter 10 — THE WIDER WORLD

Above: Jack Meyer, his wife Joyce and the kumars from the Dhrangadhra palace school.

Below: Menu of an OH dinner in Octamund, India, 1915.

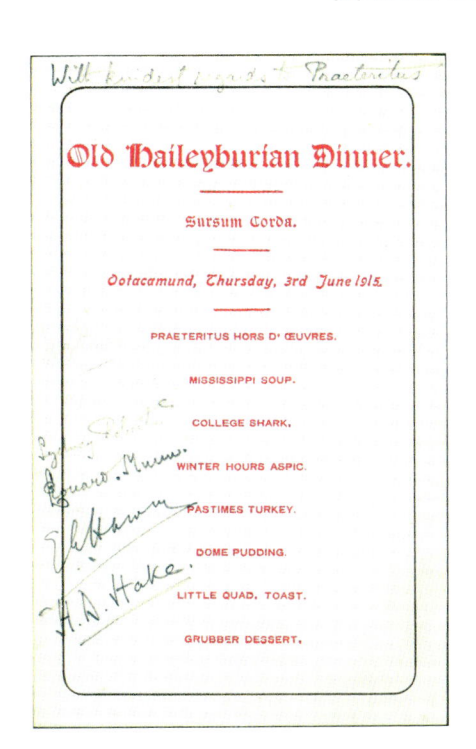

FROM HAILEYBURY TO INDIA

When John Maxwell Batten arrived at Haileybury College in the first intake of pupils on 23 September 1862, the School's connections with India and the East India College were cemented. Batten was the son of a former student at the East India College, a member of the Indian civil service, and his grandfather had been the EIC's principal. Alfred Haggard (brother of Ryder), who arrived at the same time as Batten, married a daughter of a former student of the East India College and became the first Haileyburian to serve in the Indian Civil Service. Contrary to many people's assumptions about Haileybury, however, the School was never a hothouse for the production of men for the Indian Civil Service. Compared with the numbers that Winchester, Westminster and Cheltenham produced, Haileybury's contribution was very small.

Haileybury's chief contribution to India came in the form of providing officers for the Indian Army, joining exotic-sounding regiments such as the Bengal Lancers and the Central Indian Horse. By the early 1880s there was a network of old boys in India which stretched from Kalat in the north to Mysore in the south. The dangers of soldiering in India were most commonly found on the North-West Frontier and in 1895 no less than 15 Haileyburian officers were involved in the siege and relief of Chitral. Two years later Orlando Gunning (Le B 1881.2) and Ernest Newman (BF 1881.3) found themselves at Malakand surrounded by 10,000 Pashtun tribesmen and survived to tell the tale.

The Indian Army also offered Haileyburians the chance of entering the Political Department, which assisted and administered the princely states. By the end of the 19th century Haileyburians were representing the Queen Empress in Mysore, Bhopal, Kathiawar, Jamnagar, Wadhwan, Mewar, Marwar, Nepal, Gwalior, Bharatpur, Baroda and Hyderabad, to name but a few of the states they were involved in. The Political Department and the ICS were highly sought-after posts, but they were never very far from danger. Basil Allen (M 1883.3) was attacked by 'fanatics' in Assam and A.A. Irvine (Tr 1885.1) lived on weeks' old bread during the famine in Jhelum district in 1890 because of the distance the supply carts had to travel. Haileyburians took up other roles in India as well, making a name for themselves in the Public Works Department, the Indian Medical Service and police, and as engineers for India's vast railway network. It was in these less fashionable yet vital services that Haileyburians made the most lasting contributions to India. William Appleford (M 1880.2) spent more than 30 years constructing a network of roads through Kashmir, often having to fly between projects, such was the size of his area of responsibility. While Stewart Douglas (Ha 1884.3) of the Indian Medical Service spent years investigating outbreaks of the plague for the India Office and Ernest Anson (L 1878.2), later Bursar at Haileybury, was in charge of the construction of the Calicut–Cannanore railway.

In the shadowy world of the Great Game, Haileyburians played a role, stepping in and out of the darkness of imperial intrigue. Major Ernest Redl (BF 1883.1) would appear in strategically important places along the Indian border, seemingly without any clear attachment to the military or political service, making discrete notes on Russian and tribal movements, vanishing and later popping up in another hot spot. Sir Henry McMahon (Th 1876.2), Foreign Secretary to

THE DEATH OF JAMES CADELL AND SIR PERTAB SINGH

James Dalmahoy Cadell (L 1887.2) arrived in the city of Jodhpur as a young Lieutenant in the Central India Horse, to participate in an inter-regimental polo tournament. Sadly, Cadell was stuck down with enteric fever and died on 12 January 1897 in the house of HH Maharaja Sir Pertab (Pratap) Singh, a friend of his father, and Regent of Mewar. The lack of European residents in Jodhpur at the time caused Sir Pertab and his brother to help place the body in a coffin and carry it downstairs. Sir Pertab was a Rajput of the Rathore clan, descended from the Sun. By touching a dead body he had broken the caste rules, but he believed that there was a far greater code, that of the warrior and his love for a brother officer. The news of Sir Pertab's great sacrifice for young James Cadell was eagerly taken up by papers in London and his actions were held up as a symbol of imperial chivalry. A month after Cadell's death, Sir Frederick Pollock published a poem about the event called *The Sin of Sir Pertab Singh* in the *Spectator*, which was reprinted in *The Haileyburian* the following month. Pollock was not alone in being fascinated by the creative possibilities of the tragedy – Sir Henry Newbolt, a Cliftonian, used the story of Cadell's death and Sir Pertab's kindness for his poem *A Ballad of Sir Pertab Singh*.

When Sir Pertab Singh came to Britian later that year for Queen Victoria's Diamond Jubilee he visited Haileybury on 7 July. The visit was a great success and the Maharaja was greeted ecstatically by the pupils. As he left, the entire School rushed out of the Quad to line the Avenue and cheered him on his way.

ATMP

Far left: *James Cadell.*

Below left: *The visit of Sir Pertab Singh to Haileybury in 1897.*

Below: *Sir Pertab Singh, some-time Regent of Mewar and some-time Maharaja of Idar.*

Chapter 10 — THE WIDER WORLD

the Government of India, is still remembered through the existence of the McMahon line which has been the source of considerable friction between China and India, and Arthur Hume (C 1880.1), an officer serving in the Survey of India department, was the father of military ballooning in India.

Haileybury reunions were often well attended and the menus made fond references to their alma mater. In some princely states Haileyburians made up a large part of the European community; in 1910 half of the Europeans in Tonk had been educated at Haileybury. Haileybury's relationship with India is a complicated one. The service of men like John 'Jock' Gibson (Ha 1922.1), Principal of Mayo College and the first European recipient of the Padma Shri, one of India's civil honours, to education in India is tempered by the lasting problems of Viscount Radcliffe's (L 1912.3) Partition. India was not the reason for Haileybury's foundation, but it did provide extraordinary fertile ground for many of its former pupils to flourish and leave lasting contributions to the subcontinent's history and development.

ATMP

FROM INDIA TO HAILEYBURY

Haileybury's links to the Indian subcontinent go back to the very beginnings of the School's foundation, but it was not until the Christmas term of 1912 that an Indian was educated here. In 1912, HH Maharaja Sir Pertab Singh, Regent of Mewar, entered his nephew Jagat Singh (Hi 1912.3) at Haileybury to receive a modern English education. In the first three decades of the 20th century the traditional Indian palace schools were increasingly viewed with suspicion by the political officers in the princely states as inhibiting modernisation and preventing the rulers from fully participating in the Ma-Bap relationship with Britain.

In the short period between 1912 and 1944 Haileybury had nine boys whose fathers were rulers from a number of the 350 princely states. Most of the rajkumars at Haileybury were from the west of India and the Central Province, two areas where Haileybury was strongly represented in the educational and political arenas of the Raj. John 'Jack' Meyer was one such figure, an OH with a Blue for cricket and rackets, who had made a name for himself tutoring the Rajput Jhala clan in the Western States. After teaching in Porbundar and Limbdi, Meyer was charged in 1932 with running the palace school in Dhrangadhra, one of the most important states in the region. The regime that Meyer created in the palace school was akin to an English public school; cricket was used as a vehicle to encourage confidence and where he asked the princes soul-searching questions about the responsibilities of power. In 1935 Jack Meyer returned to England with the entire Dhrangadhra palace school and founded Millfield School. In the following year Meyer sent Maharajkumar Sriraj Ghanashyamsinhji (E 1936.3), the heir to the Dhrangadhra ghadi, to Haileybury and his kinsman Kumar Shri Virendrasinhji Jorawarsinhji (A 1938.2), son of the ruler of Wadhwan, followed

Right: *Nawab Muhammad Dilawar Khanji of Junagadh, who became Haileybury's last governor on the Indian subcontinent when he was appointed Governor of Sindh in 1976.*

him two years later. One of Haileybury's international cricket players was Maharajkumar Sir Vijayananda Gajiapathi Raju (Tr 1920.3), son of the Maharaja of Vizianagaram, known simply as 'Vizzy'. After finishing his education at Haileybury and Mayo College, Vizzy went on to become an important figure in Indian cricket, captaining the national side in 1936, and later acting as President of the Board of Control for Cricket in India and a radio commentator. Vizzy, who died in 1965, remains the only cricketer to have been knighted while still an active test player. A decade later Vizzy's brothers-in-law, Hari (C 1930.1) and Raghunath (C 1930.3), sons of the Raja of Kashipur, attended Haileybury and this cricketing connection and the fact that their sister, Sita Devi, was considered one of the most beautiful women in the world at the time, gave the boys an unprecedented degree of popularity. Raghunath, a tall, handsome youth, made a name for himself as a keen sportsman and represented Colvin at rugby from his first term, while Hari became a very able boxer.

The Second World War and the Independence of India caused the steady stream of rajkumars to dry up and only one of the Haileyburian princes ever ascended the ghadi. Wali Muhammad Dilawar Khanji (Ha 1936.3), the eldest son of the eccentric and obsessive dog-fancying Nawab of Junagadh, was forced to flee the state in 1947 after his father refused to cede his state to India. A new life in Pakistan allowed Dilawar not only to succeed to his father's titles but to take an active role in political life, culminating in his appointment as Governor of Sindh in 1976. It is perhaps fitting that the last Haileyburian governor on the subcontinent should have been a native son.

ATMP

ARTHUR SHOOSMITH (Ha 1904.3)

While much has been written about Sir Herbert Baker's design for the Secretariat building in New Delhi and its relationship with the architecture of Memorial Hall, little attention has been drawn to a Haileyburian who worked on the vast project. Arthur Gordon Shoosmith was born at St Petersburg. Shoosmith trained to be an architect and, after an enforced break in his studies acting as an interpreter in the army during the First World War, he was awarded the Soane Medal by the Royal Institute of British Architects. On the back of his award of the Soane Medal, Shoosmith was employed to act as Sir Edwin Lutyens' resident architect in New Delhi. Shoosmith's job was to interpret Lutyens' designs sent over from the London office. His contributions to the fine detailing that went into the exterior and interior of the Viceregal Lodge were a testament to his understanding of the architectural traditions of India and its relevant crafts.

Although Shoosmith was a highly regarded architect he had only two of his designs built and both of those were in India. He had competed in a competition to design the Anglican and Catholic cathedrals, losing out to Henry Mead. As something of a consolation prize Shoosmith was given the commission for the garrison church of St Martin. St Martin's church on the outskirts of New Delhi was Shoosmith's masterpiece, described by one architectural historian as a 'timeless monument in brick'. The sheer physical power of the church is quite breathtaking and it is now considered to be the signal that Modernism had indeed arrived in India. After completing St Martin's and Lady Hardinge's Serail which is decorated with a huge winged heart on the central tower, Shoosmith left India in 1931 and ended his career as an inspector for the Ministry of Works.

ATMP

Below: *The brick-built Garrison church of St Martin's, New Delhi, one of only two buildings designed by Arthur Shoosmith.*

THE MAIN ROAD IN THAILAND: NAMED AFTER A HAILEYBURIAN

Sukhumvit Road is one of Thailand's main roads, covering a distance of over 400km from central Bangkok to the Cambodian border. Prasob Sukhum, after whom it is named, was born on 4 May 1899 in the south of Siam and attended Haileybury in Highfield between 1915.1 and 1916.1. His parents became increasingly concerned for his safety in war-time England, particularly after he broke his leg, and decided to move him to Phillips Exeter Academy in the United States. He later went on to MIT to study civil engineering.

In 1924, he established the American University Alumni Association in Bangkok, which gained royal patronage in 1940 and is now Thailand's oldest and most respected language-teaching centre. However, it was in the field of civil engineering that he was to make his name. In 1941 he was appointed Permanent Secretary to the Ministry of Industry and then in 1943, Secretary General to the Department of Highways, Ministry of Transport. He was bestowed with the title of Phra Bisal Sukhumvit by HM the King for his contribution to the nation as a senior government official, and the road was named after him in 1950.

Pakorn Sukhum

THE KAZAKHSTAN CONNECTION

There are only two schools in the whole of the former Soviet Union in partnership with a UK independent school and both are in Kazakhstan: Haileybury Almaty, which opened in 2008, and Haileybury Astana, which opened in 2011.

In the 1980s, whilst working at Shrewsbury School, I got to know the 'dynamo' Alister Bartholomew (Staff 1987.3–2006.2), geography teacher, Head of PE, and my predecessor as 1st XV coach, very well. In 1987, Alister left to join Haileybury, later becoming Housemaster of Edmonstone.

He later became Haileybury's Director of Development. Regular contact with Serzhan Zhumashov, a Kazakh property developer, whose eldest son had been in Edmonstone, Alister's House, had resulted in a proposal for Haileybury to open a partnership school in Almaty, with Alister subsequently working for Serzhan's company, Capital Partners.

Some considerable 'spadework' had been done before my arrival in September 2007: architect's drawings had been agreed, a promotional brochure/prospectus had been printed, an office established, and Capital Partners was in control until the big 'crash' came, which put the whole project in jeopardy. Serzhan was decisive, however: the Haileybury partnership was to go ahead and if necessary he was prepared to finance the $50m project himself.

With such great support from Capital Partners, and with Alister Bartholomew as its Director of Development, the School had to be 'launched' and a successful launch night was planned at a prestigious hotel. Haileybury UK pupils performed and Haileybury Governors were present: 200 people were expected and over 500 attended, with ensuing registrations of more than 400 for a school due to open with a maximum of 360 pupils aged 5–14 years, with accompanying kindergarten.

School fees were announced in December 2007, with a requirement to pay a further 100 per cent as a deposit. Such was the immense interest, seemingly no parents were deflected by the fee request, and in February 2008 over 400 children were assessed for the available places; this presented the difficulty of having to decline places for many children. The intention was, and still is, for Haileybury Almaty to become a co-educational school for pupils aged 5–18 years, with senior students studying for the International Baccalaureate.

The construction work appeared very slow, but recruitment of teachers and administration staff, begun in October 2007, was an ongoing consideration, with the last appointment made at the end of July 2008. During August maintenance, cleaning and security personnel were appointed and, most importantly, a catering team engaged. With the Mayor of Almaty and government education officials present, in glorious sunshine the school, only two-thirds finished, opened on 1 September 2008.

Construction work continued in an area which housed the dining hall, sports centre, swimming pool, music department, and drama studio, which necessitated sending the pupils home every day at 1pm as the School could not provide lunch during September, and postponing the extra-curricular programme until November because of the significant lack of facilities. There were internet problems, significant delays in resources and late arrival of school uniform, and demanding parents who did not fully understand the idea of Haileybury on Kazakh soil. The standard of English was universally poor, which required great patience and good teaching methods from all staff, ably supported by teaching assistants. To compound any frustrations the staff experienced at school, the accommodation arrangements on a newly completed luxury 'housing estate' proved a disappointment. Maintenance, security and the remote location made staff feel uneasy, and one by one staff moved during the year to accommodation nearer the 'bright lights' of the city.

Despite the difficulties, the staff were truly magnificent. A school routine was quickly established and pupils made aware of high expectations about their work, behaviour and dress code. A House system was introduced adopting existing Haileybury UK names: Bartle Frere, Edmonstone and Kipling, plus a new House named Attlee. The extensive extra-curricular programme included interaction between senior pupils and children from an orphanage who became weekly visitors. 'The education of the whole person' was at the heart of this school.

In December 2008 the President of Kazakhstan, Nursultan Nazarbayev, visited the School, and on his departure stated to Haileybury UK representatives: 'I like what I see; Haileybury, please open another school, in Astana.'

I was again given the pleasure, privilege and immense challenge of opening Haileybury Astana, but the timescale from drawing board to completion was going to be 17 months, with construction work beginning in earnest on 1 August 2010, and completion expected on 1 September 2011, in temperatures for at least four of these months of −20°C to −30°C.

I did not leave Haileybury Almaty until the end of 2010, so I had eight months to try to replicate the formula which had worked well in Almaty. Very similar trials and tribulations had to be faced and overcome, but on 31 August 2011, a day early, President Nazarbayev opened Haileybury Astana.

The School roll increased by over 50 per cent in its first four weeks, the staff team is very buoyant and exudes enthusiasm, teaching and learning to a good standard are happening, a 'tight' routine has been established, but 'fire fighting' continues. During a typical week in October 2011, the staff bus broke down on the way to school, the heating was still not working, rain poured into the design technology and art rooms, damaging interactive white boards and computers, significant resources were still missing, the first outbreak of nits was discovered, and many 'lost in translation' moments – some immensely frustrating but others very funny – remained a daily occurrence.

All will be well, and the link between Kazakhstan and Hertford Heath is a vibrant one, which I hope will serve countless generations of Haileyburians well in the future.

Vivat Haileyburia!

Andrew Auster
(Headmaster, Haileybury Astana 2011)

Above: *Pupils at Haileybury Astana.*

Opposite: *Opening day at Haileybury Almaty, 1 September 2008.*

Chapter 10 ∼ THE WIDER WORLD

APPENDIX

THE EAST INDIA COLLEGE: 1806–58

By the eve of the 19th century the Honourable East India Company had become a colonial power governing India. Its employees were no longer cotton traders; they were fulfilling the roles of colonial administrators, magistrates and state governors. Following criticism by Lord Cornwallis, Governor General of India from 1786 to 1793, it came under pressure to make its civil service more 'professional'. In 1800 the then Governor General Lord Wellesley founded an independent 'University of the East' to educate civil servants, prompting the East India Company to set up a 'Committee of College' in 1804 to look into the idea of its own specialised college.

The Committee's subsequent report recommended the teaching of oriental languages, histories and customs. It seemed that young 'writers' had been going out to India with little or no understanding of whom they were going to administer. The report concluded that the idea of a special college 'peculiarly adapted to the education of young men destined for India was a thing very much wanted'. A suitable site was found just north of London, in the village of Hertford Heath, previously owned by a Dr William Walker, late of the East India Service. It was there that the young architect William Wilkins designed the magnificent Quadrangle of the College. The site was not ready until 1809, so for its first three years the College was housed in Hertford Castle.

To be considered for a place, potential students had be nominated by an existing Director of the Company. More than 2,000 students passed through the College Quad between 1806 and 1858. Although their backgrounds varied, candidates all gained their nomination as a consequence of a personal relationship between the nominating director and a

Below: *The Haileybury Dilly, by Philip Charles Trench (EIC 1826) which took students at the East India College to the neighbouring towns.*

APPENDIX

Left: *The carved bench, originally placed in Big School, illustrates the strong familial connections between the East India College and Haileybury. There are at least four families (the Roberts, the Lawrences, the Hobart-Hampdens and the Saptes) who attended both institutions.*

family member or friend of the petitioner. This system was criticised for creating a closed social 'elite' which subsequently ran India. A major change occurred only with the 1853 Government of India Act, which abolished the patronage system and established the Indian Civil Service examinations for candidates from any educational establishment. Although this opened up India to non-College men, the College was still arguably the best place to train for the role. Sir Charles Wood, in a preliminary version of the Act, had considered it 'the only suitable place' for education of this kind and Trevelyan even stated that it 'furnishes a very satisfactory system of special instruction for the Indian Civil Service'.

The College had many positive features. Staff appointments were of the highest quality. Professors, such as the Reverend Thomas Malthus, were eminent in their field of study. His appointment as Professor of History and Political Economy was also innovative as it predates the establishment of such a chair at Cambridge University. With the teaching of oriental languages, the College was the first to use 'moonshees', indigenous Indian support teachers, and in 1826 it was the first to appoint a non-European professor of Persian and Arabic, Mirza Mohammed Ibrahim, a Persian. The College was some years ahead of the universities in the teaching of Indian languages, with the Boden Chair of Sanskrit being endowed at Oxford only in 1832. The curriculum was roughly divided into four subject areas that would be useful for future careers in India: oriental literature; mathematics and natural philosophy; classical and general literature; law, history and political economy.

One of the main criticisms of the College was the issue of ill-discipline. In 1817 it was reported that the principal had been chased 'by a dog with a tin kettle tied to his tail' and a tutor was allegedly beaten. The College was also criticised for not meeting the recruitment demands of the Indian Civil Service. Between 1815 and 1820 the College sent an average of 34 'writers' out to Bengal, Madras and Bombay. In 1823 the government of Bengal alone asked for 80 'writers'. It was also argued that the College was not economically viable. With the EIC itself in a precarious position by the 1850s it could not subsidise the College in the longer term. The 1855 Government of India Act, 'An Act to relieve the East India Company from the obligation to maintain the College at Haileybury', signalled the end of the College. Less than a year before its 50th birthday it was earmarked for closure and given two years to clear out its remaining students. The EIC was itself abolished in 1858.

Despite its forced closure, the general opinion was that the quality of the Indian civil service had been improving since the establishment of the College. In the 1864 Government of India, six of the 11 men were old College men, including Trevelyan and Lawrence. The last EIC governor of an Indian province was in post in 1891, more than 30 years after the closure.

Although the grounds remained derelict for four years after the closure, a local consortium, purchased the site and opened a new school in 1862. Some legacy of the College remains today in the Quadrangle buildings and the grounds. The success of the College's former pupils and service of its Principals have too been immortalised in the form of House names. Current and past pupils will be well acquainted with the names of Bartle Frere, Lawrence, Edmonstone, Colvin and Thomason and of old Principals Batten, Melvill and Le Bas. The legacy of the East India College will remain in the memory for as long as the present school survives.

David Oldridge (BF 1995.3)

EXPLANATORY NOTES ON SOME HAILEYBURY TERMS

A short guide to some of the words found in the book.
(In compiling this list the Editors are fully aware that the meaning of some of the terms change with the generations.)

Aquatics: The annual House and individual swimming competition.

Ascension Day: A *given* day (holiday) to celebrate the School's name day which began in 1897, used to explore the county. The hymn *Lift up your Hearts* was sung on this day in 1899.

Bath, the: The original Swimming Pool, dug in 1863 on the site of the Hospital Pond.

Blue's Metrical Alphabets: Annual song at the Lawrence House Entertainments which used the alphabet to sum up events in the previous year. In 1868 the song began *Haileybury brothers, I think that you may see/ Signs of the times in the A B C/ A is for All of us, and B is for the Best/ Butler was and Bradby is, The Blues make up the rest...*

Beak: Assistant master/teacher. *The Beak* was the name used for the Master at various times. The ISC used *tramp* as an alternative to *beak*.

Blood: Member of the XV, XI and VI. Also known as a *swell*.

Caesar's Grave: Large flower bed between the Study Wing (now Batten) and the road by Pavilion. Claimed to be the site of the grave of 'Pongo' Vaughan's dog, Caesar, although some people claim the dog was called Sailor. Destroyed in 2010 to make way for parking.

Cap Room: The room that stocked caps, hats, braces, ribbons, laces, neckties etc. Situated next to the Book Room close to the Lodge.

Carrying the Ball: Ceremony in which the Captain of Cock House carried the Ball around Quad followed by the House.

College: Originally the confines of the Quad (1871); those who lived in the Quad Houses were at times called *collegians*. Used as a prefix, *College* was used in the nineteenth century to denote something that was beastly, bad or sub-standard such as *College Shark*, meaning bad/dubious fish. *School* as a prefix was much more positive, while to describe some one as *Hailey House* was to label them as contemptible. To use the label *Common Room* in conjunction with food or life in general meant something was good quality/worthy of praise. *Schooo-oool* was the tolerated cry from the side of Terrace Field when the XV played in 1900.

College Bells: Bells that chimed when the College Clock (housed in Clock House) struck the quarter, half, three quarter and hour. These bells were distinct from the Secular/Lists Bell and the Chapel Bell.

Convivium: A dinner/banquet paid for and hosted by the President of the Senior Literary and Debating Society, these two conditions had to be met for it to be called a *Convivium*.

Dardanelles, the: Two passages on the east side of (Great) Quad, linking it with Little Quad. The Lower Dardanelles is between Old Studies and Big School while the Upper Dardanelles is next to Thomason Housemaster's house. The name may have derived from the narrowness of the passages being likened to the constricted straits connecting the Sea of Marmara to the Aegean Sea.

Dates: Punishment given in multiples of X3, X5 and X10. Master, Edward Lyttelton claimed to have developed the idea for the punishment while teaching at Eton but so to did 'Po-face' Milford and Wardlaw Kennedy. The miscreant had to copy out important historical dates, each date being approximately ten lines long. The *Dates Card*, developed by William Fenning, was purchased at the Book Room with **Dates Paper** which was originally the size of two pieces of foolscap. Any offender given X15 in a week was entered in the *Date Book*. A *Dates Ticket* was a chit sent to the HM by a beak who set X10 Dates or more with an explanation of the crime. To receive X10 was known as a being given a *Poem*. It was a duty of the Head of History from time to time, to revise the *Dates Card*.

DCR: Dormitory Classroom, more commonly called the DC.

Elysium: Formed by invitation with no more than nine members, the Head of the School was always a member. Originally Elysium was a room at the top of the stairs in the Porter's Lodge, then the Library gallery and finally in a private room in Hall. Members of Elysium could dine separately from the rest of the School and entertained new beaks to breakfast on Sundays and later to dinner. This institution no longer exists.

Foreign: Not one's own. Matches against other schools were called *foreign matches* while other houses were called *foreign dormitories*.

Groise: Term used to describe butter, grease and margarine. A *groiser* was a pupil who sought to ingratiate themselves with others. *Groisey* was to behave in an oily or smarmy manner. It could also be spelt *Groize* and mean to be greasy. A *groizebin* was a dustbin.

Grubber, the: The informal name for the Grub Shop or The Shop. Purveyor of grub/food to pupils. *Grubbing* was generally used to describe eating outside of formal meal times; *study grubbing* was the pooling of monies by the members of the study to buy food for cooking, something Edward Bradby could not stand, or merely the act of eating in the study. *Study grubs* was the name for these collective 'feasts. *Grub nights* were on Saturday and Sunday evenings when meals did not have to be taken in Hall. The *XV grubs* was beer, provided after matches. In the mid-nineteenth century *to grub* also meant to work hard.

Hags' Bags: Laundry bags. *Hags* were, in this case, Matrons and their rooms. Matrons were also known as *Patch Hags* to differentiate them from *Hatch Hags*, the women who served at the Dining Hall hatches, while the char-ladies were known, somewhat ironically, as *nymphs*.

Hoips: The many. Those who played games below House teams. Derived from the *Hoi Polloi*, they were also known as the *Baby Side*. The term *Hoi Polloi*, was also described by members of Elysium as everybody else.

Hour, the: Originally time put aside for private tuition. Abolished in 1974.

KBM: The Kipling, Batten and Melvill Block, constructed in 1879. The building that housed Kipling, Batten and Melvill. With the closure of the original Melvill it is also known as the KB Block.

Little Tea: Refreshments taken in the afternoon in Hall and initially by subscription only. In 1962.1 the institution was described as continuing to 'attract hordes and the problem of disorder in quad'.

Mississippi, the: The Woollensbrook. A small stream flowing below Hailey Lane.

New Gov'nor: Term used to describe those pupils in their first term. The definition of a Gov'nor may have been coined because they govern nobody and everybody governs them. A *Gov'nor* was a pupil who had not been in the School for a year. The spellings *Gov'nor*, *Guv'nor* and *Governor* are interchangeable. Owing to the hierarchical nature of school life the term *Gov'nor* was split into *First Termer*, *Second Termer* and *Third Termer* by pupils.

Plebs: Tea taken in the Dining Hall during the Half. An early version of *Plebs* that was only taken on Saturdays and Sundays was known as the *Tea fight*.

Quad: Today used to describe Main Quad, also known as Great Quad, designed by William Wilkins. New Quad later known as Little or Small Quad was created when the KBM Block was built. Allenby also had their own Little Quad which was used to play a peculiar form of cricket. Scholars' or Classics Quad (really a court) is the space between the Form Rom Block and the Lodge while Memorial Quad was created by Sir Herbert Baker behind Clock House at the same time as Memorial Dining Hall.

Shops: The workshops for woodwork and engineering.

Stripes and Whites: The rugby jerseys used at school, the stripes were in fact dark blue hoops on white. *Stites* was a much used variation on the term *Stripes and Whites* combined the three words into one. Matches were played between Houses wearing the jerseys to differentiate each other, as there were no House jerseys in the nineteenth century and first four years of the twentieth century.

Talbot's Mount: A mound of earth that has since become part of the landscape behind the Squash Courts. The earth came from the excavations to create Memorial Quad and the Dining Hall. A favoured place with smokers.

Wings: Awarded for *Aquatics*/swimming. A white fabric winged heart badge, later a tie.

LIST OF SUBSCRIBERS

This book has been made possible through the generosity of the following subscribers.

Mark Adams	Roger Bass	Martin P. Bray	Jordan Carter
Aristomenis I. Xanthopoulos Agapitos	Phoebe Bassett	Nicola Bray	Rhys Carter
Adrian Allan	Tomiris Batalova	Peter J.L. Bray	James Cassidy
Chloe Allen	Edouard Bayford	Robert Bray	Sarah Cassidy
John B. Allinson	Mark W. Beaumont	Nigel Hugh Richard Bridges	Eugenia Castro-Lago
Adil Alshinbaev	Peter G. Bennett	Charis Bridgman Baker	Dr Tina Challacombe
George Edward Alstrom	James Bentley	Livia Bridgman Baker	Natalie Caroline Cheng
Arman Amirzhan	Martyn Best	Persephone Bridgman Baker	E.E.L. Clark
R.G. Anderson	Elliot Bester	J.D.H. Briggs	E.M. Clark
Megan Olivia Andrews	John Bettinson	R.E.S. Brimelow	Barry Clarke
Stephen J.E. Angus	Henry Bexson	John Brock	W.B. Clarke
Nick Armstrong-Flemming	M.C. Black	Kathryn S. Brooks	Alice Clough
Christine Arrowsmith (née Taylor)	P.A. Blair	Calum Bryce	C.D.A. Cochran
John Atkinson	Mark Blandford-Baker	James Bryce	The Conrad Family
Nigel Atkinson	Dominic Boakes	Peter Budden	John H. Conyngham
Air Vice Marshal Don Attlee	David H.W. Bolton	Joanna Burch	Dr John B. Cook
Rotimi Awotesu	E. Bond	Simon Burrows	J.R.L. Cook
Hugo Bagnall-Oakeley	Matthew Bond	Alexander Burton	Timothy Cope
David F. Bailey	Sam Boothby	Alex Campbell	Jake Courtney
Major Michael A.B. Balcon	Jeremy Bourne Swinton Hunter	Ben Campbell	Christopher Crowder
David Baldwin	James Bowles	Hugo James Cannon	Noah Cummins
Colin T. Barber	Luke Brace	Charlie Carr	Oliver Cummins
John D. Barber	Hugh Bradley	Susannah Carr	Tristan Cummins
Hanna Bartholomew	Julia Bradley	Ben Carter	Michael Neale Dalton
Katharine Bartholomew	Katie Brasher (née Healy)	Blake Carter	Squadron Leader M.E. Dark RAF
Oliver Bartholomew	Andrew N. Bray	Gillian Carter	(Retd)

LIST OF SUBSCRIBERS

Chris Darnell
D.C. Dauban
Barnaby L. Davis
Sebastian J. Davis
Guy de Lisle Dear
Alice Death
Luigi Del Basso
Jane Digweed
Luke Dinwoodie
Simon Dodge
Revd Gerald A. Drew
Peter Duggan
N.P.W.G. Edmiston
P.A.C. Edwardes
John Edwards
Dr Mark Elliott
Eralp O.M. Ertekun
M. Evens
E. Jane Everard (née Etherington)
I.D. Everard
Henry Everest
Brian C. Fawcett
Tom Fazakerley
Ronald Feather
Peter M. Fielding
Tim Fillingham
Alex Firth
Patrick Ian FitzGerald
Nicholas Feyintola Folarin-Coker
Rory Fowler
Maisie Franklin
Michael J. Freegard
David Frere-Cook
Miguel Freudenthal
Katrin Fritz
Lars Fuhrmann
Rodney Galpin
George Garthwaite
James Garthwaite
Graham Gatenby
Stephanie Gates
The Gatward Family
Humphrey Gillott
Roland Gillott

James Gilpin
A.R. Godfrey
Natasha Godlee
Olivia Godlee
Rebecca Godlee
Helena Goodman
Katie Goodman
Michael Goodrich
Matthew Goodson
Tanya Graham
Hannah Grint
Thomas Grint
Jonathan Hall
R.C.S. Hall
Michael J. Halsey
Andrew Hambling
Linda Hambling
Ian and Elizabeth Hamilton
Maximilian R. Hamilton
Niall Hamilton
Professor Tony Harker
David Harries
Tory Hart
Duncan and Elspeth Harvey
Jessica Alice Harvey
Luke Raithe Harvey
Francesca Heaton
Georgina Heaton
R.J. Hedges
Alexander Henderson
Adrian G. Henson
Hannah Hinkelmann
Ollie Hirschfield
Konrad K.W. Holtsmark
Olav J.W. Holtsmark
A.M.D. Horne
David Horne
Edward Horne
George Horne
Jessica Horne
Emma Horsburgh
Tom Horsburgh
Mrs K.G. Hoskins
R. Anthony D. Howard

James Howlett
George Hudson
Mr and Mrs Adam J. Hughes
David Hunt
Revd I. Paton Hunter
Sir Alastair Innes Bt
Malcolm J. Innes
Panos Ioannou
William Irving
Michael Jacoby
Emily James
Richard James
Andrew Jobson
Stephen Jobson
Dale Johnson
Hugh I.L. Jones
Leanna Jones
Ian P.D. Jory
Oliver Josephs
Mr and Mrs Michael Jowett
Josephine Kau
George Langton Kendall J.P. O.St.J.
Edward Key
Amirul Khalid
Ammar Khalid
Amnan Khalid
Anushea Khalid
Sam King
Toby King
Edward Klein (in memoriam)
Harry Bruce Klein
Elisabeth Koehler
Norbert Schmitz-Koep
M. James Kondo
Natasha Kumar
Tanya Kumar
Simon Kverndal QC
Michael J. Lansdown
A.D.H. Lapidus
Richard Lawrence
Lucinda Lee-Bapty
Charlotte Lennox
Padraig Lennox
Jeremy S.L. Lenox

Phil Linnell
Ines Loeffler
Derek Longman
A.D. Low
Richard G. Low
Alexander Lunn
Christopher Lunn
Virginia E.M. Macgregor
   (née Woods)
M.A.F. MacPherson of Pitmain
Botazhan Makhambetova
David Malcolm
Emma Malcolm
Christopher G. Marks
Adam Markwell
Nicholas Markwell
Rhiannon Massey
William Massey
Jacqueline Mayer (née Wright)
Peter B. Maynard OBE
Alex McCormick
Simon McGuire
Mike McMorrow
Harry Meek
Izzy Meek
Nick Meredith
Marcus Merkenich
Moritz Merkenich
David Miles
Mrs K.L. Millar
Luke Miller
Stephen Miller
Andrew Mills
Siena Milner
Alice Moniz
Gabrielle Moniz
Sophie Moniz
Thomas Moniz
Charles Monk
Ben Morris
Paul Morris
C. Muirhead-Hernandez
Kenneth Munn
Tezay Mustafa

201

Stefanie Nacke
W.M.C. Newcomb MC
John Newham
John Nicholas
Ben Nicholls
Benjamin E.J. Nichols
John Nichols
Andrew Nolan
Fiona Rachel Norris
Sara Louise Norris
Adrian Norrman
Roger Eliphalet Nott
Thomas Philip John Oliver
Charlotte Orford
Barry Osman
Carol Osman
Geoffrey Page (in memoriam)
C.M. Parsons
John Parsons
Andreas Payne
Militsa Payne
David Pearce
Frederick E. Pearson
The Phillips Family
Ben Phillips
John E. Phillips
John M. Phillips
Max Phillips
Alistair Philpott
Matthew Philpott
Rosanna Philpott
Claudia Pittatore
Marco Pittatore
Jack William Henry Price
Katie Louise Price
Simon Nicholas Price
Richard Prickett

Andrew Prosser
Dr Laura Pugsley
M.R.J. Radley
Bill Rankin
J. Peter Rauch
Christoph Rauhut
Sir Peter Reynolds CBE
Richard Rhodes James
John Rice
Callum Richardson
Gabriella Richardson
Robin Rickman
Dr Patrick Ridsdill Smith
David Rimmer
Mark Roach
Lauren F. Parkinson Roberts
Georgina Robertson
John Romer
David John Ross
Henrike Ruehl
Fiona Rumboll
Peter Sapte
Christopher Saunders
Toby Saysell
Edward Sennett
Alexander Shambrook
Felix Sharman
J.C.P. Sharp
Rowena Sharp
Reena and Aran Shaunak
D.C. Shaw
David N. Sheasby
Yunosuke Shimizu
Nicholas Shirley
Henry S. Short
James Edward Sibley
Jack Sitwell

Louie Sitwell
Martin Skan
A.R.E. Slingsby
Angus F. Smith
James Smith
Lucy H. Smith
Tom R. Smith
Charles Sohrab
Claudia Sohrab
Louisa Rose Sorensen
Babajide Sotande-Peters
Maxim Souter
Luke South
Natasha South
Ann Spavin
Chris Spencer
Ian Springall
Katie Stanyard
Will Stanyard
Regina Steinmeyer
David (Sam) Stevens
Richard Neal Straker-Ball
N.R. Strange
María de los Ángeles Suárez-Castro
Constantino Suárez-Tobares
Michael Thacker
Berenice Thilloy
Annie Thomas
Revd R.F. Thomas
Jonathan Thompson
Mr and Mrs S.J. Thompson
James P.S. Thomson
Simon John Thwaites
Chris Topping
James Trafford
Jonathan Tritton
Edward Chi Kim Tsui

Chris Turnbull
David Turnbull
Jenny Turnbull
Rob Turnbull
David Twigg
Sam Tyler
William W. Vanderfelt
Nigel Venning
Lt Gen. Sir Richard Vickers
Lex Vis
Catherine Vooght
William Vooght
J.M. Walker
Rebecca Wall
Donald Walsh
Michael Ward
The Warlow Family
A.D. Watkinson
G.N. Watkinson
W.H. Watkinson
Major General Bryan Webster
Jemma Webster
Michael Wells
Mike Wheeler
Jeffrey H. White
Jonathan White
C.T.T. Whitehead
Robin Widdows
Jemima Willgoss
Erica Wilson
Robin F.S. Wilson
Patrick C.C. Winterburn
Tim Woffenden
Abigail Wood
Francesca Wood
Martin and Sally Woodcock
Ed Wright

INDEX

Page numbers in bold denote authorship. Those in italics indicate illustrations.

Aberdeen, Lord 70
Abraham, Alexander *144*
Adams, Charles Wilfrid 158
Adams, Paul 62
Adonis, Lord 22
Aitkens, Michael 84
Albright, C.J. *54*
Alcibiades 27
Aldenham, Lord 28
Allchin, Geoffrey 114
Allen, Basil 189
Allenby, Edmund (Viscount) 19, *19*, 114, 128, *129*, 129
Allinson, John **135**
Anderson, Alexander (Alec) 78, 79, 175
Anderson, Petri 176
Andrews, Robin **144**
Anslow-Wilson, D.S.A. *54*
Anson, Ernest 189
Anyaoku, Chief Emeka 163
Appleford, William 189
Archer, A.G. 62
Archer, Jeffrey 162
Arnold, Dr Thomas 25, 48, 52
Ash, Edward *50*
Ashcroft, Robert 46, 90, 92, 102, 129, 147, 158
Ashkenazy, Vladimir 80
Atherton, Mr 43
Athey, Neil 66, **66–7**
ATMP (*see* Parker, Toby)
Attlee, Clement 38, 95, 99, *124*, 124–5, 160, 161, 162–3
Auster, Andrew 22, 24, **193–4**

Austin, Stephen 10, 91
Ayckbourn, Sir Alan 39, 72, *73*, 73, 83–4
Ayrton, Maxwell 33, 40
Ayrton, Michael 71

Bach, J.S. 78
Bairnsfather, Bruce 158
Baker, Sir Brian *132*, 132
Baker, Sir Herbert 117, 172, 175, 192
Baker, William 10
Baker-White, Mark 62
Balcon, Michael **142**
Baldwin, Alfred 30
Baldwin, Robert 160
Balfe, Michael 100
Ballam, S.R. *54*
Band, Jonathon 137
Banes, George 107
Banks, Edward **63**
Barber, A.T. 43
Barber, Colin 137
Barber, John 114
Barett, Thomas 11
Barnett, John (*see* Stagg, John Reginald)
Barraud, Francis Phillip 172
Bartholomew, Alister 193
Bartle Frere, Sir Henry 14–18
Bartlett, Donald 178
Bartlett, Ken 53, 83, 97, 188
Barton, R.H. 165
Bass, Fontella 156
Bass, Roger 36, **97–8**

Batten, John Hallet 123
Batten, John Maxwell 189
Batten, Reverend Joseph 19, 21, 177
Baugh, John 57
Beatty, David 29
Beaumont, 'Binkie' 86
Beaumont, Reverend Martin **173**
Becker, Hugh 114
Beckett, Francis 162
Beckwith, Edward 124
Beethoven, Ludwig van 98
Beggs, Rachel 83
Behrend, John Arthur Henry 100, 101
Bell, Mr 95
Benham, Jack *135*, 135
Betjeman, John 179
Billings, Jessica 50
Billings, Sam 62, *63*
Bird, Mary *58*
Birkett, J.G.G. 46
Bishop, Robin *88*
Blackmore, Malcolm 58
Blair, Peter **164–7**
Blair, Tony 84, 163
Blakeway Smith, David *130*, **130–3**
Blomfield, Sir Arthur 11, 21, 27, 174
Blomfield, Sir Reginald 26, 37, 124, 129, 144, 172, 174, 175
Bloom, Mark Alex **119**
Blunt, Wilfrid 37, *38*, 38, 157
Blyth, William *42*, 42
Bolsover, Mike **54–5**
Bolton, David **94**, **111**
Bond, M.E.T. *54*

Bonhote, Canon Edward 28, 29, 73, 90, 106, *107*, 107, 114–5, 142, 144, 175
Bookless, Lloyd 173
Bourdillion, Francis 100
Bowen, Beth 156
Bowen, Kate **127**, *126*
Bowers, The Very Reverend George 9, *9*, 10
Boyle, Alan Reginald 134
Bradby, Mrs 27
Bradby, Captain Edward 25
Bradby, Reverend Dr Edward H. 13, 25–7, *26*, 36–7, 42, 48, 101, 102, 123, 149, 174
Bradshaw, David 183
Brain, Dennis 80
Brammer, Julian 46
Bream, Julian 80
Bretherton, James 57
Bretherton, Luke 178
Briant, Shane *86*, 86
Briggs, Reverend Chris **171–2**, *171*
Brimelow, Nick 57
Britten, Benjamin 78
Brock, John 114–6, **124**, **143–4**
Brooke, William *50*
Brooke-Popham, Henry *133*, 133
Brown, Fred 70
Brown, Freddie 43
Brown, Reverend Charles Henry 158
Bryans, Herbert 176, 179
Buchan, John 159
Buchanan, John 152
Bulmer, Andrew 114

203

Burch, Jo 118
Burchett, Ebenezer 69
Burnaby, John 178
Burne-Jones, Edward 30
Burnett, Charles 114
Burntwood, Lord 160
Burrow, E.J. 33, 37
Burton, Peter 137
Burton, Tim 86
Bushell, J.H. 54
Butler, Reverend Arthur Gray 9, *10*, 10, 11–12, *12*, 13, 19, 22–4, 25–6, 30, 37, 45, 46, 48, 93, 102, 162
Butler, Bob 39
Butler, David 162
Butler, Henry Montagu 100
Butler, Montagu 100
Butler, R.A. 'Rab' 100
Button, Mark *155*
Byrd, William 77
Bywater, Kenton 82

Cadell, James Dalmahoy *190*, 190
Caine, Michael 157
Cambridge, HRH the Duke of 27
Came, Rick 111
Camp, Bill *43*
Campbell, George 'William' 42
Campbell, Sir Ronald 136–7
Campbell-Bannerman, Sir Henry 188
Campling, John 105
Capper, Sir Thompson 176
Carlisle, Arthur 187
Carr, Charlie *51*
Carr, Simon 162
Carrington, Charles 80, 158
Casimir, Tony 76, 77
Caswell, M.B. *54*
Chaplin, Charlie 144
Chaplin, Harold 76
Chapple, Sir John 80, **80–1**, 128–9, *129*
Charlton, Cedric 'Charley' 84
Chatterton, E. *177*
Chaucer, Geoffrey 95
Chelmsford, Lord 28
Chessyre, John 12
Cheston, E.C. 46
Chick, John **92–4**
Chilcott, Bob 78
Childers, Erskine 157, *163*, 163
Childers, Molly *163*

Chitty, Thomas David **105–8**
Christian of Schleswig-Holstein, HRH Princess 124
Churcher, T.S. *54*
Churchill, Winston 135, 162, 163
Chuter, C.D. *54*
Clark, Albert Charles 158
Clark, Roly **127–8**, *128*
Clarke, Betty 152
Clarke, James 126
Clarke, 'Weary' 184
Clement-Jones, Tim **112**
Clerihew Bentley, Edmund 89
Clive, Sir Robert 136
Coates, M.O. *54*
Cobb, Colin 46, 97, 147
Cochran, C.D.A. **56**, **58**, **150**
Cogan, Jim 125
Coghill VC, Nevill 21, 89
Cohen, Philip 91
Coldham, G.J. 60
Coldham, George 47
Cole, Peter 46
Collier, Paul 179
Colvin, John 123
Conyngham, John **185–6**
Cook, Dawn *54*
Cook, Douglas 'Killer' *52*, 52–4
Cook, John **149–50**
Cook, Mrs M. *54*
Cooke, D.H. 46
Cooper, M.C. *54*
Copeland, Sergeant Major 43
Copinger, Michael 124
Copland, Aaron 78
Cornwallis, Lord 196
Cottrell, Henry 101
Couchman, Henry 16, 18, 19
Coward, Andrew *118*
Cranborne, Lord 163
Cromwell, Oliver 13
Crowder, C.M.D. *110*
Cruikshank, George 179

Dalrymple Bruce, Clarence 188
Dankworth, Johnny 80
Darbishire, David 135
Darlington, Sir Charles 95
Darnell, Chris 99, **113–4**
Daubeney, Sir Charles 27
Davies, Joe 22, **22–4**, 89, *103*, 150
Davies, John Howard 87
Davis, Peter 78, 79

Davy Burnaby, George 85
Dawes, Rhodri 63
Day, Harry 'Wings' Melville Arbuthnot 133, 137
de Bec, Geoffrey 33
de Bernières, Louis 78
de Freitas, Geoffrey 160
de Neuville, Alphonse 157
Delmar-Morgan, Curtis 138
Dempsey, Joe 82, 83
Denny, Sir Michael *138*
Denny, William *38*
Devi, Sita 192
Dexter, Lucy *154*
Dexter, Ray **48–50**
Dhar, Govind 162
Dhrangadhra, Maharajkumar Sriraj Ghanashyamsinhji of 191
Diak, Rodney (see Jones, David)
Dickinson, C.H. 49
Dickson, Sir William 128, *130*, 130–2
Dimock, Richard **121–2**
Dimsdale, Robert 10
Dixon, Andrew Graham 71
Dixon, Steve 89
Dobbie, D.C.F. *54*
Dodd, Martin 82
Doors, The 114
Dorset, George 42
Douglas, Stewart 189
Dove, Reverend Julian 69
Dowling, Paul **180**
Drury, C.A.J. *54*
du Toit, Andrew 185
Duff, P.M. *54*
Dunn, Arthur 60
Durden-Smith, Richard 86
Duruflé, Maurice 78

Edinburgh, Duke of 23, 66–7
Edmonstone, Sir George 18, *185*, 185
Edward, Prince 67
Edwards, E.B.A. (Basil) 76, 80
Eisenhower, Dwight 132
Eliot, T.S. 185
Elizabeth II, HM Queen 23, *23*, 61, 158
Elkan, Benno 18
Elliot, Kirsten *155*
Ellis, Peter 62, 90

Fair, Major 'Bull' 147

Fairbairn, Alan 62, 144, *110*
Fairlie, Mr *54*
Fairport Convention 186
Fauré, Gabriel 78
Fawcett, B.C. *54*
Fender, Percy 43
Fenning, Reverend William 46
Field, Frank 163
Firbank, Ronald 179
Fitzgibbon, G. *54*
Flemyng, Benjamin 'Robert' 85–6
Flint Cahan, Rupert 166
Ford-Robertson, Julian 150
Ford, David 59
Forest, Baron 133
Forsyth, Frederick 162
Fowkes, H.C.F. *54*
Fowler, Owen 184
Fox, William 85
Foyle, Dr 39
Francis, Clive 73
Franks, Philip 84
Fraser-Andrews, James 82
Fraser, Nicholas 48
Freegard, Michael **7**, **56**
French, Reverend Thomas Valpy 123
Frend, W.H.C. 178
Frontini, Dalia 75, *166*
Frost, Terry 71
Fullagar, Brende 72, 73
Furse, Charles Wellington 69–70, 71, 72

Gambon, Michael 73
Gandon, Amy 166
Gandon, Nick 62
Gascoyne, George 69
Gavin, Bryan 105
Gaye, Howard 85
George VI, King 23, *23*
George, Ian 46, **48**
George, Jamie 48
George, Tom 48
Gibson, John 'Jock' 191
Gilbert, D.C. *54*
Gilbert, W.S. 76
Gill, A.A. 48
Gillott, Humphrey **113**
Gladstone, William 70
Glasmacher, Barbara 151
Glover, S.P. *54*
Goatcher, J.W. *54*
Godfrey, A.R. 46

INDEX

Godfrey, M.E. *54*
Godley, Sir Alexander *129*
Golden, Ms 188
Golding, R.W. *54*
Goodman, Lord 99–100
Gosse, Phillip Henry 187
Gough, Lionel 158
Gove, Michael 22
Grainger, Stewart 85
Gray, R.F. *54*
Greatorex, Christopher 84
Greer-Walker, M. *54*
Gregory, David 48
Greig, Miranda 84
Gresford Jones, H. *177*
Groves, J.C. *54*
Gubbins, Richard 101
Guinness, Arthur 150
Gunning, Orlando 189
Gurdon, Charles 45, *46*, 46, 47
Gurdon, Edward Temple 46, *46*, 47, 47

Haggard, Alfred 11, 189
Haggard, Ryder 189
Haggard, Stephen 85
Hailsham, Lord *161*, 162
Hake, H.D. 61
Hallet, Edward Hughes 11
Hambling, Andrew 23, 45–6, 90, *91*, **91–2**, 113
Hames, Tim 163
Hamilton, Guy *86*, 87
Hamilton, Sir Hubert 28
Hammond, Wally 62
Hankin, Matthew 48
Hardcastle, M.W. *54*
Hardinge, Lady 192
Hardy, Thomas 76
Hargreaves, Harry 'Hotplate' 118, 150
Harley, Nigel 110
Harold, King 33
Harper, Anthony **117**
Harper, Gerald 84
Harris, James 136
Harris, Kenneth 162
Harris, T.G. *54*
Harrison, N.S. 62
Harrison, N.S.A. 49
Hart, C.E. *54*
Harte, H.G. 19
Hartnigk, Carmen 160

Harvey, Elspeth **158–9**, 158
Harvey, Jonathan 59
Harvie IV, J. 'Jim' B. 114
Harwood, Felicity 162
Haug, Simon **121**
Havergal, Henry 175
Havers, C.I.P. *54*
Hawdon, Kynard 188
Hawkins, Steve 40
Hawtrey, Reverend Stephen 21
Haywood, F.M. 83
Haywood, M. 101
Head, Angus **87**
Hearn, Dan 46, 84, **94–5**, 113, *161*, 160–3, 163, 185
Heath, Sir Edward *161*, 162
Hedges, Richard **108–10**
Heming, Michael 79
Henderson, Reverend W.G. 10
Hennessy, Peter 162
Henry of Battenberg, Princess *23*, 23
Hensley, Reverend Augustus 11, *12*, 13, 14, 16, 19
Herbert, Bernard Theodore 158
Herbert, Right Reverend Christopher 99
von Herkomer, Sir Herbert 26
Heron, Patrick 71
Higgins, J.D. (John) 39, 157, 188
Hill, Gerald 28
Himmler, Heinrich 137
Hindmarsh, Jack 36, *36*, 38, 76, *77*, 78, 79, 80, 118
Hitchcock, Alfred 85
Hitler, Adolf 136
Hoare, G.J. *54*
Hollington, Basil 62
Hornett, Rose 147
Hoskyns 12th Bt, Reverend Sir Edwyn *50*, 123–4
Hoskyns 13th Bt, Reverend Sir Edwyn 178
Hoste, George 9, 11, 14, 186
Hoste, Henry 'Skipper' 186
Howard, Michael 163
Howarth, Geoff 62, 90
Howe, Jack *41*
Howell, David 162
Hubback, R.P. *54*
Huckin, Tom **55–6**
Hudson, Cecil **41–3**
Hughes, Martin 39
Hughes, F.M. *54*

Hume, Arthur 191
Hunt, David 40, **95–7**
Hunt, Justin **40**, 40
Hurt, John 86
Hylton-Stewart, Bruce 174–5

Illingworth (née Short), Fiona **179**
Infantino, Antonio 49
Innes, Malcolm **52–3**, *54*
Insoll, Christopher 71
Irvine, A.A. 189
Isaacs, Sergeant 70

Jackson, John Hampden 158
Jankowski, Horst 114
Jeans, Reverend George 69
Jellicoe, Father Basil 177–8, *178*
Jenkins, Roy 162
Jewell, David *161*, 177
Johns, Peter 46
Johnston, 'Jaggers' *93*
Johnston, M.A.B. 136
Jolliffe, J.F. *54*
Jones, Benjamin 116
Jones, Sir Clement 112
Jones, David 85, 86
Junagadh, Wali Muhammad Dilawar Khanji of *191*, 192
Jupp, H. 49

Kaila, Alexia 121
Karney, A.B. *177*
Kashipur, Hari of 192
Kashipur, Raghunath of 192
Kashipur, Raja of 192
Kau, Josie *58*
Kaye, Jessica 166
Kazi, James 156
Kempthorne, J.A. *177*
Kennedy, Wardlaw *158*, 158
Kennedy Scott, Nick 76
Kent, Roger 62
Keys, Rachel 151, 156
Khalidi, T.A.S. *54*
Khan, Zayna 160
King, B.B. 151
King, Cyril 42
King, Hal 136
Kingdon, Oliver *129*
Kipling, Lockwood 30
Kipling, Rudyard 18, 21, 28, 29, *29*, 30, 31, 80–1, 186
Klais, Johannes 175

Knocker, G.M. 157
Koe, Alfred 101
Köhler, Lily *122*
Krajewski, Mathilde *122*
Kuszell, Andrzej 39
Kverndal, Ole 147

Lane, Cleo 80
Lange, David 163
Langlais, Jean 78
Lanyon, Peter 71
Lawrence, Sir Henry 14
Lawrence, Sir John (later Lord) 14, 123, 160
Lawrence, Richard **76**
Le Bas, Reverend Charles 19
Le Fanu, Henry F. *177*, 179
Le Fanu, William 157
Lea, 'Gussy' 135
Lean, David 87
Lees, Doug 150
Legge, Robert George 159
Leigh-Mallory, Sir Trafford 132
Leighton, Kenneth 78
Lempriere, Dr Lancelot 42, 91
Letts, Quentin 163
Letts, R.F.B. 62
Lewis, Andrew 60
Libeaux, André 167
Lintoff, Maria 71
Livingstone, David 187
Lloyd, Reverend W.R. 'Labby' 147
Lloyd-James, David 83
Lochtmans, Miriam 82
Lochtmans, Willy 82
Lofting, John *54*, 62
Loncaster, Hamish 82
Longman, Derek 79, *79*, 118, **174–5**
Loveridge, Emma 179
Lowe, Chris 162
Lugard, Sir Frederick 187
Lutyens, Sir Edwin 192
Lyon, Mrs E. 80
Lyon, John 179
Lyttelton, Canon Edward 23, 24, 42, 49, *55*, 55, 61, 90, 123, 174
Lyttelton, Humphrey 80

Macaulay, Rose 179
Macaulay, Thomas Babington 13
MacCorkindale, Simon 83, 84
MacDonald, Henry 30
Macpherson, Alistair 157

205

Maitland Maitland, Edward *133*, 133–4
Malim, Reverend F.B. 23
Mallett, Tony 90
Malthus, Reverend Thomas 18, 93, 163, 197
Manduell, John 38
Mangan, Stephen *84*, 84, 85
Mann, Adrien 58
Manning, Francis William 158
Manwaring, G.B. 159
Maran, Mike 78
Marconi, Guglielmo 85
Margaret, Princess 61
Marinus, Stuart 83
Marriott, Martin 152
Martinez, Cristina 75
Mary, Queen 23
Matcham, Russell **125–6**
Matthews, E.C. (Edgar) 72, *72*, 76, 83, 105, 107, 142, 158
Matthews, Molly 33
Mayhew, Lord 160, 163
Maynard, Peter B. **124**
McCarthy, John 173
McClelland, Richard 86
McLellan, D.M.C. *54*
McMahon, Sir Henry 189
McVeigh, Joe **186**
McVittie, Malcolm 59
Mead, Henry 192
Mead, Hugh 73
Medd, Nick 56
Medland, Thomas 14
Melvill, Reverend Henry 21
Melvill VC, Teignmouth 21
Mendoza, Molly *164*
Mercer, Miss Howard 116
Meyer, Joyce *191*
Meyer, R.J.O. (Jack) 61, *191*, 193
Miles, Beverly 83
Miles, Roland 83
Milford, L.S. 38, 46, 47, 90, 91, 102
Millar, E.H. *54*
Miller, Andrew 62
Miller, Arthur 73
Miller, E.J. 72
Miller, Luke **177–9**, *178*
Miller, William **76–7**
Mills, Sir John 84, 86
Milner, D.R. 110
Milton, John 73
Mitchell, R.E. *54*

Mitchell-Carruthers, Alexander 188
Montgomery, Viscount 14
Moore, C.J. *54*
Moores-Grimshaw, Andrew 83
More, J.W.C. 102
Morgan, Reverend Philip 90
Morley, Kate 82
Morris, George 13
Morris, William 31, 73
Morson, L.J. 55
Moss, Stirling *57*, 57
Mountbatten, Lord 131, 132
Mozart, Wolfgang Amadeus 38
Muir, Sir William 123
Murdoch, Ian 59
Murdoch, Peter 59
Murrell, Mick 111

Nagel, Reverend C.N. 28
Nagtegaal, Marno *118*
Nash, E.J.H. 'Bash' 180
Nash, Paul 71
Nazarbayev, Nursultan 194
Neild, Nancy 76
Nelson, Lord 85
Newbolt, Sir Henry 190
Newcombe, Bill 152
Newson, S.J.B. 62
Newman, Ernest 189
Nichols, John 79, **138–42**
Nolan, Christopher *87*, 87
Northcote, Sir Stafford 13
Nunn, Tony 55, **144–7**
Nurden, Hank 147

O'Brien, Tony 76
O'Donoghue, Scott 58
O'Flaherty, Hugh 137
Ohlenschlager, Val 105
Oldridge, David **196–7**
Olivier, Laurence 76
Osborne, Sir D'Arcy 136–7
Osman, Barry *42*
Otter-Barry, Robert 188
Ovid 11
Owen, David (Lord) *161*

Paisley, Reverend Ian 163
Pamphlion, Harold *95*, 95
Pankhurst, J.M. *54*
Pannet, Juliet 152
Parker, Toby **9–21**, 27–31, 36, 42, 69–72, 81, 85–7, 91, 100, *100*–2, 106, 111, 124–5, 128, 133–8, 156, 176–7, 186–92
Parkes, Mike 57
Parkin, Nigel 73
Parkinson, Lord 163
Parris, Matthew 162
Parrish, M.R. *54*
Parry, Hubert 78
Parsons (née Van Horne), Jennifer **53**, 154
Pearson, Frederick E. **97**
Perowne, A.W.T. *177*
Perrins, Michael **163**
Petersen, Oliver **57–60**
Pickles, Mr 143
Pidcock, G.A.H. 133
Pitts, William 177
Plummer, Rowland 11
Pollock, Sir Frederick 190
Pollock, Jeremy *50*
Powell, Anthony 179
Powell, Enoch 162
Poynter, Edward 30
Prance, Reverend Lewis 14
Prentki, Nigel 57
Price, Cormell 18, 27, 28, 29, *30*, 30–1
Prickett, Sir Thomas 132
Pringle, B.S. *54*
Proctor, Andrew 83
Proust, Marcel 118
PRW (*see* Woodburn, Roger)
Pullen, Father Jim 173
Purdy, Nigel 80
Purkiss, L.K. (Bill) *110*, 147
Purnell, Anthony 'Reg' 76

Race, Sylvie 147
Racine Jaques, Nigel 139
Radcliffe, Viscount 191
Raissis, Aris 71
Rampling, Charlotte 57
Rawlins, George 188
Read, Herbert 71
Reade, Reverend Henry 11, 16
Redl, Ernest 189
Reed, Carol 87
Regin, Nadia 86
Reinecke, Carl 100
Rendall, Charles 183
Rennie, Alasdair 71
Repton, Humphrey 34
Rhoades, James 18, 101
Rhodes, Cecil 188

Rhodes James, Richard **90–1**, 94, 113, *180*, 180
Rice, John **138**
Richards, David 90
Richards, Hoyt *85*, 85
Richardson, W.J. *54*
Richey, George *129*
Richmond, George 10
Richter, Ernest 100
Rider, T.J. *54*
Ridley, Henry Nicholas 187
Rimmer, David 60, **61–2**
Rimmer, Ken 92, 113
Robbins, Nigel 56
Roberts, 'Bloody R.' 143
Roberts, Lord 128
Roberts, M.R. *54*
Robertson, Reverend James 23, 36, 38, 101
Robertson, Max 55
Robinson, Bert 58
Robson, Stuart 57
Rodd, Sir Rennell 136
Rogers, Graham 38
Rolling Stones, The 57, 186
Rose, Sir Michael 162
Ross, David **82–3**
Ross, Jane 83
Ross, Sandy 62
Rothenstein, William 70
Roxy Music 186
Roy, Prannoy 114
Russell Dore, Frank 21
Ryder, Susan 77
Rye, Peter 80, **113**

Salisbury, Lord 128
Sandell, Ben 166
Sanders, Sir Arthur *134*, 134
Sanger, David 175
Saunders, Christopher **143**
Savile, W.H. 101
Sawbridge, Hugh 76, 186
Scarborough, Alex *151*
Schröder, Gerhard 98
Schwenk, Theodor 72
Scorer, B.R.I. *54*
Scott, Robert (Bob) *23*, 76
Seabrook, F.J. (Jim) 43, *60*, 90
Seebohm, H.E. 28, 29
Seeley, John Robert 90
Selous, Frederick Courtney 186–7
Sewell, Betty 79

INDEX

Seymour, Mark 62, 97
Seymour, Richard 62
Shakespeare, William 76, 184
Shapeero, E.N. *54*
Sharland, Peter 87
Sharpe, Sir Alfred *187*, 187–8
Shaw, P.C.M. *54*
Sheasby, D.N. *54*
Sheldon, Alec 105
Shoosmith, Arthur Gordon 192
Short, Clare 163
Sickert, Walter 70
Simcox Lea, Thomas 187
Simpson, John 33, 40
Simpson, Nigel 83
Singer Sargent, John 70
Singh, HH Maharaja Sir Pertab (Pratap) *190*, 190
Sinker, Roy 178
Skan, Martin **102**
Skelly, Richard 90
Slater, Raymond 'Twitch' 86, 142
Sleight, Tony *54*, 183
Slessor, Sir John 124, 128, *131*, 132, 133
Smallman, Neville 147
Smith, A.D. *54*
Smith, C.P.C. (Christopher) 91, *92*, 102
Smith, Robert 10
Smith, W.E. 100
Snow, Julian 160
Snowdon, W.L. (Bill) 76, *76*
Souter, J.S. *110*
Speaight, George 83
Speaight, Robert 83, *85*, 85, 159
Spears, John 59
Stafford, Robert 114
Stagg, John Reginald 81
Stalin, Joseph 162
Stanyard, Will 50
Steadman, H.W.R. *54*
Stephen, Jenny 153
Stephen, Martin 153
Stephens, Alison *78*, 78
Stephens, Philip 154
Stephenson, G.V. 46
Sterling, Bunny 59
Stewart, Bill 36, 39, 114, 149, *152*, 154
Stewart, Bob 162

Stewart, H.E.A.H. 159
Stewart, Ian *161*
Stitcher, G.R. 46
Stone, Mr 42
Stout, Henry 34
Stringer, Michael 86, *86*, 107, 140–1
Stuart-Hunt, Charles **59**
Sukhum, Pakorn **193**
Sukhum, Prasob 193
Sullivan, Arthur 76
Summerscale, David 25–7, 57, *99*, 99, 118, *130*, **152–4**
Sunderland Lewis, George H. 101
Sutherland, Graham 71
Swaby, Laura *155*
Swinburn, Algernon 31

Talbot, John 23
Talbot, N.S. 177
Taylor, Joseph 11
Tebbit, Lord 163
Temple, Reverend Henry 10
Thatcher, Margaret 162, 163
Theobald, Steve 55, 147
Thomas, Ben 48
Thomas, G.A.P. 55
Thomas, J.B.W. (Jack) 39, 76, **89**, 154
Thomas, Peter 114
Thomas, Quentin 79
Thomas, Reverend Richard *54*
Thomason, James 14, 123
Thompson, Chris 62
Thompson, David 76
Thompson, F.R. 149
Thompson, W.G. 149
Thomson, Paula 83
Thomson, A.R. 131
Thornburn, Hilary 66
Thorne, Cornelius *61*
Thorne, Marlborough 61
Thornton, Edward 123
Tonypandy, Lord 162
Townsend, Peter 61
Toyne, Mrs Cecily 79
Toyne, S.M. 61, 79, 166
Trench, Frederic 101
Trench, Philip Charles 196
Trenchard, Lord 132, 162
Trevelyan, Sir Charles *13*, 13
Trevithin and Oaksey, Lord 13

Tschaikowsky, James 131
Tsui, Edward Chi Kim 188
Turnbull, Rob *119*
Turney, Jason 82
Tyrwhitt-Drake, Bill 62, 147
Tyrwhitt-Drake, Hugh 98

Ungoed-Thomas, Sir Lynn 160

Vane-Tempest, Charles 105
Vansittart, Peter 159
Verdi, Giuseppe 79
Verne, Jules 187
Vickers, Andrew 28
Vickers, Jeremy 28
Vickers, Sir Richard **28**, 56
Vickers, Robin 28
Vickers, W.G.H. 28
Victoria, Queen 23, 37, 112
Vivaldi, Antonio 38
Vizianagaram, Maharajkumar Sir Vijayananda Gajiapathi Raju of 192
Vohora, Atul 71
Vosper, Frank 85, 86
Vyner, Neil 62

Wadhwan, Kumar Shri Virendrasinhji of 191–2
Walford, Reverend Charles 11, *12*, 14, 16
Walford, Reverend Henry 18
Walker, J.W. 174
Walker, M.J.M. *54*
Walker, Nick 62
Walker, William 33–4, 196
Walker-Arnott, Edward **72–3**, 98–100
Wallace, S.J. *54*
Walsh, Donald 42
Ware, R.I.W. *54*
Warfield, P.J. 46
Waring, M.C. *54*
Watson, Anthony 114
Watson, David 180
Weatherly, Frederic 100
Weber, Tommy 57
Webster, Bryan **128–9**, *129*
Welch, Ryan *155*
Wellesley, Lord 196

Wennink, A.G. 62
Wensley, Bert *43*, 43, 62
Westley, Roger *98*, 98
Weston, Bishop Frank 178–9
Whistler, James McNeill 70
Whistler, Rex 70–1, 72
White, 'Chalky' 186
Whitley, Sir John 133
Whyte, John 'Daddy' *95*
Widdows, Robin 57
Wilkins, J.M. *54*
Wilkins, William 11, 15, 16, 34, 157, 177, 196
Wilkinson, Lee **83–4**
William, Prince 23
Williams, Alex N. McL. 66
Williams, E.F. 76
Williams, Elizabeth **122**
Williams, Matthew *118*
Williams, Monier 10
Willis, Bishop John Jameson 178
Willoughby, Maurice 91
Wilson of Rievaulx, Lord 86, *161*, 161
Wimbush, Richard 179
Winters, Oliver 166
Woffenden, Tim **151**, **156**
Wood, Charles 197
Woodburn, Roger 33–5, 47, 56–7, 60–1, 90, 118, **160**
Woodruff, Philip 22
Wright, David **36–9**, 158, 173
Wright, Edward 43
Wright, Geoff 89
Wyatt, Matthew 33
Wyles, C.T. (Chris) 46, 48
Wynne-Willson, St J.B. *177*, 177
Wynter, Bryan *71*, 71–2

Xenophon 114

Yarnold, Ted 150
Yearsley, K.D. 136
York, HRH The Duke of 41
Young, Carmichael 79
Young, Richard **183–5**

Zagalsky, P.F. *54*
Zhumashov, Serzhan 193
Zuckerman, Sir Solly 71
Zurita, Adriana 53

ACKNOWLEDGEMENTS

PARTICULAR THANKS TO:

Petri Anderson
Neil Athey
Alan Atkinson
Mike Bamford (Society of Malawi)
Robin Bishop
LSgt Shane Brandon (Archivist, Welsh Guards)
Christopher Buyers
Pauline Cassidy
Karen Chave
Roger Cullingham (Windsor Website and Forum)
Ray Dexter
Liz Drew
Heather Edwards-Hedley
Pauline Evans
Clive Francis
Kevin Greenbank (Centre of South Asian Studies, Cambridge)
Jeff Hardcastle
Ken Hartfield (Stephen Austin)
Elspeth Harvey
Rob Inglis
Tana Macpherson Smith
Luke Miller
Val Proctor
Robin Ravilious
Andy Renwick and Peter Elliott (RAF Museum)
Marianne Rogers
Dick Shilton (Archivist, Millfield School)
Col. Umaid Singh (Jaipur Riding and Polo Club)
Rob Turnbull
Lt Gen Sir Richard Vickers
Keith White (Archivist, Haileybury Melbourne)
Rev. Dr Ben Yoo, St Martin's Garrison Church, Delhi

PICTURE CREDITS:

Unless otherwise noted, the illustrations in this book have been provided by Haileybury. Every effort has been made to contact the copyright holders of all works reproduced in this book. If any acknowledgements have been omitted, please contact Third Millennium Publishing:

Dust jacket: Building Panoramics

Building Panoramics 21
Alamy Picture Library 86
John Allinson 134
Julian Alliott 56
Petri Anderson 176
Julian Andrews 6, 20, 21, 35, 42, 47, 51, 53, 66, 68, 88, 89, 94, 103, 104, 107, 115, 116, 17, 119, 120, 142, 146, 148, 149, 153, 156–7, 166–170, 173, 175, 179, 181, 185, 197
Neil Athey 66
Peter Blair 164
David Blakeway Smith 130
Kate Bowen 127
Mark Button 155
Christopher Buyers 191
Centre for South Asian Studies, University of Cambridge 192
Roly Clark 128
Ray Dexter 54, 58, 63, 150, 154
Clive Francis 73
Getty Images 57, 124
Archive, Haileybury (Melbourne) 183, 183
Haileybury Almaty 195
Haileybury Marketing Department/ *The Haileyburian* 2, 58, 67, 122 195
Angus Head 44
Dan Hearn 161

Justin Hunt 40
Rob Inglis 178
Jaipur Riding and Polo Club 190
Robert Klaas 91
Manchester Libraries 9
Mary Evans Picture Library 55, 71
Russell Matcham 125, 126
Derek Longman 79
Luke Miller 178
Millfield School 189
Tony Nunn 55
Toby Parker 22, 41, 99, 147, 176, 183
Susan Pugsley 80, 177
John Rice 138
The Society of Malawi 185
Jonathan Spavin 145
Laura Swaby 155
Tate, London 2012 69
The Board of Trinity College, Dublin 163
Trustees of the RAF Museum, Hendon 135
Rob Turnbull 8, 32, 34, 40, 105
Sir Richard Vickers 28
Katherine Walsh 194
Bryan Webster 129
Estate of Rex Whistler 70
Windsor Website and Forum 18
Wireimage 87
Roger Woodburn 34, 85, 98, 160
www.alisonstephens.com 78